BIBLIOGRAPHY
FOR
CROSS-CULTURAL
WORKERS

Compiled By
A.R. TIPPETT

William Carey Library
CHRISTIAN MISSION BOOKS

South Pasadena, California

Copyright 1971 by
A. R. Tippett

Library of Congress Catalog Card Number: 70-176292
International Standard Book Number: 0-87808-109-7

Published by the William Carey Library
533 Hermosa Street
South Pasadena, Calif. 91030
Telephone: 213-682-2047

PRINTED IN THE UNITED STATES OF AMERICA

Contents

Bibliographical Essay   1
The Bibliographical Finding Aids   13
  Serials Cited   15
  Symposia Cited   21
  Abbreviations Used   25

General Reference Works   27
  Cyclopedias and Dictionaries   29
  Bibliographies   30
  General Anthropological Works   35
    Single Society Studies   38
    Comparative Studies   47

Anthropological Dimensions   51
  Theory of Anthropology   53
  Social Anthropology and Cultural Analysis   63
    Values   88
    Economic Anthropology   91
    Law   96
  Patterns of Leadership and Authority   99
  Acculturation, Culture Clash and Culture Change   107
  Culture and Personality   122
  Applied Anthropology   136
  Urban Anthropology   144
  Ethnolinguistics and Communication   153
  Missionary Anthropology   159

Religious Dimensions   171
  General Works on Animistic Religion   173
  Basic Concepts: The Philosophy of Animism   179
  Animistic Practitioners and Systems   189
    Religious Systems, Structures and Rituals   189
    Magic, Sorcery, Witchcraft and Divination   194
    Shamanism and Curing   198
    Spiritism, Possession, Glossolalia, Voodoo   202
    Syncretism   204
  Organized Nativistic Movements   207
  The Great Religions   217
  Christian Mission in the Animist World   228

Research Methods   233
  Anthropology, Ethnohistory, Missiology   234
    Teaching Anthropology   249

Bibliograpical Essay

1. The Nature and Function of a Bibliography

This is a bibliography - a systematic list of books and articles, indicating their authorship, publisher, date and place of publication; and a finding aid for persons who might wish to search out the material for use. This is a minimum dictionary definition, but a bibliography has far more character than that, as the following pointers indicate.

1. *A bibliography is a piece of research in progress.* It is an on-going exercise and can never be complete. Even while it is being typed for the printer it is already becoming obsolete, and as one proofs its pages he is immediately aware of serious omissions. Even in a limited field like the activity of the cross-cultural worker, completeness is an impossibility. In this present volume completeness was not the compiler's aim. He had other goals and criteria.

2. *A bibliography is a functional working tool.* Ordinary people seldom buy bibliographies. They are not the kind of volume to decorate the table in the lounge or by the bedside. A person buys a bibliography as a research tool, as a finding aid, for reference, for verification, to learn what has been done on a particular subject by other researchers, and for many similar reasons. The bibliography is essentially a functional tool for students, teachers, readers and researchers, or for people who desire to keep informed about the publications of their profession.

3. *A bibliography is a representation of available material.* One bibliography on my desk has ten thousand entries confined to the islands of Fiji and Tonga in the South Pacific, but I know many other items not listed in it. It is, at best, only a representative lot.

In this present cross-cultural bibliography the listings have been grouped around specific subjects, but selected from all regions of the world in the hope that cross-cultural workers with all ethnic groups will find it of some value. However the "world scope" of a bibliography creates a serious problem for

1

the compiler. At best one can present a representative selection. Sometimes a seemingly important work may have been neglected because a region is already overloaded. Or a seemingly insignificant tribe may have been noticed because it is the sole representative of its type and location. On the other hand some entries have been included in more than one section, where they speak significantly to two topics.

4. *A bibliography reflects the strengths, weaknesses and biases of its compiler.* This is always true but not always recognized by those who use the compilation. The assembly of a bibliography is a much more personal exercise than the standardized columns of entries might suggest to the user. Even a small bibliography of 2,500 to 3,000 entries, like this one has involved the compiler in far more than that number of decisions. The bias is reflected not only in the selection of the listed items, but also in the total structure of the volume and the precise section or sub-section where each entry is inserted.

In this present volume the compiler's anthropological and missiological specialization in the Southwest Pacific is no doubt apparent and it is precisely for that reason that the blank pages are left at the end of the sections, so the user may not only keep the volume up to date, but also insert items reflecting his own regional and topical bias. In spite of this however, a deliberate attempt has been made to distribute the entries to cover all parts of the world.

5. *A bibliography facilitates the availability of research material.* A bibliography is an assembly of infor-mation organized round a theme, a discipline, a program, an interest, a region or perhaps a race of people. It implies either an ongoing research into this subject or the compiler's conviction that research in the area is needed, and would indeed be undertaken if the available material were effectively organized for use. Much valuable information is hidden away, for example, in technical journals and never brought to light. Few people can subscribe to more than four or five of these technical journals, yet even in this small volume entries have been selected from such journals.

This raises the whole question of the *availability* of research material. When is material available? It can hardly be called available just because it has been printed, if it is in some obscure journal which the researcher would not think of consulting. Even if it is in a major technical journal of another academic discipline it is not really available, though it may be standing on the next shelf in the library where one is working.

But when the bibliographer records it under the correct sub-head it is immediately available, even if he has to send to some distant repository for a xerox copy. It is available because, first, he knows of its existence; and second, he knows where to look for it. A bibliography therefore facilitates the availability of research material.

6. *A bibliography implies the existence of unused resource material.* I remember a missionary from a Latin American country, who determined to spend his furlough studying the cultural background of the people among whom he worked. He spent the first half of his time complaining of the lack of research material: no-one had researched his area of interest. He had side-stepped my suggestion that a visit to the U.C.L.A. research library would correct his problem. At last, under pressure he did so, and found a drawer and a half of cards on his country and thereafter complained that he had too much material. He had lost much valuable time by not knowing where to go in the first place. A bibliography seeks to save this kind of lost research-time by changing search-time into research-time for a bibliographer.

Furthermore, we all know how frustrating it can be to discover, when one is completing his research, that basic work had already been done and was available all the time in published form if only we had known before. This infuriating experience cannot be fully avoided - even for the bibliographer himself - but the bibliographer hopes to reduce the frustration for researchers by making their search-time the topic of his research.

7. *The publication of a new bibliography implies an unsatisfied felt need.* A *felt need* exists and calls for the listing and organization of existing research material, as we have seen, to make it available for use. The need may be felt by the people for whom the research is being done; either those who are sponsoring the research, or those who will benefit from it when complete. This need may be met either by the new subject matter listed, or by the new bibliographical arrangement as the case may be. In the former case the bibliographer is assembling data which remains to be evaluated. In the latter he is himself making a conceptual contribution by a new combination of known data.

The bibliographer has to keep the felt needs in mind as he selects and arranges his material. Otherwise it will merely result in a published volume and not in a *working tool*.

Let us take an example. An indigenous church is an institution worthy of study either for anthropological or missiological reasons. A bibliography of books and articles on

3

this subject may be required (1) to throw light on the processes of changing structures and institutions, or (2) to help indigenous church people everywhere to understand their own structures and indigeneity, or (3) to help missionaries to know how to phase out their missions into indigenous churches, which are culturally and functionally relevant in their own localities. The first of these felt needs is anthropological and might call for a university thesis of a more objective character, sponsored by secular funds. The second might be done for the people themselves in the indigenous church, maybe by one of its own nationals as a degree research project, but something for him to take home to his people for discussion and action. The sponsor of the third could well be the mission board, which is concerned with the transition from mission to church. Or a fourth possibility could be the need of a professor of missionary anthropology who prepares it for his missionary trainees as an educational research tool in the training program, by means of which he hopes to instill the *idea of research* as a *continuum* in missionary procedure.

Thus, although the bibliographer has one precise felt need in mind, he is not unaware that his bibliography may meet other felt needs of related groups and individuals. Even so the organization and selection of material will be conditioned by the more specific felt need he himself hopes to meet.

8. *Each bibliography is a unique combination of inter-relating factors.* A bibliography is more than a list of titles. It has structure and arrangement, and usually sections and sub-sections. If you look at its "Table of Contents" it tells you something of the character and entity of the total book. The break-down of the sections indicates the parts which inter-relate in the compiler's conceptualization of the field or discipline which is the total entity of the book. In this present volume, the arrangement within the sections and sub-sections are alphabetical by author. The entries for each author are in chronological sequence so that they suggest something of the development of his ideas - a common pattern in anthropological writing. These sections however are not meant to be isolated entities. They are configurations which integrate and inter-act within the whole pattern. The reader should regard them as dynamic and relating parts rather than static isolates.

Many of the articles really belong to three or four sections - they inter-relate so! At the head of a number of sections the seeker is recommended to look also in this section or that for further material of a similar character. The total area of this bibliography holds together as an entity of research and description which might be called "Basic Material for Cross-cultural Workers".

II. The Component Parts of This Bibliography

This bibliography is broken down into four basic component parts, which may be regarded as the aspects of research and/or description for those persons in our western society who are concerned with religion in its social context in the non-western cultural setting. Although this has been assembled first of all for missionaries (including fraternal workers and partners in mission) the bibliography should speak also to medical and health workers, educationalists, agriculturalists, veterinarians, technical advisors, peace corps workers and all westerners engaged in cross-cultural contact programs, employed by governments, and even professional anthropologists.

The common ground for these persons is, first, that they are all agents of contact and of change - frequently of deliberately directed change. They are all involved in, what they may differently conceptualize as *progress*, and, however variant their conceptions of progress, nevertheless the cultural dynamics are similar. Thus, for example, Homer Barnett's *Innovation* speaks equally well to the doctor, the teacher, and the missionary. Thus also the process of group dynamics and directed change, of decision-making, of advocacy acceptance and rejection, forms a major configuration of the total pattern of this bibliography.

Second, no matter whether the researcher is a religious man or not, he cannot escape *the fact of the central place of religion* in cross-cultural situations. It is not without good cause that Radin conceived of religion as the social *integrator*, "concerned with the maintenance of life values" and "permeat (ing) every phase of existence (1937:15) and Wallace spoke of it as a re-integrator when a group found its solidarity shaken (1948:53). Yet for many doctors, teachers and even for some anthropologists, religion has been "classified out" of the study of basic social structure, like the "Religion" page in *Time Magazine*.

Nothing convinces me more of this *westernization process* in research than preparing a bibliography of the kind undertaken in this volume. The percentage of books and articles, which could and should have shown social structure and religion as integrated is far too small. We ethnocentric westerners love to segregate Church and State, but we have a great deal of 'unlearning' to do if we are to operate in most cross-cultural situations.

1. *The Reference Component of this Bibliography:*

The reference component of this bibliography comprises a list of eyclopedias and dictionaries, a catalogue of serials cited in the bibliography, a table of abbreviations and a list of symposia and other books cited as references in the main body of the bibliography. The purpose of this unit is mainly to provide a group of finding aids for the person using the main bibliography.

2. *The Anthropological Component Parts of this Bibliography:*

The fact that this volume does not concern itself with the whole of anthropology, even the whole of cultural anthropology, should not be regarded as an attempt to avoid a concept of the wholeness of man. The omission of physical anthropology, archaeology and technical linguistics, for example, is purely to allow for concentration on the precise purpose in mind - namely, to produce a bibliography of *Man in His Social Context*, where the battle for human betterment is being fought out today, whether in terms of religious conversion or of technical aid.

Some historical depth is retained with the inclusion of ethnohistorical material. This is relevant at the point where social change is being studied - some diachronic dimension being required. Some linguistic material is included under the head of Ethnolinguistics (which bears on such things as meaning, identification and rapport) and Communication.

Social Anthropology, the largest section, could have been much more diversified, but many of the case studies listed in this section are total society studies and defy diversified classification. Values, Economics and Law have been categorized because a quantity of material of this type has been isolated by specialists in anthropological writing. The compiler of this bibliography has considered it worth drawing the attention of cross-cultural workers to the quite non-western dimensions of these configurations.

Items which concern Leadership and Authroity Patterns have been given a section of their own because of their special significance for missionaries, administrators, teachers and other foreigners likely to be in leadership positions, and to be responsible for phasing in new structures and controls, that they may be indigenous rather than foreign.

The compiler of this bibliography also believes that in spite of the 'heavy weather' experienced recently in Culture and Personality, nevertheless this is essentially part of the

6

social setting where advocacy, acceptance and rejection are vital issues, and also such problems as human relations, meaning, and values. This is also an aspect of missiology which recognizes that the person is both an individual and a member of a social group. Because of the ruthlessness of western individualism the cross-cultural worker needs to be aware of persons in other cultural groups, where the values are more communal.

Applied Anthropology, Urban Anthropology, and Missionary Anthropology represent contemporary outreaches of Anthropology, bringing the science to bear on precise situations. They say that Anthropology is no longer just science for science sake, no longer merely descriptive salvaging. Human societies are not just so many guinea-pigs being observed as responding to stimuli. The science justifies itself only in so far as it contributes to human betterment.

3. *The Religious Component Parts of this Bibliography:*

In this bibliography Religion is normally Animism. When we speak of the Philosophy of Animism, we are dealing with basic religious ideas, power encounter, *mana, toh* and *taboo*, soul-force or soul-stuff, the idea of the soul, theories of sickness and so forth, which the cross-cultural worker must understand before he can come to grips with them.

This is distinguished from what we ethnocentrically speak of as 'Philosophy', instead of Western Philosophy. The Philosophy of Animism is essentially religious. The Philosophy of the West is a process of rationalization which permits the avoidance of Religion altogether. The former involves spiritual phenomena from outside the person. The latter emanates from within man. The former is experiential: the latter is theoretical. Thus in the section on The Great Religions this bibliography concentrates on the animistic bases rather than the philosophical superstructure, which belongs in another bibliographical volume of its own, and is so extensive that it would have thrown this present work out of balance.

The analysis of Animistic Systems and Practitioners is a major section, with sub-sections that are indeed classificatory. Thus, for example, items on sorcery and witchcraft are grouped together, and set off clearly from those on shamanism and curing. Discussions on various forms of enthusiasm are grouped as a corpus on their own, and likewise those entries covering writings on the phenomenon of syncretism. All these are differentiated within the section on animistic systems and practitioners to bring out their functional differences.

Organized Animism is also given an entity of its own,

and likewise the Christian Encounter with Animism.

All this, of course, is obviously vital for the missionary; but the doctor and the veterinarian also had better
acquaint themselves with the philosophy of sorcery and counter-
sorcery, for example. Their own status and acceptance depend
on it. The well-known current T.V. commercial, which claims
tribal appreciation and acceptance of a program of animal
husbandry because of its effective healing of the cattle, is
possibly merely regarded as effective counter-sorcery. I have
known an almost identical program to be rejected completely
because the cattle were so sick that the injections killed them.
The white man had his chance and failed and thereafter the door
was closed against him. The point of the incident is simply
that every cross-cultural worker needs an understanding of the
religious concepts which ramify through the social institutions
of the people to whom he goes; regardless of whether his own
personal mission is religious, or medical, or administrative,
or educative. He has to learn that acceptances and rejection
of innovations are often made on a basis of values he does not
share, and that many of these are religious.

4. *The Research Component in this Bibliography:*

The research methods of Missiology today are basically
the same as those of Anthropology and Ethnohistory. The precise goals may vary but the techniques are the same - observation, participation, experiment, comparison, interviewing,
even to the use of graphics and computers. This section of the
bibliography should serve all who are engaged in cross-cultural
research and data-collecting. The range of entries (as in
other sections) is wide - some quite simple: others technically
sophisticated. This has been deliberate to increase the value
of the volume for a greater number of users.

One serious problem in the training of missionaries is
the dearth of teachers, who have both anthropological and
missiological qualifications and perspectives. Authorities in
charge of seminaries and other training institutions usually
prefer field experience (which understands the problems from
the missionary angle) to anthropological proficiency (which
provides the interpretive competence from the cultural angle).
As a result many missionaries are trained by a professor whose
graduate degree is in some other discipline. This position is
being corrected slowly, but meantime there is sore need for
"anthropological teacher-training" among professors of missions.
To help those who are struggling to improve their competence in
this way a sub-unit has been included on "The Teaching of
Anthropology".

Recently the compiler of this bibliography was asked by

8

a professional psychologist if a missionary could involve himself in research. Today, with all the facilities for anthropological training, the answer to that question must be that a
person *dare not* be a missionary without engaging himself in
research. And that goes also for all cross-cultural agents of
change. They cannot be fully efficient without first learning
the language, understanding the customs and values, recognizing
the personal linkages and relationships, appreciating and
accepting the social structures. This involves one in continu-
ous research of some kind or other. Identification and rapport
depend on this. But it is not merely a matter of knowing all
about these things. Cross-cultural work calls for an understanding attitude and empathy. Anthropology and Missiology are
not just recording descriptions of cultural groups; one is
seeking to understand *in order to be at their disposal* -- both
the missionary and the social worker. Superior, 'big-hearted',
technical aid without empathy is highly suspect. So this
bibliography is offered to the user in the hope that it will
facilitate better cross-cultural understanding and mutual
respect between westerners and non-westerners; and that we may
the better achieve the unity of man by recognizing the diversity within that unity.

III. Some Suggestions for Using the Bibliography.

An article of interest is listed in the bibliography but
the journal where it is printed is not readily available. How
does one obtain access to it? Most of the entries in this
bibliography are available in the major university libraries.
This has been one criteria for selection. In any case you will
first acquaint yourself with the finding aids at hand in your
own city or university. Let us suppose you live in Los Angeles.
You discover an item in this bibliography. It is indicated as
in *Human Organ.*, which by reference to the list of abbreviations is found to be the journal, *Human Organization*. If your
library is a small one, which does not focus on Anthropology,
go to the *Union List of Periodicals in the Libraries of
Southern California*. Here you will find that eleven libraries
in the metropolis carry this serial, and they are scattered all
over the city. This pattern will vary in different cities, but
there always will be some procedure that is effective if you
take the trouble to seek it out.

Make use of the library facilities. Most libraries have
xeroxing machines for the use of their patrons. Do not fail to
draw on the inter-library loan system for scarcer material not
in your library, and for theses from other universities. Your
own library will have several union catalogues from major
repositories.

Many of the scarcer items listed in this bibliography - Anthropology, Sociology and Psychology - are reprinted in a superb series known as the *Bobbs-Merrill Reprints*. Your regular book-seller can order these for you at 25¢ an article. Thus, for example, suppose you want Wallaces's important article on "Revitalization Movements" which appeared in *Amer. Anth.* in 1956, and, let us say the series in your library only starts from 1960. You will be pleased to discover the item is A.230 in this reprint series. Ask your book-seller to send for the catalogue. The series has over a thousand select items -a useful bibliography in itself.

We have another very good resource in the increasing number of excellent symposia that have been published in the last few years. They range from $2.95 to $40.00. Many are in paperback and are worth buying for your own library. Some of the articles included in these come from obscure or foreign journals which are hard to get, and others have articles especially written to fill gaps in the theme of the symposium. A good many of these are listed in this bibliography, and frequently individual articles from them are also listed.

Let me illustrate the point. Some years ago I was doing research on the Solomons and I needed an article by R.C. Thurnwald on some Buin values. It had appeared in an Australian journal, *Oceania*, and I had to make a long journey to a university which had this serial and take a xerox copy. Since then that article has been reprinted in *Tribe and Peasant Economies* (Ed. Dalton) one of a fine series of symposia called *American Museum Sourcebooks in Anthropology* and published by the Natural History Press. This 584-page volume I obtained in paperback for $2.95. In this bibliography the entry would read - Dalton, 1967: 224-245, after the pattern used in anthropological literature.

Because entries of this type are scattered throughout the bibliography and are quite numerous I have included a list of these symposia in the reference section at the front of the book. It will serve as a modified index. I have also included such books, which though by a single author, have a wide range of chapter topics which I have considered worth listing like articles on independent subjects. Such books may be general studies but a good chapter on religion and another on social structure, say, seem worth listing as articles. This may have led to some repetition but I hope it increased the value of the bibliography. Such an item would be listed - Oliver, 1955: 396-410 - for example.

I would also draw the user's attention to the presence in this bibliography of a number of "Book Discussion" entries. This is a kind of presentation used by the journal, *Current Anthropology*. Some significant anthropological book is critically examined by several authorities and then the writer of the book has a rejoinder. This is like attending a lively seminar and very profitable.

Now I return to my starting point. A bibliography is a piece of research in progress, an on-going task which is never complete. I have included items up to June 1971 and have made it as representative as possible within a limit of 3000 entries. Primarily the bibliography has been assembled to meet the needs of men doing graduate degrees in Missiology at the Fuller Theological Seminary, to cover the comprehensive exam in "Mission Across Cultures", but I hope that all cross-cultural agents of change will find the volume of value.

Pasadena
July 1971   A.R. Tippett

The Bibliographical Finding Aids

SERIALS CITED

SYMPOSIA CITED

ABBREVIATIONS USED

SERIALS CITED IN THIS BIBLIOGRAPHY

Administrative Science Quarterly. Ithica, Cornell University

Africa. London, Oxford University Press

African Affairs. London, Royal African Society

African Studies. Johannesburg, Witwatersrand University Press

America Indigena. Mexico, Instituto Indigenista Interamericano

American Anthropologist. Washington, D.C., American Anthropological Association

American Behavioral Scientist. Beverly Hills,Sage Publications

American Catholic Sociological Review (now *Sociological
Analysis*) Worcester, Heffernan Press

American Journal of Sociology. Chicago, Chicago University
Press

American Quarterly. Philadelphia, University of Pennsylvania

American Sociological Review. Washington, D.C., American
Sociological Association

Annals of the American Academy of Political and Social Science.
Philadelphia

Anthropological Forum. Perth, University of Western Australia
Press

Anthropological Quarterly. Washington, D.C., Catholic
University of America

Anthropos. Fribourg, Imprimerie St. Paul

Archives de Sociologie des Religions. Paris, Groupe de
Sociologie des Religions

15

Background Information for Church and Society. Geneva, World
Council of Churches

Bible Translator. London, United Bible Societies

British Journal of Sociology. London, London School of
Economics

Bulletin of the History of Medicine. Baltimore, Johns Hopkins
Institute of the History of Medicine

Bureau of American Ethnology Memoirs. Washington, D.C.,
Smithsonian Institution

Cahiers d'Etudes Africaines. Sorbonne, Ecole Pratique des
Hautes Etudes

Catholic Educational Review. Washington, D.C., Catholic
University of America

Christian Century. Chicago, Christian Century Foundation

Christian Life. Wheaton, Christian Life Publications

Church Growth Bulletin. Pasadena, School of World Mission &
Institute of Church Growth

Columbia Law Review. New York, Columbia Law Students

Comparative Studies in Society and History. The Hague, The
Society for Comparative Study in Society and
History

Crozer Quarterly. Crozer, Crozer Theological Seminary

Current Anthropology. Chicago, University of Chicago

Daedalus. Boston, American Academy of Arts and Sciences

Diogenes. New York, International Council for Philosophy and
Humanistic Studies

Economic Development & Cultural Change. Chicago, University of
Chicago

Economic Journal. Cambridge, Royal Economic Society

Encounter. Indianapolis, Christian Theological Seminary

Ethics. Chicago, University of Chicago Press

Ethnohistory. Bloomington, American Society for Ethnohistory

Ethnology. Pittsburgh, Dept. of Anthropology, University of
Pittsburgh

Ethnos. Stockholm, Stateus Etnografiska Museum

Etudes Mélanésiennes. Noumea, Société d'études Mélanésiennes

Evangelical Missions Quarterly. Springfield, Evangelical
Missions Information Service

Folk-lore. London, Folk Lore Society

Folklore. Carcassonne, Société du folklore francais et du
folklore colonial

Frankfurter Berträge Zur Soziologie. Frankfurt am Main,
Europaische Verlagsanstalt GmbH.

Frontier. London, Wynn Williams (Publishers) Ld.

Hibbert Journal. London, George Allen & Unwin

History of Religions. Chicago, University of Chicago Press

Human Organization. Lexington, Society for Applied Anthropology

Human Relations. London, Plenum Publishing Co.

Humanités Cahiers. Paris, Institut de Science Economique
Appliquee

India Cultures Quarterly. Jabalpur, School of Research

International Journal of Social Psychiatry. London, The Avenue
Publishing Co.

International Review of Missions. Geneva, World Council of
Churches

International Social Science Bulletin. (Journal since 1958)
Paris, UNESCO

Journal de la Société des Océanistes. Paris, Musée de l'Homme

Journal of Abnormal & Social Psychology. Provincetown, The
Journal Press

Journal of African History. London, Cambridge University Press

Journal of American Folklore. Philadelphia, American Folklore Society

Journal of the American Statistical Association. Washington, D.C., American Statistical Association

Journal of Applied Psychology. Washington,D.C., American Psychological Association

Journal of Applied Sociology (now *Sociology and Social Research*) Los Angeles, University of California

Journal of Educational Sociology (now *Sociology of Education*). Washington, D.C., American Sociological Ass'n.

Journal of General Psychology. Provincetown, The Journal Press

Journal of Modern African Studies. London, Cambridge University Press

Journal of the Polynesian Society. Wellington, The Polynesian Society

Journal of Religion in Africa. Leiden, E.J. Brill

Journal of the Royal Asiatic Society. London, Royal Asiatic Society of Great Britain & Ireland

Journal of the Royal Anthropological Institute of Great Britain and Ireland. London, Royal Anthropological Institute of Great Britain and Ireland

Journal of Social Issues. Ann Arbor, Society for the Psychological Study of Social Issues

Journal of Social Psychology. Provincetown, The Journal Press

Kroeber Anthropological Society Papers. Berkeley, University of California, Dept. of Anthropology

Man. London, Royal Anthropological Institute of Great Britain and Ireland

Mankind. Sydney, Anthropological Society of Australia

Ministry. Lesotho, All African Conference of Churches and other sponsoring bodies

Monde Non Cretien. Paris, Leenhardt

Moslem World (Muslim World) Hartford, Hartford Seminary Foundation

National Lutheran (ceased publication)

National Taiwan University Journal of Sociology. Teipei,
 National Taiwan University

Occasional Bulletin. New York, Missionary Research Library

Oceania. Sydney, University of Sydney

Pacific Affairs. Vancouver, University of British Columbia

Pacific Islands Monthly. Sydney, Pacific Publications

Pacific Journal of Theology. Apia, Conference of Pac. Churches

Plains Anthropologist. Topeka, Plains Anthropologist Corp.

Practical Anthropology. Tarrytown, Practical Anthropology

Présence Africaine. Paris, Presence Africaine

Proceedings of the American Philosophical Society. Philadelphia

Psychiatry. Washington, D.C., White Psychiatric Foundation

Public Administration Review. Washington, D.C., American
 Society for Public Administration

Public Opinion Quarterly. Princeton, Princeton Univ. Press

Quarterly Review of Biology. Washington, D.C., American
 Institute of Biological Sciences

Reformed Journal. Grand Rapids, Wm. B. Eerdmans

Religion and Society. Bangalore, Christian Institute for the
 Study of Religion and Society

Religion in Life. Nashville, Abingdon Press

Review of Religion. New York, Columbia University Press

Review of Religious Research. New York, Religious Research Assn.

Rhodes-Livingstone Institute Journal (now *African Social
 Research*) Manchester, Manchester University Press

Rural Sociology. Madison, Rural Sociology Society, University
 of Wisconsin

Science. Lancaster, Amer. Assn. for the Advancement of Science

Science News. Washington. D.C., Science Service Inc.

Scientific American. New York, Scientific American Inc.

Scientific Monthly. Washington, D.C., American Association for the Advancement of Science

Social Forces. Chapel Hill, University of North Carolina Press

Social Process. Honolulu, Univ. of Hawaii Sociology Club

Social Research. New York, New York School for Social Research

Sociological Review. London, Sociological Society

Sociologus. Berlin, Duncker & Humbolt

Sociology and Social Research. Los Angeles, University of California

Sociometry. Washington, D.C., American Sociological Ass'n.

South African Journal of Science. Johannesburg, South African Association for the Advancement of Science

South East Asia Journal of Theology. Singapore, Association of Theological Schools in South East Asia

South Pacific. Sydney, Australian School of Pac. Administration

Southwestern Journal of Anthropology. Albuquerque, University of New Mexico

Student World. Geneva, World Student Christian Federation

The Writer. Washington, D.C., The American University

Thoria. Lund, C.W.K. Gleerups Forlag

Transactions of the Fiji Society. Suva,

Union List of Periodicals in Libraries of Southern California. Riverside, Central Magazine Co.

World Dominion (now *Frontier*) London, World Dominion Press

World Today. London, Oxford University Press

World Vision Magazine. Monrovia, World Vision International

REFERENCE LIST OF SYMPOSIA AND OTHER WORKS
CITED IN THIS BIBLIOGRAPHY

Anderson 1964 — *Urbanism and Urbanization*, Leiden, E. J. Brill

Baëta 1968 — *Christianity in Tropical Africa*, London, Oxford University Press

Banton 1965 — *The Relevance of Models for Social Anthropology*, New York, F. Praeger

Banton 1966 a — *The Social Anthropology of Complex Societies*, New York, F. Praeger

Banton 1966 b — *Anthropological Approaches to the Study of Religion*, New York, F. Praeger

Bascom & Herskovits 1959 — *Continuity and Change in African Societies*, Chicago Univ. of Chicago Press

Beattie & Middleton 1969 — *Spirit Mediumship and Society in Africa*, New York, Africana Publishing Corporation

Boas 1938 — *General Anthropology*, Boston, D. C. Heath

Boas 1940 — *Race, Language and Culture*, New York, Macmillan Co.

Bohannan and Dalton 1965 — *Markets in Africa*, New York, Natural History Library

Bohannan & Plog 1967 — *Beyond the Frontier*, New York, Natural History Press

Bohannan & Middleton 1968 — *Marriage, Family and Residence*, New York, Natural History Press

Calverton 1931 — *The Making of Man*, New York, Modern Library

Cohen 1968 — *Man in Adaptation: The Cultural Present*, Chicago, Aldine Publishing Co.

Coughlin 1960 — *Double Identity: The Chinese in Modern Thailand*, Hong Kong, Hong Kong Univ. Press

Dalton 1967 — *Tribal and Peasant Economies*, New York, Natural History Press

Dalton 1971 — *Economic Development & Social Change*, New York, Natural History Press

Diamond 1964 — *Culture in History*, New York, Columbia Univ. Press

Dundes 1968 — *Every Man His Way*, Englewood Cliffs, Prentice-Hall

Evans-Pritchard 1954 · *The Institutions of Primitive Society,* Oxford, Blackwell

Fortes & Dieterlen 1965 · *African Systems of Thought,* London, Oxford Univ. Press

Freedman 1967 · *Social Organization,* Chicago, Aldine Publishing Co.

Goldenweiser 1946 · *Anthropology,* New York, F. S. Crofts & Co.

Gutkind 1970 · *The Passing of Tribal Man in Africa,* Leiden, E. J. Brill

Hammond 1964 · *Cultural & Social Anthropology,* New York, Macmillan Co.

Harding & Wallace 1970 · *Cultures of the Pacific,* New York, The Free Press

Haring 1956 · *Personal Character and Cultural Milieu,* Syracuse, Syracuse University Press

Hayward 1963 · *African Independent Church Movements,* London, Edinburgh House Press

Hoebel, Jennings & Smith 1955 · *Readings in Anthropology,* New York, McGraw-Hill Book Co.

Hormann 1956 · *Community Forces in Hawaii,* Honolulu, Univ. Sociol. Club

Hunt 1967 · *Personalities & Cultures,* New York, Natural History Press

Hymes 1961 · *Language in Culture and Society,* New York, Harper & Row

Kaplan 1961 · *Studying Personality Cross-Culturally,* New York, Harper & Row

Keesing 1963 · *Cultural Anthropology,* New York, Holt, Rinehart & Winston

Kluckhorn & Murray 1969 · *Personality in Nature, Society & Culture,* New York, A. A. Knopf

Kroeber 1953 · *Anthropology Today,* Chicago, Univ. of Chicago Press

Kroeber & Waterman 1946 · *Source Book in Anthropology,* New York, Harcourt, Brace & Co.

Leacock 1958 · "Social Stratification & Evolutionary Theory" *Ethnohistory* 5 (Whole of No. 3)

Lessa & Vogt 1958 · *Reader in Comparative Religion,* Evanston, Row Peterson & Co. (1st Ed)

Lessa & Vogt 1965 · *Reader in Comparative Religion,* New York, Harper & Row (2nd Ed)

Lewis 1965 · *French-Speaking Africa: The Search for Identity,* New York, Walker & Co.

Linton 1945 · *The Science of Man in the World Crisis,* New York, Columbia Univ. Press

Madan & Sarana 1962	*Indian Anthropology,* Bombay, Asia Publishing Co.
Mandelbaum 1958	*Selected Writings of Edward Sapir in Language, Culture & Personality,* Berkeley, Univ. of California Press
Mandelbaum et al 1963 a	*The Teaching of Anthropology,* Berkeley, Univ. of California Press
Mandelbaum et al 1963 b	*Resources for the Teaching of Anthropology,* Berkeley, Univ. of California Press
Manners 1964	*Process & Pattern in Culture,* Chicago, Aldine Publishing Co.
Marriott 1955	*Village India,* Chicago, University of Chicago Press
Middleton 1967 a	*Gods & Rituals,* New York, Natural History Press
Middleton 1967 b	*Myth & Cosmos,* New York, Natural History Press
Middleton 1970 a	*Magic, Witchcraft and Curing,* New York, Natural History Press
Middleton 1970 b	*From Child to Adult,* New York, Natural History Press
Miner 1967	*The City in Modern Africa,* New York, F. A. Praeger
Naroll & Cohen 1970	*A Handbook of Method in Cultural Anthropology,* New York, Natural History Press
Nijhoff 1968	*Urbanization in Developing Countries,* The Hague, International Union of Local Authorities
Ottenberg 1960	*Cultures and Societies in Africa,* New York, Random House
Redfield 1962	*Papers of Robert Redfield,* Chicago, Univ. of Chicago Press
Shapiro 1956	*Man, Culture & Society,* New York, Oxford Univ. Press
Spencer 1954	*Method & Perspective in Anthropology,* Minneapolis, Univ. of Minnesota
Spier 1960	*Language, Culture & Personality,* Salt Lake City, Univ. of Utah Press
Spiro 1965	*Context and Meaning in Cultural Anthropology,* New York, The Free Press
Srinivas 1960	*Indian's Villages,* Bombay, Asia Publishing House
Swartz 1968	*Local Level Politics,* Chicago, Aldine Publishing Co.
Tax 1964	*Horizons of Anthropology,* Chicago, Aldine Publishing Co.
Tippett 1967	*Solomon Islands Christianity,* London, Lutterworth Press

Tippett 1968   *Fiji Material Culture*, Honolulu,
                        Bishop Museum Press
Tippett 1970   *Peoples of Southwest Ethiopia*, South
                        Pasadena, William Carey Library
van den Berghe 1965   *Africa: Social Problems of Change &
                        Conflict*, San Francisco, Chandler
                        Publishing Co.
Vayda 1968   *People & Cultures of the Pacific*,
                        New York, Natural History Press
Vayda 1969   *Environment and Cultural Behavior*,
                        New York, Natural History Press
Whiteford 1960   *Teaching Anthropology*, Beloit, Logan
                        Museum of Anthropology
Wolstenholme & O'Conner *Man & Africa*, Boston, Little, Brown
   1965   & Co.
Yinger 1957   *Religion, Society & the Individual*,
                        New York, Macmillan Co.

ABBREVIATIONS

The following abbreviations will be found
mainly in the titles of journals cited.

Abnorm.	Abnormal	Mod.	Modern
Afr.	Africa(n)	Nat.	National
Amer.	American	Op.	Opinion
Anth.	Anthropology,	Organ.	Organization
	Anthropological	Pac.	Pacific
Appl.	Applied	Philos.	Philosophical
Assn.	Association	Pol.	Politics, Political
Behav.	Behavior,	Prac.	Practical
	Behavioral	Proc.	Proceedings,Process
Bib.	Biblical	Psych.	Psychology,
Brit.	British		Psychological
Bull.	Bulletin	Pub.	Public
Bur.	Bureau	Qr.,Quar.	Quarterly
Cath.	Catholic	Rel.	Religion(s)
Ch.	Chapter		Relations
Chg.	Change	Res.	Research
CICOP	Catholic Inter-	Rev.	Review
	American Cooperat-	Roy.	Royal
	ion Program	Sci.	Science
Compar.	Comparative	S.C.M.	Student Christian
Cult.	Culture		Movement
Curr.	Current	Soc.	Social, Society
Dept.	Department	Sociol.	Sociology,
Devel.	Development		Sociological
Econ.	Economic	S.P.C.K.	Society for the Pro-
Ed.	Editor		motion of Christian
E.M.Q.	Evangelical Missions		Knowledge
	Quarterly	Stud.	Student
Gen.	General	SW.	Southwestern
Hist.	History, Historical	Theol.	Theology
H.R.A.F.	Human Relations Area	Trans.	Translator,
	Files		Transactions
Hum.	Human	U.C.L.A.	University of Calif-
Inst.	Institute		ornia,Los Angeles
Inter.	International	U.C.P.A.A.E.	University of
I.R.M.	International Review		California Piblic-
	of Missions		ations in American
Isl.	Islands		Arcgaeology and
Journ.,Jr.	Journal		Ethnology
M.I.T.	Massachusetts Insti-	Univ.	University
	tute of Technology		

General Reference Works

CYCLOPEDIAS AND DICTIONARIES

BIBLIOGRAPHIES

GENERAL ANTHROPOLOGICAL WORKS

Single Society Studies
Comparative Studies

CYCLOPEDIAS AND DICTIONARIES

ASHMORE, H.S. (ed.)
1962   *Encyclopedia Britannica.* Chicago, Encyclopaedia
Britannica Inc. 24 Vols.

COMMITTEE ROYAL ANTHROPOLOGICAL INSTITUTE
1964   *Notes and Queries on Anthropology.* London,
Routledge & Kegan Paul (Bibliography 369-385)

FERM, VERGILIUS (ed.)
1964   *An Encyclopedia of Religion.* Paterson, Littlefield, Adams & Co.

FUNK & WAGNALL
1949   *Funk & Wagnall's Standard Dictionary of Folklore,
Mythology and Legend.* New York, Funk & Wagnall
2 Vol.

HASTINGS, J. (ed.)
1925   *Encyclopedia of Religion and Ethics.* Edinburgh,
T. & T. Clark 13 Vols.

1951   *Encyclopedia of Religion & Ethics.* New York,
Scribners 3 Vols.

JOBES, G.
1961   *Dictionary of Mythology, Folklore and Symbols.*
New York, Scarecrow Press

MANDELBAUM, D.G., G.W. LASKER & E.M. ALBERT (eds.)
1963   *Resources for Teaching Anthropology.* Berkeley,
University of California Press (See Beckham)

MURDOCK, G.P.
1958   *Outline of World Cultures.* New Haven, Human
Relations Area Files

1961   *Outline of Cultural Materials.* New Haven, Human
Relations Area Files

PIKE, E.R.
1951   *Encyclopedia of Religion and Religions.* London,
Allen & Unwin

ROBBINS, R.H.
1959   *The Encyclopedia of Witchcraft and Demonology.*
New York, Crown Publishers

ROBINSON, M.S. & K. WILSON
1962   *The Encyclopedia of Myths and Legends of All
Nations.* London, Ward & Co.

SELIGMAN, E.R.A. (ed.)
1948   *Encyclopaedia of the Social Sciences.* London,
The Macmillan Co. 15 Vols.

SILLS, D.L.
1968   *International Encyclopedia of the Social Sciences.*
New York, The Macmillan Co. and Free Press 13 Vol.

SPENCE, L.
1960   *An Encyclopedia of Occultism.* New Hyde Park, New
York University

WINICK, CHAS.
1958   *Dictionary of Anthropology.* Ames, Littlefield,
Adams & Co.

ZAEHNER, R.C. (ed.)
1959   *The Concise Encyclopedia of Living Faiths.*
London, Hutchinson

BIBLIOGRAPHIES

AMERICAN UNIVERSITIES FIELD STAFF
1960   *A Select Bibliography: Asia, Africa, Eastern
Europe, Latin America.* New York, No. Amer. Univ.
Field Staff

BAYITCH, S.A.
1967   *Latin America and the Caribbean: A Bibliographical
Guide to Works in English.* Coral Gables, Univ.
of Miami Press

BECKHAM, R.S. & M.P.
1963   "Basic List of Books and Periodicals" in
Mandelbaum et al., 1963   85-316

BERKOWITZ, M.I. & J.E. JOHNSON
　　1967　　*Social Scientific Studies of Religion: A Bibliography*. Pittsburg, Univ. of Pittsburg Press

BLEEKER, C.J. & S. ALICH
　　1964　　*International Bibliography of the History of Religions*. Leiden, E.J. Brill

BOHANNAN, P. & F. PLOG (eds.)
　　1967　　*Beyond the Frontier: Social Process and Culture Change*. New York, Natural History Press, Bibliography 381-400

CAMMACK, F.M. & S. SAITO
　　1962　　*Pacific Island Bibliography*. New York, The Scarecrow Press

COMMITTEE COMMEMORATING HANAYAMA'S 65th BIRTHDAY
　　1960　　*Bibliography on Buddhism*. Tokyo, Hokuseido

CONOVER, HELEN F.
　　1963　　*Africa South of the Sahara: A Selected, Annotated List of Writings*. Washington, D.C., Library of Congress

COUNCIL OF THE AFRICAN-AMERICAN INSTITUTE
　　　　　　See "Matthews"

CURRENT ANTHROPOLOGY
　　　　　　"Current Publications" - Regular feature, geographically classified and covering articles in major international journals

DALTON, GEORGE (ed.)
　　1967　　*Tribal and Peasant Economies*. New York, Natural History Press, Bibliographical Essay, 539-546, Bibliography, 547-564

　　1971　　*Economic Development and Social Change*. New York, Natural History Press, Bibliography, 619-651

DEVANANDAN, PAUL
　　1961　　*A Bibliography on Hinduism*. Bangalore, Christian Institute for the Study of Religion and Society

DUIGNAN, PETER
　　1967　　*Handbook of American Resources for African Studies*. Stanford, Stanford University

FORDE, DARYLL
　　1956　　*Select Annotated Bibliography of Tropical Africa*. New York, Survey of Tropical Africa

GIBSON, G.D.
1960   "A Bibliography of Anthropological Bibliographies"
            Curr. Anth. 1   61-75

GLAZIER, K.M.
1969   *Africa South of the Sahara: A Select and Annotated
            Bibliography, 1954-1968.* Stanford, Hoover Insti-
            tution Press

GROPP, A.E.
1968   *A Bibliography of Latin American Bibliographies.*
            Metuchen, N.J., The Scarecrow Press

HANDBOOK OF LATIN AMERICAN STUDIES
            Gainesville, University of Florida Press.
            Bibliographical Serial.

HOBBS, CECIL
1956   *Indochina: A Bibliography of the Land and People.*
            New York, Greenwood Press

HONIGMAN, JOHN J.
1967   *Personality in Culture.* New York, Harper & Row,
            Bibliography 427-474

HUNT, ROBT. (ed.)
1967   *Personality and Cultures.* New York, Natural
            History Press, Bibliography 400-420

HYMES, DELL
1964   *Language in Culture and Society.* New York, Harper
            & Row, Bibliography 711-749

INTERNATIONAL BIBLIOGRAPHY OF THE HISTORY OF RELIGIONS
            Leiden, E.J. Brill.   This is a serial.

KEESING, FELIX M.
1953   *Culture Change: An Analysis and Bibliography of
            Anthropological Sources to 1952.* Stanford,
            Stanford University Press

1963   *Cultural Anthropology.* New York, Holt, Rinehart &
            Winston, Bibliography 433-456, also a useful
            Glossary 426-432

KENNEDY, RAYMOND
1945   *Bibliography of Indonesian Peoples and Cultures.*
            New Haven, Human Relations Area Files (Revised in
            1962 by Maretzki & Fischer)

LA BARRE, WESTON
1971   "Materials for a History of Studies of Crisis
        Cults: A Bibliographic Essay" with critical
        comment, *Curr. Anth.* 12   3-44

LEESON, I.
1952   *Bibliography of Cargo Cults & Other Nativistic
        Movements in the South Pacific.* Noumea, South
        Pacific Commission

LESSA, WM. A. & E.Z. VOGT (eds.)
1965   *Reader in Comparative Religion: An Anthropological
        Approach.* New York, Harper & Row, "Selected Mono-
        graphs on Non-western Systems" and "General Bibli-
        ography" 640-653

LUZBETAK, L.J.
1963   *The Church and Cultures.* Techny, Divine Word
        Publishers, Topical and General Bibliographies
        357-409

MARETZKI & FISCHER
        See Raymond Kennedy

MATTHEWS, D.G. (ed.)
1967   *African Affairs for the General Reader: A Selected
        and Introductory Bibliographical Guide.* New York,
        Council of the African-American Institute

MIDDLETON, JOHN (ed.)
1967   *Gods and Rituals.* New York, Natural History Press,
        Bibliography   437-450

1970   *From Child to Adult.* New York, Natural History
        Press, Bibliography   327-344

MITCHELL, R.C. & H.W. TURNER
1966   *A Bibliography of Modern African Religious Move-
        ments.* Evanston, Northwestern University Press

MURDOCK, G.P.
1960   *Ethnographic Bibliography of North America.* New
        Haven, Human Relations Area Files

O'LEARY, T.J.
1963   *Ethnographic Bibliography of South America.* New
        Haven, Human Relations Area Files

1970   "Ethnographic Bibliographies" in Naroll & Cohen
        1970   128-146

SHULMAN, F.J.
1970   *Japan & Korea: Annotated Bibliography of Doctoral Dissertations*. Chicago, American Library Ass'n.

SIMMS, RUTH P.
1965   *Urbanization in West Africa: A Review of Current Literature*. Evanston, Northwestern University Press, Annotated Bibliography 63-109

SMALLEY, WM. A.
1960   *Selected and Annotated Bibliography of Anthropology for Missionaries. Occas. Bull.* 11, whole number

STEWARD, JULIAN H. (ed.)
1963   *Handbook of South American Indians*. New York, Cooper Square Publishers, for Smithsonian Institution, Bureau of American Ethnology 7 Vols. Each volume has a bibliography.

STUCKI, C.W.
1963   *American Doctoral Dissertations on Asia, 1933-1962*. Ithica, Cornell University

TAYLOR, C.R.H.
1965   *A Pacific Bibliography*. Wellington, Polynesian Society

Union List of Periodicals in Libraries of Southern California. Riverside, Central Magazine Co.

VERHAEGEN, P.
1962   "Bibliographie de l'Urbanisation de l'Afrique Noire: Son cadre ses causes et ses consequences economique, sociale et culturelles" *Enquetes Bibliographiques*, 9 (Centre de Documentation Economique et Sociale Africaine)

VON FURER HAIMENDORF, E.
1958   *An Anthropological Bibliography of South Africa*. The Hague, Mouton

WALLACE, ANTHONY F.C.
1966   *Religion: An Anthropological View*. New York, Random House   Bibliography 271-290

GENERAL ANTHROPOLOGICAL WORKS

BARNETT, H.G.
  1953   *Innovation: The Basis of Cultural Change.* New
           York, McGraw-Hill Book Co.   Now in paperback

BEALS, R.L. & H. HOIJER
  1954   *An Introduction to Anthropology.* New York, The
           Macmillan Co.

BEALS, ALAN R.
  1967   *Culture in Process.* New York, Holt, Rinehart &
           Winston

BOAS, FRANZ et al.
  1938   *General Anthropology.* Boston, D.C. Heath & Co.

BROWN, INA CORINNE
  1963   *Understanding Other Cultures.* Englewood Cliffs,
           Prentice-Hall Inc.

CALVERTON, V.F.
  1931   *The Making of Man: An Outline of Anthropology.*
           New York, Random House (The Modern Library)

CHAPPLE, E.D. & C.S. COON
  1946   *Principles of Anthropology.* New York, Henry Holt
           & Co.

COHEN, YEHUDI A.
  1968   *Man in Adaptation: The Biosocial Background and
           The Cultural Present.* Chicago, Aldine Publishing
           Co.   2 Vols.

COON, CARLTON S.
  1963   *A Reader in General Anthropology.* New York, Holt,
           Rinehart and Winston.

EVANS-PRICHARD, E.E.
   1964   *Social Anthropology and Other Essays*. Glencoe,
              Free Press (Combines *Social Anthropology* and
              Essays in Social Anthropology in paperback ed.)

EVANS-PRITCHARD, E.E. (ed.)
   1954   *The Institutions of Primitive Society*. Oxford,
              Basil Blackwell

FIRTH, RAYMOND
   1958   *Human Types: An Introduction to Social Anthro-
              pology*. New York, Barnes & Noble

   1963   *Elements of Social Organization*. Boston, Beacon
              Press   Paperback BP153

GILLIN, JOHN
   1948   *The Ways of Men: An Introduction to Anthropology*.
              New York, D. Appleton-Century Co.

GOLDENWEISER, ALEXANDER
   1922   *Early Civilization: An Introduction to Anthro-
              pology*. New York, F.S. Crofts & Co.

   1946   *Anthropology: An Introduction to Primitive Culture*.
              New York, F.S. Crofts & Co.

GOLDSCHMIDT, WALTER
   1964   *Exploring the Ways of Mankind*. New York, Holt,
              Rinehart & Winston

HERSKOVITS, MELVILLE J.
   1951   *Man and His Works: The Science of Cultural Anthro-
              pology*.   New York, Alfred A. Knopf

HOEBEL, E. ADAMSON
   1958   *Man in the Primitive World: An Introduction to
              Anthropology*. New York, McGraw-Hill Book Co.

   1966   *Anthropology: The Study of Man*. New York, McGraw-
              Hill Book Co.

HOLMES, LOWELL D.
   1965   *Anthropology: An Introduction*. New York, The
              Ronald Press

HONIGMANN, JOHN J.
   1963   *Understanding Culture*. New York, Harper & Row

KEESING, FELIX
   1963   *Cultural Anthropology: The Science of Custom*.
              New York, Holt, Rinehart & Winston

KLUCKHOHN, CLYDE
  1969   *Mirror for Man: The Relation of Anthropology to Modern Life*. New York, Whittlesey House

KROEBER, A.L.
  1948   *Anthropology*. New York, Harcourt, Brace & Co.

KROEBER, A.L. & T.T. WATERMAN
  1931   *Sourcebook in Anthropology*. New York, Harcourt, Brace & Co.

LINTON, RALPH
  1936   *The Study of Man*. New York, Appleton-Century-Crofts

  1955   *The Tree of Culture*. New York, Alfred A. Knopf

LOWIE, ROBT. H.
  1920   *Primitive Society*. New York, Horace Liveright

  1946   *An Introduction to Cultural Anthropology*. New York, Rinehart & Co. Inc.

  1961   *Primitive Society*. New York, Harper & Bros. Torchbook Edition   Originally printed 1920

MARETT, R.R.
  n/d   *Anthropology*. New York, Henry Holt

MORGAN, LEWIS HENRY
  1963   *Ancient Society*. Cleveland, World Publishing Co. Originally published 1877

MURDOCK, GEORGE PETER
  1965   *Culture and Society*. Pittsburgh, Univ. of Pittsburgh Press

RAPPORT, SAMUEL & HELEN WRIGHT (eds.)
  1967   *Anthropology*. New York, New York Univ. Press

SHAPIRO, HARRY L.
  1960   *Man, Culture and Society*. New York, Oxford Univ. Press

SMITH, ALLAN H. & JOHN L. FISCHER (eds.)
  1970   *Anthropology*. Englewood Cliffs, Prentice-Hall,Inc.

TAX, SOL (ed.)
  1964   *Horizons of Anthropology*. Chicago, Aldine Publishing Co.

TITIEV, MISCHA
1958   *Introduction to Cultural Anthropology*. New York,
          Holt, Rinehart & Winston

WOLF, ERIC R.
1964   *Anthropology*. Englewood Cliffs, Prentice-Hall Inc.

SELECT   LIST

OF

SINGLE SOCIETY STUDIES

ASHTON, HUGH
1952   *The Basuto*. London, International African Inst.

BANTON, MICHAEL P.
1957   *West African City: A Study of Tribal Life in
          Freetown*. London, Oxford Univ. Press

BARNETT, H.G.
1960   *Being a Palauan*. New York, Holt, Rinehart &
          Winston

BASCOM, WILLIAM
1969   *The Yoruba of Southwestern Nigeria*. New York,
          Holt,Rinehart & Winston

BATESON, GREGORY
1958   *Naven, a Survey of Problems....of a New Guinea
          Tribe, drawn from three points of view*. Stanford,
          Stanford Univ. Press

BEALS, ALAN R.
1965   *Gopalpur: A South Indian Village*. New York, Holt,
          Rinehart & Winston

BEATTIE, JOHN
1966   *Bunyoro: An African Kingdom*. New York, Holt,
          Rinehart & Winston

BEIDELMAN, T.O.
1971   *The Kaguru: A Matrilineal People of East Africa*.
          New York, Holt, Rinehart & Winston

BELO, JANE
1949   *Bali: Rangda and Barong*. New York, Augustin
          American Ethnol. Soc. Monograph 16

BOISSEVAIN, JEREMY F.
1969   *Hal-farrug: A Village in Malta.* New York, Holt,
          Rinehart & Winston

BUCK, P.H.
1954   *Vikings of the Sunrise.* Christchurch, Whitcombe &
          Tombs (In U.S.:*Vikings of the Pacific.* Chicago,
          Univ. of Chicago Press 1959)

BUECHER, HANS C.
1971   *Bolivian Aymara.* New York, Holt, Rinehart &
          Winston

BUNZEL, RUTH
1952   *Chichicastenango: A Guatemalan Village.* Seattle,
          Univ. of Washington Press

CHAGNON, N.A.
1968   *Yanomano: The Fierce People.* New York, Holt,
          Rinehart & Winston

CHANCE, N.A.
1966   *The Eskimo of North Alaska.* New York, Holt,
          Rinehart & Winston

CODRINGTON, R.H.
1891   *The Melanesians: Studies in their Anthropology &
          Folk-lore.* Oxford, Clarendon Press

COHEN, RONALD
1967   *The Kanuri of Bornu.* New York, Holt, Rinehart &
          Winston

CULSHAW, W.J.
1949   *Tribal Heritage: A Study of the Santals.* London,
          Lutterworth Press

DENTAN, R.K.
1968   *The Semai: A Non-Violent People of Malaya.*
          New York, Holt, Rinehart & Winston

DIAMOND, NORMA
1969   *K'un Shen: A Taiwan Village.* New York, Holt,
          Rinehart & Winston

DIAZ, M.N.
1970   *Tonala: Conservatism, Responsibility & Authority
          in a Mexican Town.* Berkeley, Univ. of California
          Press

DOWNS, JAMES F.
1966   *The Two Worlds of the Washo.* New York, Holt,
            Rinehart & Winston

DOZIER, EDWARD P.
1966   *Hano: A Tewa Indian Community in Arizona.* New
            York, Holt, Rinehart & Winston

1967   *The Kalinga of North Luzon.* New York, Holt,
            Rinehart & Winston

DUBE, S.C.
1967   *Indian Village.* New York, Harper & Row

DU BOIS, CORA
1944   *The People of Alor: A Socio-Psychological Study of
            an East Indian Island.* Minneapolis, Univ. of
            Minnesota Press (Harvard Univ. Press update: 1960)

DU PRE, CAROLE
1968   *The Luo of Kenya: An Annotated Bibliography.*
            Washington, D.C., Inst. of Cross-Cultural Research

DUNN, STEPHEN P. & E.
1967   *The Peasants of Central Russia.* New York, Holt,
            Rinehart & Winston

EDEL, MAY
1957   *The Chiga of Western Uganda.* New York, Oxford
            Univ. Press

EKVALL, ROBERT B.
1968   *Fields on the Hoof: Nexus of Tibetan Nomadic
            Pastoralism.* New York, Holt, Rinehart & Winston

ELKIN, A.P.
1954   *The Australian Aborigines and How to Understand
            Them.* Sydney, Angus & Robertson

EMBREE, JOHN FEE
1939   *Suye Mura: a Japanese Village.* Chicago, Univ. of
            Chicago Press

EVANS-PRITCHARD, E.E.
1940   *The Nuer: A Description of the Modes of Livelihood
            and Political Institutions of a Nilotic People.*
            Oxford, Clarendon Press

FARON, LOUIS C.
1968   *The Mapuche of Chile.* New York, Holt, Rinehart
            & Winston

FIRTH, RAYMOND
1957   *We, the Tikopia: A Sociological Study of Kinship in Primitive Polynesia.* London, Allen & Unwin

FOSTER, GEORGE M.
1967   *Tzintzuntzan: Mexican Peasants in a Changing World.* Boston, Little, Brown & Co.

FRASER, THOS. M. JR.
1966   *Fishermen of South Thailand.* New York, Holt, Rinehart & Winston

FRIEDL, ERNESTINE
1964   *Vasilika: A Village in Modern Greece.* New York, Holt, Rinehart & Winston

FUKUTAKE, TADASHI
1967   *Japanese Rural Society.* Tokyo, Oxford Univ.Press

GAMST, FREDERICK C.
1969   *The Qemant: A Pagan:Hebraic Peasantry in Ethiopia.* New York, Holt, Rinehart & Winston

GEDDES, W.R.
1957   *Nine Dyak Nights.* Melbourne, Oxford Univ. Press

GREEN, M.M.
1947   *Ibo Village Affairs, chiefly with reference to the Village of Umueke Agbaja.* London, Sidgwick & Jackson

HALPERN, J.M.
1956   *A Serbian Village.* New York, Columbia Univ. Press

HART, C.W.M., & ARNOLD R. PILLING
1962   *The Tiwi of North Australia.* New York, Holt, Rinehart & Winston

HENRY, JULES
1964   *Jungle People: A Kaingang Tribe of the Highlands of Brazil.* New York, Vintage Books

HERSKOVITS, M.J.
1971   *Life in a Haitian Valley.* New York, Doubleday & Co. (Originally published: 1937)

HITCHCOCK, JOHN T.
1966   *The Magyars of Banyan Hill.* New York, Holt, Rinehart & Winston

HOEBEL, A. ADAMSON
1966   *The Cheyennes: Indians of the Great Plains.* New
            York, Holt, Rinehart & Winston

HOGBIN, IAN
1964   *A Guadalcanal Society: The Koaka Speakers.* New
            York, Holt, Rinehart & Winston

HOSTETLER, J.A. & G.E. HUNTINGTON
1967   *The Hutterites of North America.* New York, Holt,
            Rinehart & Winston

HUNTINGFORD, G.W.B.
1953   *The Nandi of Kenya: Tribal Control in a Pastoral
            Society.* London, Routledge & Kegan Paul

1955   *The Galla of Ethiopia: the Kingdoms of Kafa and
            Janjero.* London, International African Institute

HUXLEY, FRANCIS
1957   *Affable Savages: An Anthropologist Among the Urubu
            Indians of Brazil.* New York, Capricorn Books

JENNESS, DIAMOND
1959   *People of the Twilight.* Chicago, Chicago Univ.
            Press

JUNOD, HENRI ALEXANDRE
1927   *The Life of a South African Tribe.* London, Mac-
            millan Co. Reprint:1962,New York, University Books

KEISER, R. LINCOLN
1969   *The Vice Lords: Warriors of the Streets.* New York,
            Holt, Rinehart & Winston

KLIMA, GEORGE J.
1970   *The Barabaig: East African Cattle-Herders.* New
            York, Holt, Rinehart & Winston

KLUCKHOHN, C. & D. LEIGHTON
1946   *The Navaho.* Cambridge, Harvard Univ. Press

KROEBER, A.L.
1928   *Peoples of the Philippines.* New York, American
            Museum of Natural History

1953   *Handbook of the Indians of California.* Berkeley,
            California Book Co.

KUPER, HILDA
1964   *The Swazi: A South African Kingdom.* New York,
            Holt, Rinehart & Winston

LA BARRE, WESTON
   1948   *The Aymara Indians of the Lake Titicaca Plateau, Bolivia.* Menasha, Amer. Anth. Assn. Memoir 68

LESSA, WM. A.
   1966   *Ulithi: A Micronesian Design for Living.* New York, Holt, Rinehart & Winston

LEWIS, OSCAR
   1951   *Life in a Mexican Village: Tepoztlan Restudied.* Urbana, Univ. of Illinois Press

   1960   *Tepoztlan: A Village in Mexico.* New York, Holt, Rinehart & Winston

   1965   *Village Life in North India: Studies in a Delhi Village.* New York, Vintage Books

LEYBURN, J.G.
   1941   *The Haitian People.* New Haven, Yale Univ. Press

LITTLE, K.L.
   1951   *The Mende of Sierra Leone: A West African People in Transition.* London, Routledge & Kegan Paul

LOWIE, R.H.
   1956   *The Crow Indians.* New York, Rinehart (Originally published 1935)

LYSTAD, ROBERT A.
   1958   *The Ashanti: A Proud People.* New Brunswick, N.J., Rutgers Univ. Press

MADSEN, WM.
   1964   *The Mexican-Americans of South Texas.* New York, Holt, Rinehart & Winston

MARRIOT, McKIM (ed.)
   1955   *Village India: Studies in the Little Community.* Chicago, Univ. of Chicago Press (Amer. Anth. Assn. Memoir 83)

MARWICK, BRIAN A.
   1940   *The Swazi: An Ethnographic Account of the Natives of the Swaziland Protectorate.* Cambridge, The University Press

MESSENGER, JOHN C.
   1969   *Inis Beag: Isle of Ireland.* New York, Holt, Rinehart & Winston

MIDDLETON, JOHN
   1965   *The Lugbara of Uganda,* New York, Holt, Rinehart & Winston

MINER, H.M.
1949   *St. Denis: A French-Canadian Parish.* Chicago,
           Univ. of Chicago Press

NEWMAN, PHILIP L.
1965   *Knowing the Gururumba.* New York, Holt, Rinehart
           & Winston

NORBECK, EDWARD
1954   *Takashima, a Japanese Fishing Community.* Salt
           Lake City, Univ. of Utah Press

1966   *Changing Japan.* New York, Holt, Rinehart &
           Winston

NURGE, ETHEL
1965   *Life in a Leyte Village.* Seattle, Univ. of
           Washington Press

OLIVER, D.L.
1955   *A Solomon Island Society: Kinship and Leadership
           among the Siuai of Bougainville.* Cambridge,
           Harvard Univ. Press

OPLER, MORRIS E.
1969   *Apache Odyssey: A Journey Between Two Worlds.*
           New York, Holt, Rinehart & Winston

OSGOOD, CORNELIUS
1951   *The Koreans and Their Culture.* New York, Ronald
           Press

PIERCE, JOE. E.
1964   *Life in a Turkish Village.* New York, Holt,
           Rinehart & Winston

POSPISIL, LEONARD
1963   *The Kapauku Papauans of West New Guinea.* New York,
           Holt, Rinehart & Winston

POWDERMAKER, H.
1971   *Life in Lisu: The Sutdy of a Melanesian Society in
           New Ireland.* New York, Norton & Co. (Originally
           published 1933)

RADIN, PAUL
1923   *The Winnebago Tribe.* Washington,D.C., U.S. Bur.
           of Amer. Ethn.

RADCLIFFE-BROWN, A.R.
    1948   *The Andaman Islanders.* Glencoe, Free Press
                (Originally published 1922)

RATTRAY, R.S.
    1956   *Ashanti.* Oxford, Clarendon Press (Originally
                published 1923)

REDFIELD, ROBT.
    1930   *Tepoztlan, a Mexican Village: A Study of Folk Life.*
                Chicago, Univ. of Chicago Press

    1941   *The Folk Culture of Yucatan.* Chicago, Univ. of
                Chicago Press

    1950   *A Village that Chose Progress: Chan Kom Revisited.*
                Chicago, Univ. of Chicago Press

RICHARDSON, MILES
    1970   *San Pedro, Colombia: Small Town in a Developing
                Society.* New York, Holt, Rinehart & Winston

RIVERS, W.H.R.
    1906   *The Todas.* London, Macmillan & Co.

    1914   *The History of Melanesian Society.* Cambridge,
                The University Press

SASAKI, TOM
    1960   *Fruitland, New Mexico: A Navaho Community in
                Transition.* Ithica, Cornell Univ. Press

SCOTT, SIR J.G.
    1910   *The Burman: His Life and Notions.* by Shway Yoe,
                London, Macmillan & Co.

SERVICE, E.R. & H.S.
    1954   *Tobati: Paraguayan Town.* Chicago, Univ. of
                Chicago Press

SHEPARDSON, MARY & BLODWEN HAMMOND
    1970   *The Navajo Mountain Community.* Berkeley, Univ. of
                California Press

SMITH, THOMAS L.
    1954   *Brazil: People and Institutions.* Baton Rouge,
                Louisiana State Univ. Press

SPENCER, BALDWIN & F.J. GILLEN
    1927   *The Arunta: A Study of a Stone Age People.* London,
                Macmillan & Co.

SPENCER, PAUL
1965   *The Samburu: A Study of Gerontocracy in a Nomadic
            Tribe.* Berkeley, Univ. of California Press

SPIRO, MELFORD E.
1956   *Kibbutz: Venture in Utopia.* Cambridge, Harvard
            Univ. Press

1958   *Children of the Kibbutz.* Cambridge, Harvard Univ.
            Press

STERN, THEODORE
1965   *The Klamath Tribe, A People and Their Reservation.*
            Seattle, Univ. of Washington Press

SUGGS, R.C.
1960   *The Island Civilizations of Polynesia.* New York,
            The American Library

TRIGGER, BRUCE G.
1969   *The Huron: Farmers of the North.* New York, Holt,
            Rinehart & Winston

TSCHOPIK, HARRY
1951   *The Aymara of Chucuito, Peru.* New York, Anthrop.
            Papers of the Amer. Museum of Nat. Hist. 44

UCHENDU, VICTOR C.
1965   *The Igbo of Southeast Nigeria.* New York, Holt,
            Rinehart & Winston

UNDERHILL, RUTH
1956   *The Navajos.* Norman, Univ. of Oklahoma Press

VOGT, EVON Z.
1970   *The Zinacantecos of Mexico: A Modern Maya Way of
            Life.* New York, Holt, Rinehart & Winston

VON FÜRER-HAIMENDORF, CHRISTOPH
1969   *The Konyak Nagas: An Indian Frontier Tribe.*
            New York, Holt, Rinehart & Winston

WAGLEY, CHARLES
1941   *Economics of the Guatemalan Village.* Menasha,
            Amer. Anth. Assn. Memoir 58

1953   *Amazon Town: a Study of Man in the Tropics.*
            New York, Macmillan & Co.

1959   *The Social and Religious Life in a Guatemalan
            Village.* Menasha, Amer. Anth. Assn. Memoir 71

WARNER, W.L.
1958   *A Black Civilization: A Social Study of an Australian Tribe.* New York, Harper & Row

WILLIAMS, F.E.
1930   *Orokaiva Society.* London, Oxford Univ. Press

WILLIAMS, THOMAS RHYS
1966   *The Dunsun: A North Borneo Society.* New York, Holt, Rinehart & Winston

WILSON, MONICA
1951   *Good Company: A Study of Nyakusa Age-Villages.* Boston, Beacon Press

WISDOM, CHARLES
1940   *The Chorti Indians of Guatemala.* Chicago, Univ. of Chicago Press

WYLIE, LAURENCE W.
1957   *Village in Vaucluse.* Cambridge, Harvard Univ. Press

YANG, CH'ING KUN
1959   *A Chinese Village in Early Communist Tradition.* Cambridge, Mass., M.I.T. distributed by Harvard Univ. Press

YANG, MOU CH'UN
1948   *A Chinese Village: Taitou, Shantung Province.* New York, Columbia University Press

ZEKIYE, ELGAR
1960   *A Punjabi Village in Pakistan.* New York, Columbia Univ. Press

COMPARATIVE STUDIES OF PEOPLES

BENEDICT, RUTH
1959   *Patterns of Culture.* Boston, Houghton Mifflin Co. Sentry Ed. SE8

BIRKET-SMITH, KAJ
1960   *Primitive Man and His Ways: Patterns of Life in Some Societies.* Cleveland, The World Publishing Co.

DOZIER, EDWARD P.
1970   *The Pueblo Indians of North America.* New York, Holt, Rinehart & Winston

FIRTH, RAYMOND
    1958   *Human Types*. New York, Barnes & Noble Inc.
                (Available in paperback)

FORDE, C. DARYLL
    1963   *Habitat, Economy and Society: A Geographical
                Introduction to Ethnology*. New York, E.P. Dutton
                & Co.

HONIGMANN, J.J.
    1958   *Three Pakistan Villages*. Chapel Hill, Inst. for
                Soc. Sci., Univ. of North Carolina

KRADER, LAWRENCE (ed.)
    1956   *Handbook of Central Asia*. New Haven, Human Rela-
                tions Area Files

KRISHNA IYER, L.A. & L.K. BALA RATNAM
    1961   *Anthropology in India*. Bombay, Bharatiya Vidya
                Bhavan

LISITZKY, GENE
    1963   *Four Ways of Being Human*. London, Dennis Dobson
                (Available in paperback)

MEAD, MARGARET
    1963   *People and Places*. New York, Bantum Books
                Pathfinder paperback HP42

MEAD, MARGARET & N. CALAS
    1953   *Primitive Heritage*. New York, Random House

MEEK, C.K.
    1925   *The Northern Tribes of Nigeria*. London, Oxford
                Univ. Press

MURDOCK, G.P.
    1947   *Our Primitive Contemporaries*. New York, The
                Macmillan Co.

SCHAPERA, ISAAC (ed.)
    1937   *The Bantu-speaking Tribes of South Africa*.
                London, Routledge

SELIGMAN, C.G.
    1957   *Races of Africa*. London, Oxford Univ. Press

SERVICE, ELMAN R.
    1958   *A Profile of Primitive Culture*. New York, Harper
                & Bros.

TAUFA, LOPETI
    1968   "Change and Continuity in Oceania" M.A. thesis,
                 School of World Mission, Fuller Theological
                 Seminary, Pasadena   (Three Oceanic Societies.
                 Applied to Mission)

TIPPETT, A.R.
    1970   *Peoples of Southwest Ethiopia.*   South Pasadena,
                 William Carey Library

TURNBULL, COLIN M.
    1971   *Tradition and Change in African Tribal Life.*
                 New York, Camelot Books   (Four Societies)

WEYER, ED. JR.
    n/d   *Primitive Peoples Today.*   New York, Doubleday &
                 Co.   Dolphin paperback C200

Anthropological Dimensions

THEORY OF ANTHROPOLOGY

SOCIAL ANTHROPOLOGY AND CULTURAL ANALYSIS

Values
Economic Anthropology
Law

PATTERNS OF LEADERSHIP AND AUTHORITY

ACCULTURATION, CULTURE CLASH AND CULTURE CHANGE

CULTURE AND PERSONALITY

APPLIED ANTHROPOLOGY

URBAN ANTHROPOLOGY

ETHNOLINGUISTICS AND COMMUNICATION

MISSIONARY ANTHROPOLOGY

BARNETT, HOMER G.
1953   *Innovation: Basis of Cultural Change.* New York,
            McGraw-Hill Book Co.

BARRETT, DAVID
1968   *Schism and Renewal in Africa.* Nairobi, Oxford
            Univ. Press

BEALS, ALAN R.
1967   *Culture in Process.* New York, Holt, Rinehart &
            Winston

BEATTIE, J.H.M.
1955   "Contemporary Trends in British Social Anthropo-
            logy" *Sociologus* 5   1-14

1964   *Other Cultures: Aims, Methods and Achievements in
            Social Anthropology.* New York, The Free Press of
            Glencoe

BENEDICT, RUTH
1934   *Patterns of Culture.* Boston, Houghton Mifflin Co.

BENNETT, JOHN W.
1944   "The Development of Ethnological Theory as illus-
            trated by Studies of the Plains Sun Dance" *Amer.
            Anth.* 46   162-181

BIDNEY, DAVID
1960   *Theoretical Anthropology.* New York, Columbia
            Univ. Press

BOAS, FRANZ (ed.)
1938   *General Anthropology.* Boston, D.C. Heath & Co.

1940   *Race, Language and Culture.* New York, Macmillan
            Co.

CALVERTON, V.F. (ed.)
1930   *The Making of Man: An Outline of Anthropology.*
            New York, The Modern Library

COHEN, YEHUDI A.
1968   *Man in Adaptation: The Cultural Present.* Chicago,
            Aldine Publishing Co.

COOPER, JOHN M.
1941   *Temporal Sequences and Marginal Cultures.*
            Washington, D.C., Catholic Univ. of America

CURRENT ANTHROPOLOGY
1971   "Urgent Anthropology" (Report of Working Group)
            Curr. Anth. 12   243-254

DIAMOND, S. (ed.)
1960   *Culture in History: Essays in Honour of Paul Radin.*
            New York, Columbia Univ. Press

DORSON, R.M.
1963   "Current Folklore Theories" *Curr. Anth.* 4 93-112

DRIVER, H.E.
1966   "Geographical-Historical versus Psycho-Functional
            Explanations of Kin Avoidances" *Curr. Anth.* 7
            131-182

DU BOIS, CORA (ed.)
1960   *Lowie's Selected Papers in Anthropology.* Berkeley,
            Univ. of California Press

DUNDES, ALAN (ed.)
1968   *Every Man His Way.* Englewood Cliffs, Prentice-
            Hall Inc.

DURKHEIM, EMILE
1938   *Rules of Sociological Method.* Chicago, Free Press
            of Glencoe

ERASMUS, CHARLES J.
1961   *Man Takes Control: Cultural Development and Ameri-*
            can Aid. Minneapolis, Univ. of Minnesota Press

EVANS-PRITCHARD, E.E.
1952   *Social Anthropology and Other Essays.* New York,
            Free Press of Glencoe

1965   *Theories of Primitive Religion.* Oxford, Clarendon
            Press

FIRTH, RAYMOND
1956   *Human Types: An Introduction to Social Anthropo-*
            logy. New York, Barnes & Noble

FIRTH, RAYMOND
1963 *Elements of Social Organization*. Boston, Beacon
    Press (Originally issued 1951)

FOSTER, G.M.
1953 "What is Folk Culture?" *Amer. Anth.* 55 159-173

1965 "Peasant Society and the Image of the Good" *Amer.*
    Anth. 67 293-315

1969 *Applied Anthropology*. Boston, Little Brown & Co.

FRAZER, JAMES G.
1951 *The Golden Bough: A Study in Magic*. New York,
    Macmillan Co., or New York, Criterion 1959

FREEDMAN, MAURICE
1967 *Social Organization: Essays Presented to Raymond*
    Firth. Chicago, Aldine Publishing Co.

GEORGES, ROBT. A.
1968 *Studies on Mythology*. Homewood, The Dorsey Press

GOLDENWEISER, ALEXANDER
1948 *Anthropology: An Introduction to Primitive Culture*.
    New York, F.S. Crofts & Co.

GOLDKIND, V.
1965 "Social Stratification in the Peasant Community:
    Redfield's Chan Kom Reinterpreted" *Amer. Anth.*
    67 863-884

GOLDSCHMIDT, WALTER
1966 *Comparative Functionalism*. Berkeley, Univ. of
    California Press

HAEKEL, JOSEF
1970 "Source Criticism in Anthropology" Naroll & Cohen
    1970 147-164

HAMMOND, PETER B.
1964 *Cultural and Social Anthropology: Selected*
    Readings. New York, The Macmillan Co.

HEINE-GELDERN, R.
1964 "One Hundred Years of Ethnological Theory in the
    German-Speaking Countries: Some Milestones" *Curr.*
    Anth. 5 407-418

HERSKOVITS, MELVILLE
1964 *Cultural Dynamics*. New York, Alfred A. Knopf

HOWELLS, WILLIAM
1962   *The Heathens: Primitive Man and His Religions.*
            New York, Doubleday & Co.

HOYT, ELIZABETH E.
1961   "Integration of Culture: A Review of Concepts"
            Curr. Anth. 2   407-426

HSU, F.L.K.
1964   "Re-thinking the Concept 'Primitive' " *Curr.*
            Anth. 5   169-178

1971   "Psychosocial Homeostasis and Jen: Conceptual
            Tools for Advancing Psychological Anthropology"
            Amer. Anth. 73   23-44

HUIZER, GERRIT
1970   " 'Resistance to Change' and Radical Peasant Mobi-
            lization: Foster and Erasmus Reconsidered" with
            comments by Foster and Erasmus and a Rejoinder
            Human. Organ. 29   303-322

HULTKRANTZ, AKE
1970   "Anthropological Approaches to Religion" *Hist. of*
            Relig. 9   337-352

JARVIE, I.C.
1967   *The Revolution in Anthropology.*   London, Routledge
            & Kegan Paul

JONES, DELMOS J.
1970   "Towards a Native Anthropology" *Human. Organ.* 29
            251-259

KARDINER, ABRAM & EDWARD PREBLE
1961   *They Studied Man.*   New York, Mentor Books

KEESING, FELIX M.
1953   *Culture Change: An Analysis and Bibliography of*
            Anthropological Sources to 1952.   Stanford,
            Stanford Univ. Press

1963   *Cultural Anthropology: The Science of Culture.*
            New York, Holt, Rinehart & Winston

KEESING, ROGER M.
1970   "Toward a Model of Role Analysis" Naroll & Cohen
            1970   423-453

KENNEDY, J.G.
1966   " 'Peasant Society and the Image of the Limited
            Good': A Critique" *Amer. Anth.* 68 1212-1225

KLUCKHOHN, C. & W.H. KELLY
1945   "The Concept of Culture" Linton 1945   78-106

KROEBER, A.L.
1948   *Anthropology*. New York, Harcourt Brace & Co.

1952   *The Nature of Culture*. Chicago, Univ. of Chicago
             Press

KROEBER, A.L. (ed.)
1953   *Anthropology Today: An Encyclopedic Inventory*.
             Chicago, Univ. of Chicago Press

KROEBER, A.L. & CLYDE KLUCKHOHN (et al)
1963   *Culture: A Critical Review of Concepts and Defi-
             nitions*. New York, Vintage Books (Random House)

LEACH, EDMUND & I.C. JARVIE
1966   Discussion on "Frazer and Malinowski" *Curr. Anth.*
             7   560-576

LESSA, WM. A. & EVON Z. VOGT
1958 &   *Reader in Comparative Religion: An Anthropological*
1965   *Approach*. New York, Harper & Row

LÉVI-STRAUSS, CLAUDE
1963   *Structural Anthropology*. New York, Basic Books Inc

1966   "The Scope of Anthropology" *Curr. Anth.* 7 112-123
             "Anthropology: Its Achievements and Future" *Curr.*
             Anth. 7   124-129

LEVY-BRUHL, LUCIEN
1925   *How Natives Think*. New York, Alfred A. Knopf

LINTON, RALPH
1936   *The Study of Man*. New York, Appleton-Century-
             Crofts

LINTON, RALPH (ed.)
1945   *The Science of Man in the World Crisis*. New York,
             Columbia Univ. Press

LOWIE, R.H.
1920   *Primitive Society*. New York, Horace Liveright
             (New York, Harpers   1961)

1937   *History of Ethnological Theory*. New York, Farrer
             & Rinehart

57

LUZBETAK, LOUIS
1967   "International Cultural Problems" *CICOP* Working
            Paper C34-67

MAIR, LUCY
1965   *An Introduction to Social Anthropology.* Oxford,
            Clarendon Press

MALINOWSKI, BRONISLAW
1931   "Culture" *Encyclopedia of the Social Sciences.*
            Vol. 4 (Originally issued 1944)

1939   "The Group & the Individual in Functional Analysis"
            Amer. Journ. of Sociol. 44   938-964

1945   *The Dynamics of Culture Change.* New Haven, Yale
            Univ. Press

1948   *Magic, Science and Religion.* New York, Doubleday
            & Co.

1960   *A Scientific Theory of Culture and Other Essays.*
            New York, Oxford Univ. Press

1961 a   *A Scientific Theory of Culture.* New York, Oxford
            Univ. Press

1961 b   *The Dynamics of Culture Change.* New Haven, Yale
            Univ. Press (Originally issued 1945)

MANDELBAUM, DAVID
1958   *Selected Writings of Edward Sapir in Language,
            Culture and Personality.* Berkeley, Univ. of
            California Press

MANNERS, ROBERT A. (ed.)
1964   *Process and Pattern in Culture.* Chicago, Aldine
            Publishing Co.

MARETT, R.R.
1908   "A Sociological View of Comparative Religion"
            Sociol. Rev. 1   48-60

1914   *The Threshold of Religion.* London, Macmillan Co.

MEAD, MARGARET
1961   *Cooperation and Competition Among Primitive
            Cultures.* Boston, Beacon Press (Orig. issue: 1937)

1964 a   *Anthropology: A Human Science.* Princeton, D. Van
            Nostrand Co.

MEAD, MARGARET
1964 b   *Continuities in Cultural Evolution.*   New Haven,
           Yale Univ. Press

1966   "Continuities in Cultural Evolution" (Book Dis-
           cussion) *Curr. Anth.* 7   67-82

METGE, JOAN
1967   "Christ and Culture" *SE Asia Journ. Theol.* 8 19-33

MILLER, D.R.
1970   "The Personality as a System" Naroll & Cohen
           1970   509-526

MINER, HORACE
1952   "The Folk-Urban Continuum" *Amer. Soc. Rev.* 17
           529-537

MITCHELL, ROBT. C.
1970   "Towards the Sociology of Religious Independency"
           (Critique of Barrett's *Schism & Renewal*) *Journ.
           of Relig. in Afr.* 3   2-21. Reply by Barrett
           "Analytical Methods of Studying Religious Expan-
           sion" 22-44

MORGAN, LEWIS HENRY
1877 &   *Ancient Society.*   London, Routledge and Kegan Paul
1959   (1959)

MURDOCK, G.P.
1945   "The Common Denominator in Cultures" Linton   1945
           123-142

1949   *Social Structure.*   New York, The Free Press (1965)

1965   *Culture and Society.* Pittsburgh, Univ. of
           Pittsburgh Press

NADEL, S.F.
1958   *The Foundations of Social Anthropology.*   London,
           Cohen & West

OGBURN, WM. F.
1957   "Cultural Lag as Theory" *Sociol. & Soc. Res.* 41
           167-174

OPLER, MORRIS E.
1946   "Themes as Dynamic Forces in Culture" *Amer. Journ.
           of Soc.* 51   198-206

1964   "The Human Being in Culture Theory" *Amer. Anth.*
           66   507-528

ORENSTEIN, HENRY
1968   "The Ethnological Theories of Henry Sumner Maine"
            Amer. Anth. 70   264-276

PELTO, PERTTI J.
1966   *The Nature of Anthropology*. Columbus, Charles E.
            Merrill Publishing Co.

PIKER, STEVEN
1966   "The Image of the Limited Good" *Amer. Anth.* 68
            1202-1211

PRESTON, R.J.
1966   "Edward Sapir's Anthropology: Style, Structure &
            Method" *Amer. Anth.* 68   1105-1128

RADCLIFFE-BROWN, A.R.
1961   *Structure and Function in Primitive Society*.
            Glencoe, The Free Press

RADIN, PAUL
1927   *Primitive Man as a Philosopher*. New York,
            D. Appleton & Co. (Dover Publications 1957)

1932   *Social Anthropology*. New York, McGraw-Hill Book Co.

1933   *Method and Theory of Ethnology*. New York, McGraw-
            Hill Book Co.

REDFIELD, MARGARET PARK (ed.)
1962   *The Papers of Robert Redfield: Human Nature and
            the Study of Society*. Chicago, Univ. of Chicago
            Press

REDFIELD, ROBERT
1947   "The Folk Society" *Amer. Journ. of Soc.* 52
            293-308

1953   *The Primitive World and its Transformations*.
            Ithica, Cornell Univ. Press   Paperback 1965

1955   *The Little Community: Viewpoints for the Study of
            a Human Whole*. Chicago, Univ. of Chicago Press

1956   *Peasant Society and Culture: An Anthropological
            Approach to Civilization*. Chicago, Univ. of
            Chicago Press

REDFIELD, ROBT. & M.S. SINGER
1954   "The Cultural Role of Cities" *Econ. Devel. &
            Cult. Chg.* 3   53-77

REYBURN, WM. D.
1970   "Review of Barrett's Schism & Renewal in Africa"
            Prac. Anth. 17   137-144

REYNOLDS, HARRIET R.
1971   "Religious Implications of the Social Sciences"
            Prac. Anth. 18   177-180

RIVERS, W.H.R.
1910   "The Genealogical Method of Anthropological
            Inquiry" *The Sociol. Rev.*   1-12

1924   *Social Organization.* New York, Alfred A. Knopf

SAPIR, EDWARD
1917   "Do We Need a Superorganic?" *Amer. Anth.*   19
            331-337

1924   "Culture, Genuine and Spurious" *Amer. Journ. of
            Sociol.* 29   401-429

SCHOLTE, BOB
1966   "Epistemic Paradigms: Some Problems in Cross-
            Cultural Research on Social Anthropological Histo-
            ry and Theory" *Amer. Anth.* 68   1192-1201

SEWELL, W.H.
1956   "Some Observations on Theory Testing" *Rural
            Sociology* 21   1-12

SPIRO, MELFORD E.
1954   "Is the Family Universal?" *Amer. Anth.* 56   839-46

STEINER, FRANZ
1956   *Taboo.* London, Cohen & West

STEWARD, J.H.
1955   *Theory of Culture Change: The Methodology of
            Multilinear Evolution.* Urbana, Univ. of Illinois
            Press

STOCKING, GEO. W.JR.
1966   "Franz Boas and the Culture Concept in Historical
            Perspective" *Amer. Anth.* 68   867-882

TAX, SOL, et al
1955   *An Appraisal of "Anthropology Today 1953".*
            Chicago, Univ. of Chicago Press

TAX, SOL (ed.)
1964   *Horizons of Anthropology.* Chicago, Aldine Pub. Co.

TAYLOR, JOHN V.
1963   *The Primal Vision*. London, S.C.M. Press

TEMPELS, R.P. PLACIDE
1949   *La Philosophie Bantou*. Paris, Présence Africaine.
            English edition 1959

TYLOR, E.B.
1871   *Primitive Culture*. 2 Vols. (1.Origine 2.Religion)
            republished 1958, New York Harper

VAN GENNEP, ARNOLD
1908   *Les rites de passage*. Republished in English
            1960 Chicago, Univ. of Chicago Press

VASINA, JAN
1970   "Cultures Through Time" Naroll & Cohen   1970
            165-179

WEBER, MAX
1947   *Theory of Social and Economic Organization*.
            Republished 1957 New York, Free Press of Glencoe

1964   *The Theory of Social and Economic Organization*.
            New York, Free Press of Glencoe

WHITE, LESLIE A.
1949   *The Science of Culture: A Study of Man and Civili-
            zation*. New York, Grove Press Inc.

WILSON, GODFREY & MINICA
1968   *The Analysis of Social Change*. Cambridge,
            University Press

WISSLER, CLARK
1923   *Man and Culture*. New York, Thos. Y. Crowell

WOLF, ERIC
1964   *Anthropology*. Englewood Cliffs, Prentice-Hall,Inc.

                        SUPPLEMENTARY

BANTON, MICHAEL
1966   *The Relevance of Models for Social Anthropology*.
            New York, F.A. Praeger

MARTINDALE, DON
1965   *Functionalism in the Social Sciences*. Philadelphia,
            The Amer. Academy of Pol. & Soc. Science

SOCIAL ANTHROPOLOGY AND CULTURAL ANALYSIS

See also works on single societies and comparative studies under "General Anthropology". Many items listed under "Acculturation, Culture Clash and Culture Change", under "Leadership and Authority" and under "Applied Anthropology" might well have been listed here as they reflect social patterns and cultural analysis.

This unit also contains sub-units on Law, Values and Economics.

ANDERSON, T.A. & B.G.
1965   *Bus Stop to Paris: The Transformation of a French Village*. New York, Doubleday & Co.

BAILEY, F.G.
1955   "An Oriya Hill Village" Srinivas 1960 122-146

BALANDIER, GEORGES
1966   *Ambiguous Africa: Cultures in Collision*. New York, Pantheon Books

BANTON, MICHAEL
1957   *West African City: A Study of Tribal Life in Freetown*. London, Oxford Univ. Press

BARNETT, H.G.
1949   *Palauan Society: A Study of Contemporary Native Life in the Palau Islands*. Eugene, Univ. of Oregon Publications (Multigraphed)

BATESON, GREGORY
1958   *Naven*. Stanford, Stanford Univ. Press (New Guinea) (Original edition 1936)

BEAGLEHOLE, E. & P.
1941   *Pangai: Village in Tonga*. Wellington, Polynesian Society   Memoir 18

BEALS, A.R.
1955   "Interplay among Factors of Change in a Mysore Village" Marriott 1955 78-101

63

BEALS, R.L.
1966   *Community in Transition: Nayon, Ecuador.*
            Los Angeles, Latin American Center, U.C.L.A.

BEARDSLEY, R.K., J.W. HALL & R.E. WARD
1959   *Village Japan.* Chicago, Univ. of Chicago Press

BENDER, DONALD R.
1967   "A Refinement of the Concept of Household:
            Families Co-residence and Domestic Functions"
            Amer. Anth. 69   493-504

BENNETT, W.C. & J.B. BIRD
1949   *Andean Culture History.* New York, American
            Museum of Natural History, Handbook 15

BERNDT, R.M. & C.H.
1964   *The World of the First Australians: ...Traditional
            Life of the Australian Aborigines.* Chicago, Univ.
            of Chicago Press

1967   *The First Australians.* Sydney, Ure Smith (First
            Edition 1952)

BERREMAN, GERALD D.
1960   "Caste in India and the United States" *Amer.
            Journ. Sociol.* 66   120-127

BEST, ELSDON
1952   *The Maori As He Was: A brief account of Maori life
            as it was in pre-European days.* Wellington,
            Government Printer (First published 1924)

BETEILLE, ANDRE
1965   "Social Organization of Temples in a Tanjore
            Village" *Hist. of Relig.* 5   74-92

BOCK, P.K.
1969   *Modern Cultural Anthropology.* New York, Alfred A.
            Knopf

BOE, PETER
1971   "Growing Up in the Bille Tribe" *Prac. Anth.* 18
            29-42

BOHANNAN, P. & J. MIDDLETON (eds.)
1968   *Marriage, Family and Residence.* New York, The
            Natural History Press   Symposium

BOWEN, E.S. (Laura Bohannan)
1964   *Return to Laughter.* New York, Doubleday & Co.
            (Anthropological Novel)

BROOKFIELD, H.C. & PAULA BROWN
1963   *Struggle for Land: Agriculture and Group Terri-
            tories Among the Chimbu of the New Guinea High-
            lands*. Melbourne, Oxford Univ. Press

BROOKS, R. & E.
1965   *The Barrios of Manta*. New York, The New American
            Library

BUCHANAN, K.M. & J.C. PUGH
1955   *Land and People in Nigeria*. London, Univ. of
            London Press

BUCK, PETER H.
1950   *The Coming of the Maori*. Wellington, Whitcombe &
            Tombs (Maori Purposes Fund Board)

BURLING, ROBBINS
1965   *Hill Farms and Padi Fields: Life in Mainland
            Southeast Asia*. Englewood Cliffs, Prentice-Hall

BURROWS, EDWIN G.
1941   "Culture-Areas in Polynesia"   *Polynesian Society
            Memoir* 17   161-175

CHEVALIER, FRANCOIS
1966   *Land and Society in Colonial Mexico: The Great
            Hacienda*. Berkeley, Univ. of California Press

COLEMAN, JAMES S.
1956   "Social Cleavage and Religious Conflict" *Journ.
            Social. Issues* 12   44-56

COOLEY, FRANK L.
1968   "Altar and Throne in Central Moluccan Societies"
            Prac. Anth. 15   118-137

COON, CARLTON S.
1951   *Caravan: The Story of the Middle East*. New York,
            Henry Holt & Co.

COUGHLIN, RICHARD J.
1960   *Double Identity: The Chinese in Modern Thailand*.
            Hong Kong, Hong Kong Univ. Press

COWAN, MARION M.
1962   "A Christian Movement in Mexico" *Prac. Anth.* 9
            193-204

CULSHAW, WESLEY J.
1965   "The Christian Mission among Tribal Minorities in
            India" *Prac. Anth.* 12   152-157

DAVIDSON, J.W.
1967   *Samoa Mo Samoa: The Emergence of the Independent
            State of Western Samoa.* Melbourne, Oxford Univ.
            Press

DE VOS, G. & H. WAGATSUMA
1967   *Japan's Invisible Race: Caste in Culture and
            Personality.* Berkeley, Univ. of California Press

DIAMOND, STANLEY
1964   *Primitive Views of the World.* New York, Columbia
            Univ. Press   Symposium

DIAZ, MAY N.
1970   *Tonala: Conservatism, Responsibility and Authority
            in a Mexican Town.* Berkeley, Univ. of California
            Press

DODD, W.C.
1923   *The Tai Race.* Cedar Rapids, The Torch Press

DOLLARD, J.
1939   "Culture, Society, Impulse and Socialization"
            Amer. Journ. of Sociol. 45   50-63

DOWLING, JOHN H.
1968   "A 'Rural' Indian Community in an Urban Setting"
            (U.S.) *Human Organ.* 27   236-240

DRUCKER, PHILIP
1963   *Indians of the Northwest Coast.* New York, The
            Natural History Press

DUBE, S.C.
1967   *Indian Village.* New York, Harper and Row

DU BOIS, CORA
1961   *The People of Alor: A Social-Psychological Study
            of an East Indian Island.* 2 Vols. New York,
            Harper & Bros. (Originally issued 1944. "Two
            Generations Later" written 1960)

DUMONT, LOUIS
1966   "Une Sous-Caste d'Inde du Sud and Hierarchy and
            Marriage Alliance in South Indian Kinship" *Curr.
            Anth.* 7   327-346   Book Discussion

EBEL, ROLAND H.
1969   *Political Modernization in Three Guatemalan Indian
            Communities.* New Orleans, Middle American
            Research Institute

EGLAR, ZEKIYE
1960   *A Punjabi Village in Pakistan*.   New York,Columbia
            Univ. Press

ELKIN, A.P.
1961   *The Australian Aborigines: How to Understand Them*.
            Sydney, Angus & Robertson (First edition 1938)

EPTON, NINA
1958   *Saints and Sorcerers: A Moroccan Journey*.   London,
            Cassell & Co.

ETZIONI, AMITAI
1964   *Modern Organizations*.   Englewood Cliffs, Prentice-
            Hall

EVANS-PRITCHARD, E.E.
1952   *Social Anthropology*.   London, Cohen & West

1961   "Zande Clans and Totems"   *Man*.   61   116-121

1962   *Social Anthropology and Other Essays*.   New York,
            Free Press of Glencoe

EVANS-PRITCHARD, E.E. (ed.)
1954   *The Institutions of Primitive Society*.   Oxford,
            Basil Blackwell

FALLERS, LLOYD A.
1965   *Bantu Bureaucracy*.   Chicago, Univ. of Chicago
            Press   (Basoga of Uganda)

FIRTH, RAYMOND
1956   *Human Types: An Introduction to Social Anthro-
            pology*.   London, Thomas Nelson

FISK, E.K.
1968   *New Guinea on the Threshold*.   Pittsburgh, Univ. of
            Pittsburgh Press

FORCE, ROLAND W.
1960   *Leadership and Cultural Change in Palau*.   Chicago,
            Chicago Natural History Museum (Fieldiana:
            Anthropology 50)

FORTES, MEYER
1953   "Structure of Unilineal Descent-Groups"   *Amer.
            Anth*.   55   17-41   (Also in Ottenberg 1960 163-89)

1969   *Kinship and the Social Order: the Legacy of Lewis
            Henry Morgan*.   Chicago, Aldine Publishing Co.

FOSTER, GEORGE M.
    1967   *Tzintzuntza: Mexican Peasants in a Changing World.*
                Boston, Little, Brown & Co.

FOX, C.E.
    1924   *The Threshold of the Pacific.* (San Cristoval,
                Solomon Islands) London, Kegan Paul, Trench,
                Trubner & Co.

FOX, ROBERT B.
    1959   "The Function of Religion in Society" *Prac. Anth.*
                6   212-218

FRASER, DONALD
    1968   *Village Planning in the Primitive World.* New York,
                George Braziller

FREEDMAN, MAURICE
    1967   *Social Organization: Essays Presented to Raymond
                Firth.* Chicago, Aldine Publishing Co.

FREEMAN, S.T.
    1968   "Religious Aspects of the Social Organization of a
                Castilian Village" *Amer. Anth.* 70   34-49

FREYRE, GILBERTO
    1963   *New World in the Tropics: The Culture of Modern
                Brazil.* New York, Vintage Books

FRIEDERICH, R.
    1959   *The Civilization and Culture of Bali.* Calcutta,
                Sisil Gupta (India) Private Ltd

FUKUTAKE, TADASHI
    1967   *Japan's Rural Society.* (Translated by R.P. Dore)
                Tokyo, Oxford Univ. Press

FULLER, A.H.
    1966   *Buarij: Portrait of a Lebanese Muslim Village.*
                Cambridge, Harvard Univ. Press

GALDAS, ADIB
    1959   "Village Reborn" *Prac. Anth.* 6   198-211

GATHERU, R. MUGO
    1965   *Child of Two Worlds: A Kikuyu's Story.* New York,
                Doubleday & Co.

GEERTZ, CLIFFORD
    1965   *The Social History of an Indonesian Town.*
                Cambridge, The M.I.T. Press

GELLNER, ERNEST
1969   *Saints of the Atlas*. London, Weidenfeld &
            Nicholson

GERASSI, JOHN
1965   *The Great Fear in Latin America*. New York,
            Collier Books

GHAI, DHARAM P.
1965   *Portrait of a Minority: Asians in East Africa*.
            Nairobi, Oxford Univ. Press

GIBBS, JAMES L., JR.
1964   "Social Organization" Tax 1964   160-170

GIBBS, JAMES L, JR. (ed.)
1965   *Peoples of Africa*. New York, Holt, Rinehart &
            Winston

GILLION, K.L.
1962   *Fiji's Indian Migrants*. Melbourne, Oxford Univ.
            Press

GILSON, R.P.
1970   *Samoa 1830-1900: The Politics of a Multi-cultural
            Community*. Melbourne, Oxford Univ. Press

GLICK, P.B.
1970   "Melanesian Mosaic: The Plural Community of Vila"
            Plotnicov & Tuden 1970   95-117

GLUCKMAN, MAX
1967   *Custom and Conflict in Africa*. New York, Barnes &
            Noble

GLUCKMAN, MAX (ed.)
1964   *Closed Systems and Open Minds: The Limits of
            Naivety in Social Anthropology*. Chicago, Aldine
            Publishing Co.

GOFFMAN, ERVING
1961   *Encounters: Two Studies in the Sociology of Inter-
            action*. Indianapolis, Bobs-Merrill Co.

GOODE, WM. J.
1957   "Community within a Community: The Professions"
            Amer. Sociol. Rev. 22   194-200

1964   *The Family*. Englewood Cliffs, Prentice Hall

GOODENOUGH, WARD H.
1970   *Description and Comparison in Cultural Anthro-
            pology.* Chicago, Aldine Publishing Co.

GOODY, JACK
1961   "The Classification of Double Descent Systems"
            Curr. Anth. 2   3-25

GOUGH, E.K.
1955   "The Social Structure of a Tanjore Village"
            Marriott 1955   36-52

GOVERNMENT OF INDIA
1960   *The Adivasis.* Delhi, Govt. of India, Publications
            Division

GRATTAN, F.J.H.
1948   *An Introduction to Samoan Custom.* Apia, Samoa
            Printing & Publishing Co.

GREER, SCOTT A.
1955   *Social Organization.* New York, Random House

GULLIVER, P.H.
1953   "Jie Marriage" *African Affairs* 52   149-155
            (Also in Ottenberg 1960   190-198)

HALL, EDWARD T.
1959   *The Silent Language.* Greenwich, Conn., Fawcett
            Publications

HAMMOND, PETER B. (ed.)
1964   *Cultural and Social Anthropology: Selected
            Readings.* New York, The Macmillan Co.

HANDELMAN, DON & J.H. WEAKLAND
1968   "Replies to Silverman 1968" *Amer. Anth.* 70 352-56

HARDING, T.G. & B.J. WALLACE (eds.)
1970   *Cultures of the Pacific: Selected Readings.*
            New York, The Free Press   Symposium

HARRIES, LYNDON
1945   "Bishop Lucas and the Masai Experiment" *I.R.M.*
            34   389-396

HENNIG, EDGAR
1967   "Reflections on Observing a Sagada Rite" *Prac.*
            Anth. 14   92-94

HERSKOVITS, M.J.
1971   *Life in a Haitian Valley*. New York, Doubleday &
            Co. (Originally published 1937)

HIEBERT, PAUL G.
1969   "Caste and Personal Rank in an Indian Village: An
            Extension in Techniques" *Amer. Anth.* 71   434-53

HILLMAN, EUGENE
1970   "Polygyny Reconsidered" *Prac. Anth.* 17   60-74

HOCART, A.M.
1950   *Caste: A Comparative Study*. London, Methuen & Co.

HOLMES, L.D.
1969   "Samoan Oratory" *Journ. Amer. Folklore* 82 342-52

HORMANN, BERNARD L.
1956   *Community Forces in Hawaii*. Honolulu, Univ. Soci-
            ology Club   Symposium

HSU, F.L.K.
1967   *Under the Ancestor's Shadow: Kinship, Personality
            and Social Mobility in Village China*. New York,
            Doubleday & Co.

HUNTER, GUY
1962   *The New Societies of Tropical Africa: A Selective
            Study*. London, Oxford Univ. Press

HUNTINGFORD, G.W.B.
1953   "Nandi Age-sets" (Ch. 3 in *The Nandi of Kenya*)
            Reprinted in Ottenberg 1960   214-226

HUTTON, J.H.
1963   *Caste in India: Its Nature, Function and Origins*.
            London, Oxford Univ. Press

HUXLEY, FRANCIS
1956   *Affable Savages*. New York, Capricorn Books

IYER, L.A.K. & L.K.B. TATNAM
1961   *Anthropology in India*. Bombay, Bharatiya Vidya
            Bhavan

JAYASINGHAM, W.L.
1963   "Intercaste Relations in the Church in Kerala"
            Rel. & Soc. 10   58-78

JENNESS, DIAMOND
1959   *The People of the Twilight*. Chicago, Univ. of
            Chicago Press

JOHNSON, ERWIN
1964 "The Stem Family and its Extension in Present Day Japan" *Amer. Anth.* 64 839-851

1968 "Social Stratification in Rural Japan" *Ethno-history* 15 328-351

JUNOD, HENRI A.
1962 *The Life of a South African Tribe. (Thonga)* 2 Vols. New York, University Books (First published 1912)

JUNOD, VIOLAINE I. (ed.)
1963 *The Handbook of Africa.* New York, New York University Press

KAKWONSA, LD.
1960 *Korea: Its Land, People and Culture of all Ages.* Seoul, Kakwonsa Ld.   Symposium

KEEN, R. HUNTER
1964 "Dakota Patterns of Giving" *Prac. Anth.* 11 273-76

KEESING, FELIX M.
1934 *Modern Samoa: Its Government and Changing Life.* London, George Allen & Unwin

1941 *The South Seas in the Modern World.* New York, John Day & Co.

1953 *Culture Change: An Analysis and Bibliography of Anthropological Sources to 1952.* Stanford, Stanford Univ. Press

1955 "Bontok Social Organization" Hoebel. Jennings & Smith, 1955 173-189

KEESING, F.M. & M.M.
1956 *Elite Communication in Samoa: A Study of Leadership.* Stanford, Stanford Univ. Press

KENYATTA, JOMO
1962 *Facing Mount Kenya: The Tribal Life of the Gikuyu.* New York, Vintage Books

KLUCKHOHN, CLYDE
1962 *Culture and Behavior.* New York, The Free Press

KOESTLER, ARTHUR
1960 *The Lotus and the Robot.* New York, Harper & Row

KROEBER, A.L.
1938   "Basic and Secondary Patterns of Social Structure"
            Journ. Roy. Anth. Inst. 68 299-309

1944   *Configurations of Cultural Growth.* Berkeley, Univ.
            of California Press

KUPER, HILDA
1947   *The Uniform of Colour: A Study of White-Black
            Relationships in Swaziland.* Johannesburg,
            Witwatersrand Univ. Press

1960   *Indian People in Natal.* Pietermaritzburg, Natal
            Univ. Press

LAMPHERE, LOUISE
1970   "Ceremonial Co-operation and Networks: A Re-
            analysis of the Navaho Outfit" *Man.* 5   39-59

LATOURETTE, K.S.
1946   *The Chinese: Their History and Culture.* Vol. 2
            495-832   New York, Macmillan Co.

LAYARD, JOHN
1954   "The Family and Kinship" Ch. 5 in Evans-Pritchard
            (ed.) *The Institusions of Primitive Society.* 50-65

LEACH, E.R.
1954   *Political Systems of Highland Burma: A Study of
            Kachin Social Structure.* Cambridge, Harvard Univ.
            Press

1961   *Pul Eliya, a Village in Ceylon: A Study of Land
            Tenure and Kinship.*   Cambridge, The University
            Press

LEACOCK, ELEANORE, et al
1958   "Social Stratification and Evolutionary Theory"
            Ethnohistory 5   193-249   Symposium

LEBAR, F.M., et al
1964   *Ethnic Groups of Mainland Southeast Asia.* New
            Haven, Human Relations Area Files

LEHMAN, F.K.
1963   *The Structure of Chin Society: A Tribal People of
            Burma Adapted to a Non-Western Civilization.*
            Urbana, Univ. of Illinois Press

LEIGHTON, DOROTHEA & CLYDE KLUCKHOHN
1969   *Children of the People (Navaho)* New York, Octagon
            Books   (First published 1947)

73

LEITH-ROSS, S.
1956   "The Rise of a New Elite amongst the Women of
            Nigeria" van den Berghe 1965   221-229
            (Reprinted from *Inter. Soc. Sci. Bull.* 8   481-488)

LÉVI-STRAUSS, CLAUDE
1953   "Social Structure" Kroeber   1953   524-553

1963   *Structural Anthropology.* New York, Basic Books

1964   *Tristes Tropiques: An Anthropological Study of
            Primitive Societies in Brazil.* New York, Atheneum

LEVY, M.J.
1952   *The Structure of Society.* Princeton, Princeton
            Univ. Press

LEWIS, OSCAR
1955   "Peasant Culture in Mexico and India: A Compara-
            tive Analysis" Marriott   1955   145-170

1959   *Five Families: Mexican Case Studies in the Culture
            of Poverty.* New York, Basic Books Inc.

1965   *Village Life in Northern India.* New York, Vintage
            Books

1967   "The Children of Sanchez, Pedro Martinez and La
            Vida" *Curr. Anth.* 8   480-500 (Book Discussion)

LEWIS, WM. H.
1965   *French-Speaking Africa: The Search for Identity.*
            New York, Walker & Co.   Symposium

LIENHARDT, GODFREY
1964   *Social Anthropology.* London, Oxford Univ. Press

LISPET, S.M. & A. SOLARI
1967   *Elites in Latin America.* New York, Oxford Univ.
            Press

LOEWEN, JACOB A.
1967   "Lengua Festivals and Functional Substitutes"
            Prac. Anth. 14   15-36

1968   "The Indigenous Church and Resocialization" *Prac.
            Anth.* 15   193-204

LOWIE, R.H.
1947   *Primitive Society.* New York, Horace Liveright

1950   *Social Organization.* London, Routledge & Kegan Paul

74

LUKE, P.Y. & J.B. CARMAN
1968   *Village Christians and Hindu Culture.* London,
            Lutterworth Press

MAC IVER, R.M.
1964   *Social Causation.* New York, Harper & Row

MADAN, T.N. & G. SARANA (eds.)
1962   *Indian Anthropology.* Bombay, Asia Publishing House

MAIR, LUCY
1965   *An Introduction to Social Anthropology.* London,
            Oxford Univ. Press

MAJUMDAR, D.N.
1958   *Caste and Communication in an Indian Village.*
            Bombay, Asia Publishing House

MALINOWSKI, B.
1939   "The Group and Individual in Functional Analysis"
            Amer. Jour. Sociol. 44   938-964

1944   *A Scientific Theory of Culture and other Essays.*
            Chapel Hill, Univ. of North Carolina Press

1961   *Argonauts of the Western Pacific.* (Archipelagoes
            of Melanesian New Guinea) New York, Dutton & Co.
            (Originally published 1922)

1965   *Coral Gardens and Their Magic.* Bloomington,
            Indiana Univ. Press 2 Vols. Vol. 1:*Soil-Tilling
            and Agricultural Rites in the Trobriand Islands.*
            Vol. 2:*The Language of Magic and Gardening.*

MANDELBAUM, D.G.
1962   "Role Variations in Caste Relations" Madan &
            Sarana 1962   310-324

MANNERS, R.A. & J.H. STEWARD
1954   "The Cultural Study of Contemporary Societies:
            Puerto Rico" *Amer. Jour. Sociol.* 59   123-130

MARRIOTT, McKIM
1955   *Village India: Studies in the Little Community.*
            Chicago, Univ. of Chicago Press   Symposium

MARRIS, PETER
1962   *Family and Social Change in an African City: A
            Study of Rehousing in Lagos.* Chicago, North-
            western Univ. Press

MAYBURY-LEWIS, D.
1965   *The Savage and the Innocent.*   London, Evans Bros.

MAYER, ADRIAN C.
1961   *Peasants in the Pacific: A Study of Fijian Indian*
            Rural Society.   Berkeley, Univ. of Calif. Press

1963   *Indians in Fiji.*   London, Oxford Univ. Press

MAYER, PHILIP
1963   *Townsmen or Tribesmen: Conservatism and the*
            Process of Urbanization in a South African City.
            Cape Town, Oxford Univ. Press

MC ARTHUR, NORMA
1968   *Island Populations of the Pacific.*   Canberra,
            Australian National Univ. Press

MC CALL, A.G.
1949   *Lushai Chrysalis.*   London, Luzac and Co.

MC CORKLE, THOMAS
1965   *Fajardo's People: Cultural Adjustment in Venezuela,*
            etc.   Los Angeles, Latin American Center, U.C.L.A.

MEAD, MARGARET
1950   *Sex and Temperament in Three Primitive Societies.*
            New York, The New American Library (Mentor)

1954   *Coming of Age in Samoa.*   London, Penguin Books
            Originally published 1928

1955   *Male and Female: A Study of the Sexes in a Chang-*
            ing World.   New York, The New American Library

1970   *Culture and Commitment: A Study of the Generation*
            Gap.   New York, Natural History Press

METRAUX, R. & M. MEAD
1954   *Themes in French Culture: A Preface to the Study*
            of the French Community.   Stanford, Univ. of
            Stanford Press

MILLER, E.J.
1955   "Village Structure in North Kerala" Srinivas 1960
            42-55

MISRA, S.C.
1964   *Muslim Communities in Gujarat: Preliminary Studies*
            in Their History & Social Organization.   New York,
            Asia Publishing House

MONTAGUE, M.F. ASHLEY (ed.)
1956   *Marriage: Past and Present.* (Debate between
            Briffault and Malinowski) Boston, Porter Sargent

MORGAN, LEWIS HENRY
1959   *Ancient Society, or Researches in the Lines of
            Human Progress from Savagery, through Barbarism to
            Civilization.* London, Routledge & Kegan Paul
            First published 1877

MORRIS, H.S.
1968   *The Indians in Uganda: A Study of Caste and Sect
            in a Plural Society.* Chicago, Univ. of Chicago
            Press

MOSK, SANFORD A.
1954   *Industrial Revolution in Mexico.* Berkeley, Univ.
            of California Press

MPHAHLELE, EZEKIEL
1962   *The African Image.* New York, Frederick Praeger

MURDOCK, G.P.
1959   *Africa: Its Peoples and Their Culture History.*
            New York, McGraw-Hill Book Co.

1965 a   *Culture and Society.* Pittsburgh, Univ. of
            Pittsburgh Press

1965 b   *Social Structure.* New York, The Free Press
            Paperback Edition

MURRA, JOHN F.
1968   "An Aymara Kingdom in 1567" *Ethnohistory* 15
            115-151

NADEL, S.F.
1958   *The Foundations of Social Anthropology.* London,
            Cohen & West

NAIR, KUSUM
1961   *Blossoms in the Dust: The Human Factor in Indian
            Development.* New York, Frederick Praeger

NAKANE, CHIE
1967   *Kinship and Economic Organization in Rural Japan.*
            New York, Althone Press

NICHOLSON, IRENE
1965   *The X in Mexico: Growth within Tradition.* London,
            Faber & Faber

NIDA, EUGENE A.
  1958   "The Relation of Social Problems to Evangelism in
              Latin America" *Prac. Anth.* 5   101-123

  1960   "The Roman Catholic, Communist and Protestant
              Approach to Social Structure" *Prac. Anth.* Supp.
              21-26

  1962   "Akamba Initiation Rites and Cultural Themes"
              Prac. Anth. 9   145-155

OLDEROGGE, D.A.
  1961   "Several Problems in the Study of Kinship Systems"
              Curr. Anth. 2   103-107

OLIVER, DOUGLAS L.
  1951   *The Pacific Islands.*   Cambridge, Harvard Univ.Press

OSGOOD, CORNELIUS
  1951   *The Koreans and Their Culture.*   New York, The
              Ronald Press

OSWALT, WENDELL
  1963   *Napaskiak: An Alaskan Eskimo Community.*   Tuscon,
              Univ. of Arizona Press

OTTENBERG, SIMON & PHOEBE (eds.)
  1960   *Cultures and Societies of Africa.*   New York,
              Random House   Symposium

PASTERNAK, BURTON
  1968   "Athropy of Patrilineal Bonds in a Chinese Village
              in Historical Perspective" *Ethnohistory*   15
              293-327

PAZ, OCTAVIO
  1961   *The Labyrinth of Solitude: Life and Thought in
              Mexico.*   New York, Grove Press

PETERS, JOHN FRED.
  1971   "Mate Selection Among the Shirshana" *Prac. Anth.*
              18   19-23

PIDDINGTON, RALPH
  1950-   *An Introduction to Social Anthropology.* Edinburgh,
  1957   Oliver & Boyd   2 Vols.

PIDDINGTON, RALPH (ed.)
  1965   *Kinship and Geographical Mobility.*   Leiden,
              E.J. Brill

PLOTNICOV, LEONARD
1967   *Strangers to the City: Urban Man in Jos, Nigeria.*
            Pittsburgh, Univ. of Pittsburgh Press

PLOTNICOV, L. & A. TUDEN (eds.)
1970   *Essays in Comparative Social Stratification.*
            Pittsburgh, Univ. of Pittsburgh Press

PORTEUS, STANLEY D.
1962   *A Century of Social Thinking in Hawaii.*   Palo Alto,
            Pacific Books

POWDERMAKER, H.
1962   *Copper Town: Changing Africa.* New York, Harper &
            Row

PRETORIUS, PAULINE
1950   "An Attempt at Christian Initiation in Nyasaland"
            I.R.M.   39   284-291

PRICE, WILLIAM J.
1965   "Getting Married in Todos Santos" *Prac. Anth.*   12
            281-286

1966   "Birth, Childhood and Death in Todos Santos"
            Prac. Anth.   13   85-89

QUEEN, S.A., R.W. HABENSTEIN & JOHN B. ADAMS
1961   *The Family in Various Cultures.* Chicago, J.B.
            Lippincott Co.

RADCLIFFE-BROWN, A.R.
1951   "The Comparative Method in Social Anthropology"
            Journ. Roy. Anth. Inst.   81   15-22

1952   *Structure and Function in Primitive Society.*
            London, Cohen & West

1958   *Method in Social Anthropology: Selected Essays by
            A.R. Radcliffe-Brown.*   (M.N. Srinivas, ed.)
            Chicago, Univ. of Chicago Press

1964   *The Andaman Islanders.* New York, Free Press of
            Glencoe

RADCLIFFE-BROWN, A.R. & C.D. FORDE
1950   *African Systems of Kinship and Marriage.*   London,
            Oxford Univ. Press.

RADIN, PAUL
1932   *Social Anthropology.* New York, McGraw-Hill Book Co.

RAMOS, SAMUEL
1962   *Profile of Man and Culture in Mexico.* Austin,
            Univ of Texas Press

RATTRAY, R.S.
1923   *Ashanti.* Oxford, Clarendon Press

1932   *The Tribes of the Ashanti Hinterland.* Oxford,
            Clarendon Press, 2 Vols.

READ, KENNETH E.
1965   *The High Valley (New Guinea Central Highlands)*
            New York, Charles Scribner's Sons

REAY, MARIE
1964   "Present-day Politics in the New Guinea Highlands"
            Amer. Anth. 66   240-256   Special number on
            New Guinea

REDFIELD, ROBERT
1947   "The Folk Society" *Amer. Journ. Sociol.* 52
            293-308

1955   *The Little Community: Viewpoints for the Study of
            a Human Whole.* Chicago, Univ. of Chicago Press

RELIGION AND SOCIETY
1958   Symposium - "Caste in Church and Nation" *Relig. &
            Soc.* 5 (Double number)

REYBURN, WM. D.
1958   "Kaka Kinship, Sex and Adultery" *Prac. Anth.* 5
            1-21

1963   "Christianity and Ritual Communication" *Prac.
            Anth.* 10   145-159

REYNOLDS, HARRIET R.
1962   "The Filipino Family in its Cultural Setting"
            Prac. Anth. 9   223-234

RIVERS, W.H.R.
1924   *Social Organization.* London, Kegan Paul, Trench,
            Trubner & Co.

1968   *The History of Melanesian Society.* Oosterhout N.
            B. Netherlands, Anthropological Publications, 2
            Vols.   Originally published 1914

ROSE, CAROLINE B.
1965   *Sociology: the Study of Man in Society*. Columbus,
            C.E. Merrill Books

ROSEN, BERNARD C.
1971   "Industrialization, Personality and Social Mobility
            in Brazil" *Human Organ.* 30   137-148

RUSSELL, R.V.
1969   *Tribes and Castes of the Central Provinces of
            India*. Oosterhout, Anthropological Publications,
            4 Vols. (Reproduction of 1916 Edition)

RYCROFT, W.S. & M.M. CLEMMER
1962   *A Factual Study of Sub-Saharan Africa*. New York,
            Comm. on Ecumenical Mission & Relations, United
            Presbyterian Church in U.S.A.

SAHLINS, MARSHALL D.
1958   *Social Stratification in Polynesia*. Seattle,
            Univ. of Washington Press

SCHEFFLER, H.W.
1965   *Choiseul Island Social Structure*. Berkeley, Univ.
            of California Press

1966   "Ancestor Worship in Anthropology, or Observations
            in Descent and Descent Groups" *Curr. Anth.* 7
            541-551

SCHRIEKE, B.
1966   *Indonesian Sociological Studies: Selected Writings
            of B. Schrieke*. (Edited by Committee) The Hague,
            W. van Hoeve Publishers

SCHURZ, W.L.
1962   *Brazil: The Infinite Country*. London, Robert Hale

SEBRING, JAMES M.
1969   "Caste Indicators and Caste Identification of
            Strangers" *Human Organ.* 28   199-207

SELIGMAN, C.G.
1966   *Races of Africa*. London, Oxford Univ. Press

SERVICE, E.R. & H.S.
1954   *Tobati: Paraguan Town*. Chicago, Univ. of Chicago
            Press

SHAFER, ROBT. J.
1966   *Mexico: Mutual Adjustment Planning*. Syracuse,
            Syracuse Univ. Press

SILVERMAN, S.F.
1966   "An Ethnographic Approach to Social Stratification:
            Prestige in a Central Italian Community" *Amer.*
            Anth. 68   899-921

1968   "Agricultural Organization, Social Structure &
            Values in Italy: Amoral Familism Reconsidered"
            Amer. Anth. 70   1-20   (For reactions, see
            Handelman & Weakland 1968)

SILVERT, K.H.
1963   *Expectant Peoples: Nationalism and Development.*
            New York, Vintage Books

SIMPSON, L.B.
1964   *Many Mexicos.*   Berkeley, Univ. of California Press

SKLARE, MARSHALL
1957   "The Function of Ethnic Churches: Judaism in the
            U.S." Yinger's *Religion, Society and the Indi-*
            vidual.   258-263

SLOTKIN, JAMES S.
1950   *Social Anthropology: the Science of Human Society*
            and Culture.   New York, Macmillan Co.

SMITH, ARTHUR D.
1894   *Chinese Characteristics.*   New York, Fleming H.
            Revell

1899   *Village Life in China: A Study in Sociology.*   New
            York, Fleming H. Revell

SMITH, M.G.
1960   "Social and Cultural Pluralism" in van den Berghe
            1965   58-76 (Reprinted from *Annals of the New*
            York Academy of Science 83   763-777)

SMITH, M.W.
1955   "Social Structure in the Punjab" Srinivas   1960
            161-179

SMITH, R.J. & R.K. BEARDSLEY
1962   *Japanese Culture: Its Development and Character-*
            istics.   Chicago, Aldine Publishing Co.

SMITH, T. LYNN
1970   *Studies of Latin American Societies.*   New York,
            Doubleday & Co.

SMITH, W.C.
1965   *Modernization of a Traditional Society.* London,
            Asia Publishing House

SMITH, W. ROBERTSON
n/d   *Kinship and Marriage in Early Arabia.* Boston,
            Beacon Press (Originally written 1885, published
            1903)

1914   *Lectures on the Religion of the Semites.* London,
            Adams & Charles Black

SOVANI, N.V.
1966   *Urbanization and Urban India.* New York, Asia
            Publishing House

SPENCER, PAUL
1965   *The Samburu: A Study of Gerontocracy in a Nomadic
            Tribe.* Berkeley, Univ. of California Press

SPIRO, MELFORD E.
1963   *Kibbutz: Venture in Utopia.* New York, Schocken
            Books

SPROTT, W.J.H.
1958   *Human Groups.* Baltimore, Penguin Books

SRINIVAS, M.N.
1955   "The Social Structure of a Mysore Village"
            Marriott 1955   1-35

1960   "The Social Structure of a Mysore Village" from
            India's Villages.   New York, Asia Publishing
            House

SRINIVAS, M.N. (ed.)
1960   *India's Villages.* New York, Asia Publishing
            House   Symposium

STENNING, DERRICK J.
1957   "Transhumance, Migratory Drift, Migration:
            Patterns of Pastoral Fulani Nomadism" *Journ. Roy.
            Anth. Inst.* 87   57-73 (Also in Ottenberg 1960
            139-159)

STEWARD, J.H.
1951   "Levels of Sociocultural Integration: an Oper-
            ational Concept" *SW Journ. of Anth.* 7   374-390

STIRLING, PAUL
1965   *Turkish Village.* New York, John Wiley & Sons

STRATTON, ARTHUR
1964 *The Great Red Land.* New York, Charles Scribner's
Sons (Madagascar)

SUMNER, WM.G.
1960 *Folk-ways.* New York, The New American Library
(Mentor) (Originally published 1940)

SWARTZ, MARC J.
1968 *Local Level Politics: Social and Cultural Perspectives.* Chicago, Aldine Publishing Co. Symposium

TAYLOR, JACK E.
1962 *God's Messengers to Mexico's Masses: A Study of
the Religious Significance of the Braceros.*
Eugene, Institute of Church Growth

THOMAS, E.M.
1965 *The Harmless People.* (SW Africa Bushmen) New
York, Vintage Books

THOMPSON, LAURA
1969 *The Secret of Culture.* New York, Random House

THURNWALD, R.D.
1955 "The Banaro" Kroeber & Waterman 1931 284-296

TIPPETT, A.R.
1955 "The Survival of an Ancient Custom Relative to the
Pig's Head, Bau, Fiji" Suva, *Transactions*, Fiji
Society

1963 "Initiation Rites and Functional Substitutes"
Prac. Anth. 10 66-70

1965 "Shifting Attitudes to Sex and Marriage in Fiji"
Prac. Anth. 12 85-91

1967 "The Relevance of Anthropological Dimensions"
Tippett 1967 137-216

1968 *Fijian Material Culture: A Study of Cultural Context, Function and Change.* Honolulu, Bishop
Museum Press

1970 a *Peoples of Southwest Ethiopia.* South Pasadena,
William Carey Library

1970 b "Polygamy as a Missionary Problem: The Anthropological Issues" *Church Growth Bulletin* 5,4 60-3

TROBISCH, WALTER
1966   "Engagement without Courtship and Confidence"
            Prac. Anth. 13   241-251

TUMIN, MELVIN M.
1967   *Social Stratification: The Forms and Functions of
            Inequality.* Englewood Cliffs, Prentice-Hall Inc.

TURNBULL, COLIN M.
1962   *The Forest People: A Study of the Pigmies of the
            Congo.* New York, Doubleday & Co.

1963   *The Lonely African.* New York, Doubleday & Co.

TURNER, HAROLD W.
1965   "Pagan Features, in West African Independent
            Churches" *Prac. Anth.* 12   145-151

TURNER, P.R.
1967   "Part Societies" *Prac. Anth.* 14   110-113

TYLOR, E.B.
1946   *Anthropology: an Introduction to the Study of Man
            and Civilization.* London, Watts & Co. (Origi-
            nally published 1881)

1958   *Primitive Culture.* New York, Harper Torchbooks
            2 Vols. (Originally published 1871)

UNDERHILL, RUTH M.
1958   *Ceremonial Patterns in the Greater Southwest.*
            Seattle, Univ. of Washington Press

VAN DEN BERGHE, PIERRE L.
1965   *Africa: Social Problems of Change and Conflict.*
            San Francisco, Chandler Publishing Co.   Symposium

VAN ESS, DOROTHY L.
1959   "Arab Customs" *Prac. Anth.* 6   219-222

VAN GENNEP, ARNOLD
1960   *The Rites of Passage.* Chicago, Univ. of Chicago
            Press. (Originally published in French as *Les
            Rites de Passage* 1908)

VAYDA, ANDREW P. (ed.)
1968   *Peoples and Cultures of the Pacific: An Anthropo-
            logical Reader.* New York, The Natural History
            Press

VIDYARTHI, L.P.
1964   *Cultural Contours of Tribal Bihar*. Calcutta,
            Punthi Pustak

1967   *Leadership in India*. Bombay, Asia Publishing
            House

VILAKAZI, A.
1962   *Zulu Transformations: A Study of the Dynamics of
            Social Change*. Pietermaritzburg, Univ. of Natal
            Press

VOGEL, EZRA
1965   *Japan's New Middle Class*. Berkeley, Univ. of
            California Press

WAGLEY, CHARLES
1949   *Social and Religious Life of a Guatemalan Village*.
            Amer. Anth. 51 (#4 Part 2)

WAGLEY, CHARLES & M. HARRIS
1958   *Minorities in the New World: Six Case Studies*.
            New York, Columbia Univ. Press

WALLACE, A.F.C. & JOHN ATKINS
1960   "The Meaning of Kinship Terms" *Amer. Anth.* 62
            58-80

WARNER, W. LLOYD
1958   *A Black Civilization: A Study of an Australian
            Tribe*. New York, Harper & Row (Revision of
            original 1937 edition)

WATERS, FRANK
1963   *Book of the Hopi*. New York, Ballantine Books

1970   *Masked Gods: Navaho & Pueblo Ceremonialism*. New
            York, Ballantine Books

WEBER, MAX
1946   *From Max Weber: Essays in Sociology*. New York,
            Oxford Univ. Press   (Translation)

WEDGEWOOD, CAMILLA
1930   "The Nature and Function of Secret Societies"
            Oceania 1   129-145

WEISS, HERBERT F.
1965   "Comparisons in the Evolution of Pre-independence
            Elites in French-Speaking Africa and the Congo"
            Lewis 1965   139-142

WELBOURN, F.B.
1968   "Keyo Initiation" *Journ. of Relig. in Africa* 1
            212-232

WHITEFORD, ANDREW H.
1964   *Two Cities of Latin America: A Comparative Description of Social Classes.* New York, Doubleday & Co.

WILLIAMS, F.E.
1930   *Orokaiva Society.* London, Oxford Univ. Press

WILLIAMSON, R.W.
1937   *Religion and Social Organization in Central Polynesia.* (Edited by Ralph Piddington) Cambridge, The University Press

WILSON, MONICA
1963   *Good Company: A Study of Nyakusa Age-Villages.* Boston, Beacon Press

WILSON, MONICA & ARCHIE MAFEJE
1963   *Langa: A Study of Social Groups in an African Township.* Cape Town, Oxford Univ. Press

WINTER, E.H.
1965   *Beyond the Mountains of the Moon: The Lives of Four Africans.* Urbana, Univ. of Illinois Press

WISER, WM. & C.
1965   *Behind Mud Walls: 1930-1960.* Berkeley, Univ. of California Press

WISSLER, CLARK
1966   *Indians of the United States.* New York, Doubleday & Co. (Revised by L.W. Kluckhohn)

WITHERSPOON, GARY
1970   "A New Look at Navajo Social Organization" *Amer. Anth.* 72   55-65

WOLF, ERIC R.
1955   "Types of Latin American Peasantry: A Preliminary Discussion" *Amer. Anth.* 57   452-471

1956   "Aspects of Group Relations in a Complex Society in Mexico" *Amer. Anth.* 58   1065-1078

1957   "Closed Corporate Peasant Communities in Mesoamerica and Central Java" *SW Journ.Anth.* 13   1-18

1966   *Peasants.* Englewood Cliffs, Prentice Hall

YANG, C.K.
1959   *Chinese Communist Society: The Family and the Village.* Cambridge, The M.I.T. Press

YANG, M.C.
1945   *A Chinese Village: Taitou, Shantung Province.* New York, Columbia Univ. Press

ZBOROWSKI, M. & E. HERZOG
1965   *Life is with People: The Culture of the Shteti.* New York, Schocken Books

ZINKIN, TAYA
1962   *Caste Today.* London, Oxford Univ. Press

VALUES

Cultural values ramify through most sections of this bibliography, but see especially the sections on "Culture and Personality", "Anthropology and the Missionary" and "Culture Clash".

ALBERT, E.M.
1956   "The Classification of Values" *Amer. Anth.* 58 221-248

BENEDICT, RUTH F.
1934 a   "Anthropology and the Abnormal" *Journ. Gen. Psych.* 10   59-80 (Also in Haring 1956   183-201

1934 b   *Patterns of Culture.* Boston, Houghton, Mifflin Co.

1946   *The Chrysanthemum and the Sword.* Boston, Houghton Mifflin Co.

BROWN, INA CORINE
1963   *Understanding Other Cultures.* Englewood Cliffs, Prentice-Hall

DIAMOND, STANLEY
1964   *Primitive Views of the World.* New York, Columbia Univ. Press

DUNDES, ALAN
1968   *Every Man His Way.* Englewood Cliffs, Prentice-Hall (Especially 381-536)

FEHDERAU, HAROLD W.
    1963   "Keys to Cultural Insights" (Congo) *Prac. Anth.*
                10   193-199

FIRTH, RAYMOND
    1953   "The Study of Values by Social Anthropologists"
                Man 53   146-153

FORDE, DARYLL (ed.)
    1954   *African Worlds: Studies in the Cosmological Ideas
                and Social Values of African Peoples.* London,
                Oxford Univ. Press

GRIAULE, MARCEL
    1960   "The Idea of Person Among the Dogon" (Written
                1947 and translated) Ottenberg 1960   365-371

HANDELMAN, DON & J.H. WEAKLAND
    1968   Replies to Silverman 1968, *Amer. Anth.* 70 352-356

HOLMES, L.D.
    1965   "Understanding Other Cultures" in *Anthropology: An
                Introduction.* 344-360 New York, Ronald Press

KAUNDA, KENNETH
    1966   *A Humanist in Africa: Letters to Colin Morris.*
                Nashville, Abingdon Press

KLUCKHOHN, CLYDE
    1951   "Values and Value Orientations in a Theory of
                Action" in Parsons and Shils (ed.) *Towards a Gen-
                eral Theory of Action.* Cambridge, Harvard Univ.
                Press

    1956   "Toward a Comparison of Value-Emphases in Differ-
                ent Cultures" in White (ed.) *The State of the
                Social Sciences.* Chicago

LINTON, RALPH
    1937   "One Hundred Percent American" *The American
                Mercury* 40   427-429

LIVINGSTONE, DAVID
    1858   "Dialogue Shewing Rain Maker's Arguments" in
                Livingstone's Private Journals, 1853. (Schapera,
                ed.) 239-243 (Originally published in *Travels
                1858   22-27)*

MEAD, MARGARET
  1964   "The Comparative Study of Culture and the Purpos-
                ive Cultivation of Democratic Values" in *Anthro-*
                pology: A Human Science. 92-104

                "The Application of Anthropological Techniques to
                Cross-National Communication" in *Anthropology: A*
                Human Science 105-125

NEWFELD, ELMER & DONALD R. JACOBS
  1963   "Voids, Values and Christian Fulfillment" *Prac.*
                Anth. 10   190-192

OPLER, MORRIS EDWARD
  1946   "Themes as Dynamic Forces in Culture" *Amer. Journ.*
                Sociol. 51   198-206

RADIN, PAUL
  1957   *Primitive Man as a Philosopher.* New York, Dover
                Publications (Originally published 1927)

SILVERMAN, S.F.
  1968   "Agricultural Organization, Social Structure &
                Values in Italy: Amoral Familism Reconsidered"
                Amer. Anth. 70   1-20 (For reactions, see
                Handelman & Weakland 1968)

TIPPETT, A.R.
  1967   "Feud and Reconciliation" Tippett 1967   190-200

  1968   "A Case Study of Fijian Clubs" Tippett   1968
                35-80

  1968   "A Case Study of Fijian Canoes and Boats" Tippett
                1968   81-116

  1970   "Murder and Justice" (Masongo) Tippett 1970 38-43

  1970   "Social Symbiosis and Honey-Gathering" (Masongo)
                Tippett 1970   44-49

TURNER, JONATHAN
  1971   "Patterns of Value Change During Economic Develop-
                ment: An Empirical Study" *Human Organ.* 30   126-36

VOGT, EVON Z. & ETHEL M. ALBERT (eds.)
  1966   *People of Rimrock: A Study of Values in Five Cul-*
                tures. Cambridge, Harvard Univ. Press

WALLIS, W.D.
  1952   "Values in a World of Cultures" *Amer. Anth.*   58
                143-146

WILSON, GODFREY
  1960   "An African Morality" Ottenberg 1960   345-364

WILSON, PETER J.
  1967   *A Malay Village and Malaysia: Social Values and*
              Rural Development. New Haven, HRAF Press

ECONOMIC ANTHROPOLOGY

ADAMS, J. & U.L. WOLTEMADE
  1970   "Village Economy in Traditional India: A Simplifi-
              ed Model" *Human Organ.* 29   49-56

ALKIRE, W.H.
  1965   *Lamotrek Atoll and Inter-island Socio-economic*
              Ties. Urbana, University of Illinois Press

AMES, DAVID W.
  1959   "The Wolof Co-operative Work Groups" Bascom &
              Herskovits 1959   224-237

BANDALIER, GEORGES
  1960   "Traditional Social Structures and Economic
              Changes" van den Berghe 1965   385-395 (Trans-
              lated from the French by van den Berghe)

BELSHAW, CYRIL S.
  1954   *Changing Melanesia: Social Economics of Culture*
              Contact. Melbourne, Oxford Univ. Press

  1965   *Traditional Exchange and Modern Markets*. Engle-
              wood Cliffs, Prentice-Hall

BENEDICT, BURTON
  1963   "Sociological Characteristics of Small Territories
              and their Implications for Economic Development"
              Banton 1966   23-36

BOHANNAN, P. & G. DALTON
  1965   *Markets in Africa: Eight Subsistence Economies in*
              Transition. New York, Doubleday & Co.

CANCIAN, FRANK
  1965   *Economics and Prestige in a Maya Community: The*
              Religious Cargo System in Zinacantan. Stanford,
              Stanford Univ. Press

COMHAIRE, JEAN L.
1956   "Economic Change and the Extended Family" van den
             Berghe 1965   117-127 (Reprinted from *Annals of
             the American Academy of Pol. & Soc. Science* 305
             45-52)

COUGHLIN, R.J.
1960   "Economic Organization and Interests" (Chinese in
             Thailand) Coughlin 1960   116-143

DALTON, GEORGE
1967   *Tribal and Peasant Economies: Readings in Economic
             Anthropology.* New York, The Natural History Press
             Symposium   (Good Bibliography 547-564)

1971   *Economic Development and Social Change: The
             Modernization of Village Communities.* New York,
             The Natural History Press Symposium (Good
             Bibliography 619-651)

DOUGLAS, MARY
1965   "The Lele - Resistance to Change" Bohannan &
             Dalton 1965   183-213

DUPIRE, MARGUERITE
1965   "The Fulani - Peripheral Markets of a Pastoral
             People" Bohannan & Dalton 1965   93-129

FINNEY, BEN R.
1965   *Polynesian Peasants and Proletarians: Socio-Econo-
             mic Change among the Tahitians of French Polynesia.*
             Wellington, Polynesian Society (Reprint Series 9)

FIRTH, RAYMOND
1946   *Malay Fishermen: Their Peasant Economy.* London,
             Kegan Paul, Trench and Trubner

1954   "Orientations in Economic Life" Evans-Pritchard
             1954   12-24

FORDE, D. & M. DOUGLAS
1956   "Primitive Economics" Shapiro 1956   330-344
             (Also in Dalton 1967 13-28)

FURTADO, CELSO
1963   "The Development of Brazil" *Scientific American*
             209   208-220

1965   *The Economic Growth of Brazil.* Berkeley, Univ.
             of California Press

GALARZA, ERNESTO
1964   *Merchants of Labor: The Mexican Bracero Story.*
            Charlotte, McNally & Loftin

GAMBLE, S.D.
1963   *North China Villages: Social, Political & Economic
            Activities before 1933.* Berkeley, Univ. of Calif-
            ornia Press

GEERTZ, CLIFFORD
1963   *Peddlers and Princes: Social Change and Economic
            Modernization in Two Indonesian Towns.* Chicago,
            University of Chicago Press

GITLOW, ABRAHAM L.
1947   *Economics of the Mount Hagen Tribes, New Guinea.*
            Seattle, Univ. of Washington Press

GRAY, ROBERT F.
1965   "The Sonjo: A Marketless Community" Bohannan &
            Dalton 1965   35-66

GULLIVER, P.H.
1965   "The Arusha - Economic and Social Change"
            Bohannan & Dalton 1965   250-284

HAMILTON, JAMES W.
1963   "Effects of the Thai Market on Karen Life" *Prac.
            Anth.* 10   209-215

HAMMOND, PETER B.
1959   "Economic Change and Mossi Acculturation" Bascom
            & Herskovits 1959   238-256

HARDING, THOMAS G.
1967   *Voyagers of the Vitiaz Strait: A Study of a New
            Guinea Trade System.* Seattle, Univ. of Washington
            Press

HERSKOVITS, M.J.
1952   *Economic Anthropology: A Study in Comparative
            Economics.* New York, Alfred A. Knopf

HORNER, GEORGE R.
1965   "Selected Cultural Barriers to the Modernization
            of Labor" Lewis 1965   166-175

KAPP, K.W.
1963   *Hindu Culture, Economic Development and Economic
            Planning in India.* Bombay, Asia Publishing House

KARP, MARK
1965   "The Legacy of French Economic Policy in Africa"
            Lewis   1965   145-153

KAST, EDWARD L.
1963   "Comments on 'Church, Plaza and Marketplace' "
            Prac. Anth. 10   175-178

LARSON, DONALD N.
1963   "Church, Plaza and Marketplace" *Prac. Anth.* 10
            167-174

MANDELBAUM, D.G.
1955   "Technology, Credit and Culture in a Nilgiri
            Village" Srinivas 1960   103-105

MANNERS, R.A.
1965   "The Kipsigis - Change with Alacrity" Bohannan &
            Dalton 1965   214-240

MAUSS, MARCEL
1967   *The Gift: Forms & Functions of Exchange in Archaic
            Societies.* New York, W.W. Norton & Co.

MAZZOCCO, WILLIAM J.
1965   "External Tensions: Resulting Development" Lewis,
            1965   154-165

MEILLASSOUX, CLAUDE
1965   "The Guro - Peripheral Markets Between the Forest
            and the Sudan" Bohannan & Dalton 1965   67-92

MILLER, WALTER B.
1971   "Sub-culture, Social Reform and the 'Culture of
            Poverty' " *Human Organ.* 30   111-125

MIRACLE, MARVIN P.
1965   "The Copperbelt - Trading and Marketing" Bohannan
            & Dalton 1965   285-341

NASH, MANNING
1961   "The Social Context of Economic Choice in a Small
            Society" *Man* 219   186-191 (Also in Dalton 1967
            524-538)

1964   "The Organization of Economic Life" Tax 1964
            171-180 (Also in Dalton 1967 3-11)

94

OKIGBO, PIUS
1956   "Social Consequences of Economic Development in
            West Africa" van den Berghe 1965 415-426 (Re-
            printed from *Annals of Amer. Academy of Pol. and
            Soc. Science* 305   125-133)

OTTENBERG, P.V.
1959   "The Changing Economic Position of Women among the
            Afikpo Ibo" Bascom & Herskovits 1959   205-223

PANT, PITAMBAR
1963   "The Development of India" *Scientific Amer.* 209
            189-206

REINING, CONRAD C.
1959   "The Role of Money in Zande Economy" *Amer. Anth.*
            61 39-43 (Also in van den Berghe 1965   409-414)

ROWLEY, CHARLES
1966   *The New Guinea Villager: The Impact of Colonial
            Rule on Primitive Society and Economy.* New York,
            Frederick Praeger

SAKSENA, R.N.
1962   *Social Economy of a Polyandrous People.* New York,
            Asia Publishing House

SALISBURY, R.F.
1962   "Early Stages of Economic Development in New
            Guinea" *Journ. Polynesian Soc.* 71   328-339
            (Also in Vayda 1968)

SHEARER, JOHN C.
1960   *High-Level Manpower in Overseas Subsidiaries:
            Experience in Brazil and Mexico.* Princeton,
            Princeton Univ. Dept. of Economics and Sociology

SINHA, D.P.
1968   *Cultural Change in an Intertribal Market (India).*
            New York, Asia Publishing Co.

SMITH, M.G.
1965   "The Hausa - Markets in a Peasant Economy"
            Bohannan & Dalton 1965   130-179

STOLPER, WOLFGANG F.
1963   "The Development of Nigeria" *Scientific Amer.*
            209   168-184

TIPPETT, A.R.
1967   "Exchange Economy and Christian Innovation"
            Tippett 1967   171-189

TIPPETT, A.R.
1970   "Ethiopian Markets" Tippett 1970   110-115

VAYDA, ANDREW P.
1966   "Pomo Trade Feasts" *Humanités, Cahiers d l'Institut de Science Économique Appliquée* (Also in Dalton 1967   494-500)

WAGLEY, CHARLES
1941   *Economics of a Guatemalan Village.* Menasha, American Anthropological Association

WEBER, MAX
1957   *Theory of Social and Economic Organization.* Glencoe, Free Press (Translation)

WELDON, PETER D. & M.V. MORSE
1970   "Market Structure in a Highland Peruvian Community" *Human Organ.* 29   43-48

YANG, MARTIN C.
1945   "The Family as a Primary Economic Group (China)" Yang 1945   73-85 (Also in Dalton 1967   333-346)

LAW

BARTON, R.F.
1969   *Ifugao Law.* Berkeley, Univ. of California Press (First printed 1910)

BOHANNAN, PAUL J.
1964   "Anthropology and the Law" Tax 1964   191-199

CAIRNS, HUNTINGTON
1931   "Law and Anthropology" from *Columbia Law Review* Slightly modified in Calverton 1931   331-362

COLE, C. DONALD
1967   "The Trial of Sachilamba" *Prac. Anth.* 14   228-31

DIAMOND, A.S.
1935   *Primitive Law.* London, Longmans, Green

ELIAS, TASLIM OLAWALE
1956   *The Nature of African Customary Law.* Manchester, Manchester Univ. Press

GLUCKMAN, MAX
1965   *Politics, Law and Ritual in Tribal Society.* Chicago, Aldine Publishing Co.

HAAR, BAREND TER
1948   *Adat Law in Indonesia.* New York, Inst. of Pacific
            Relations

HOGBIN, H.I.
1934   *Law and Order in Polynesia: a Study of Primitive
            Legal Institutions.* New York, Harcourt, Brace Co.

HOEBEL, E.A.
1954   *The Law of Primitive Man: A Study in Comparative
            Legal Dynamics.* Cambridge, Harvard Univ. Press

MAINE, SIR HENRY J.S.
1917   *Ancient Law, its Connection with the Early History
            of Society and its Relation to Modern Ideas.*
            London, J. Dent & Sons

MAIR, LUCY
1962   *Primitive Government.* Baltimore, Penguin Books

MALINOWSKI, B.
1926   *Crime and Custom in Savage Society.* New York,
            Harcourt, Brace & Co.

MOLLEMAN, J.F.
1952   *Shona Customary Law, with reference to Kinship,
            Marriage, the Family and the Estate.* Cape Town,
            Oxford Univ. Press

MUNTSCH, ALBERT
1936   "Primitive Law and Ethics" in *Cultural Anthro-
            pology.* New York, Bruce Publishing Co. 181-197

PERISTIANY, J.G.
1954   "Law" in Evans-Pritchard 1954   39-49

POSPISIL, LEOPOLD
1958   *Kapauku Papuans and Their Law.* New Haven, Yale
            Univ. Dept. of Anthropology

RADCLIFFE-BROWN, A.R.
1944   "Primitive Law" *Encyclopaedia of the Social
            Sciences.* London, The Macmillan Co.

RATTRAY, R.S.
1929   *Ashanti Law and Constitution.* Oxford, Clarendon
            Press

SCHAPERA, ISAAC
1955   *A Handbook of Tswana Law and Custom.* London,
            Oxford Univ Press
1967   *Government and Politics in Tribal Societies.*
            New York, Schocken Books

SOCIAL ANTHROPOLOGY AND CULTURAL ANALYSIS

(Including Values, Law and Economics)

Supplementary

BANTON, MICHAEL (Ed.)
   1966   *The Relevance of Models for Social Anthropology*.
             New York, F.A. Praeger

ELIAS, T.O.
   1954   *Groundwork of Nigerian Law*. London, Routledge &
             Kegan Paul

ISHWARAN, K. (Ed.)
   1966   "Politics and Social Change" *Inter. Journ. of
             Compar. Sociol.* 7 Special Number Symposium

LINTON, RALPH
   1954   "The Problem of Universal Values" Spencer 1954
             145-168

SAHLINS, MARSHALL D.
   1963   "On the Sociology of Primitive Exchange"
             Banton 1966 b: 139-236

SPENCER, ROBT. F. (Ed.)
   1954   *Method and Perspective in Anthropology: Papers in
             Honor of Wilson D. Wallis*, Minneapolis, Univ. of
             Minnesota Press

THOMAS, FRANKLIN
   1929   *The Environmental Basis of Society*. New York,
             The Century Co (Johnson Reprint 1965)

PATTERNS OF LEADERSHIP AND AUTHORITY

APTHORPE, RAYMOND (ed)
1960   "From Tribal Rule to Modern Government"   Rhodes-
            Livingstone Inst. for Soc. Research, Lusaka
            Proc. 13th Conference

BEALS, A.R.
1960   "Change and Leadership of a Mysore Village" in
            M.N. Srinivas (ed.) 1960 147-160

BEE, ROBERT L.
1970   " 'Self-Help' at Fort Yuma: A Critique" *Hum.*
            Organ. 29   155-161

BETLEY, BRIAN J.
1971   "Otomi Juez: An Analysis of a Political Middleman"
            Hum. Organ. 30   57-63

BRANDEURE, ERNEST
1971   "The Place of the Big Man in Traditional Hagan
            Society in the Central Highlands of New Guinea"
            Ethnology 10   194-210

BRAUN, N.
1971   *Laity Mobilized: Reflections on Church Growth in*
            Japan and Other Lands. Grand Rapids, Wm.
            Eerdmans Publishing Co.

BROKENSHA, DAVID and MARION PEARSALL (eds.)
1969   *The Anthropology of Development in Sub-Saharan*
            Africa. Lexington, Society for Applied Anthro-
            pology Monograph No. 10

BROWN, PAULA
1951   "Patterns of Authority in West Africa" *Africa* 21
            261-278

CHADWICK, N.K.
1936   "Shamanism Among the Tartars of Central Asia" *J.*
            Roy. Anth. Inst. 66   75-112

COHEN, YEHUDI A.
1964   "The Establishment of Identity in a Social Nexus:
            The Special Case of Initiation Ceremonies and
            their Relation to Value and Legal Systems" *Amer.
            Anth.* 66 529-552

d'EPINAY, C. LALIVE
1967   "The Training of Pastors and Theological Education:
            The Case of Chile" *I.R.M.* 56 185-192

DRUCKER, P.
1955   "Rank, Wealth and Kinship in Northwest Coast
            Society" in E.A. Hoebel, et al. (eds.) 214-221

ELLINGSWORTH, P.
1964   "Christianity and Politics in Dahomey, 1843-67"
            J. Afr. Hist. 5 209-220

EMERY, J.
1963   "The Preparation of Leaders in a Ladino-Indian
            Church" *Pract. Anth.* 10 127-134

ETZIONI, A.
1964   *Modern Organizations.* Englewood Cliffs, Prentice-
            Hall Inc. Ch.6 58-67

FALLERS, L.
1955   "The Predicament of a Modern African Chief: An
            Instance from Uganda" *Amer. Anthro.* 57 290-305
            (also in a Bobs-Merrill reprint A62)

FARGHER, BRIAN L.
1970   "Tribal Power Structure and Church Government"
            Pract. Anth. 17 280-284

FATHI, ASGHAR
1968   "Marginality, Leadership and Directed Change" *Hum.
            Organ.* 27 143-146

FIRTH, RAYMOND
1960   "Succession to Chieftainship in Tikopia" *Oceania*
            30 161-180

FORCE, R.W.
1960   *Leadership and Cultural Change in Palau.* Chicago,
            Chicago Natural History Museum

FORD, C.S.
1955   "The Role of a Fijian Chief" in E.A. Hoebel, et al.
            (eds.) 226-233

FORTES, M. and E.A. EVANS-PRITCHARD
  1961   *African Political Systems*. London, Oxford Univ.
            Press for International African Institute

FREEMAN, DERECK
  1964   "Some Observations on Kinship and Political
            Authority in Samoa" *Amer. Anth.* 66   553-568

FREYE, G.
  1964   *The Masters and the Slaves*. New York, Alf. A.
            Knopf

GARINA, F.S.
  1957   *Leadership in Community Development in Under-
            developed Areas*. Washington, D.C., Catholic Univ.
            Press

GLUCKMAN, H.
  1965   *Politics, Law and Ritual in Tribal Society*.
            Chicago, Aldine Pub. Co. 3-5   81-215

GOLDBERG, HARVEY
  1968   "Elite Groups in Peasant Communities: A Comparison
            of Three Middle East Villages" *Amer. Anth.* 70
            718-731

HAGOPIAN, E.C.
  1964   "The Status and Role of the Marabout in Pre-
            Protectorate Morroco" *Ethnology* 3   42-52

HAEBERLIN, H.
  1918   "Sbetetda'q: A Shamanistic Performance of the
            Coast Salish" *Amer. Anth.* 20   249-257

HIEBERT, PAUL G.
  1969   "Caste and Personal Rank in an Indian Village: An
            Extension in Techniques" *Amer. Anth.* 71   434-453

HILL, JAMES E.
  1969   "Theological Education for the Church in Mission"
            (Argentine) M.A. Thesis in Missions, School of
            World Mission, Fuller Theological Seminary,
            Pasadena

HOEBEL, E.A.; J.D. JENNINGS and E.R. SMITH
  1955   *Readings in Anthropology*. New York, McGraw-Hill
            Book Co.

HOLMES, LOWELL D.
  1964   "Leadership and Decision-Making in American Samoa"
            Cur. Anth. 5   446-449

HOPKINS, NICHOLAS S.
1969   "Leadership and Consensus in Two Malian Co-opera-
        tives" in Society for Applied Anthropology
        Monograph No. 10 64-69

HOWEGAWA, C.
1963   "The Hongwanji Buddhist Minister in Hawaii: A
        Study of an Occupation. *Soc. Proc.* 26 73-79

JOHNSON, C.C.
1964   "A Study of Modern Southwestern Indian Leadership"
        Ph.D. dissertation, Univ. of Colorado.

KAEPPLER, A.L.
1971   "Rank in Tonga" *Ethnology* 10 174-193

KEESING, F.
1941   *The South Seas in the Modern World.* New York,
        John Day & Co. for the Institute of Pacific Rela-
        tions 8-9 141-199

KEESING, F. and M.
1956   *Elite Communication in Samoa: A Study in Leader-
        ship.* Stanford, Stanford Univ. Press

KOPYTOFF, IGOR
1971   "Ancestors as Elders in Africa" *Africa* 41 129-
        142

KRADER, LAWRENCE
1968   *Formation of the State.* Englewood Cliffs,
        Prentice-Hall Inc.

KUPER, ADAM
1970   "Gluckman's Village Headman" *Amer. Anth.* 72
        355-358

LEEDS, ANTHONY
1969   "Ecological Determinates of Chieftainship Among
        the Yaruro Indians of Venezuela" in *Environment
        and Cultural Behavior* (ed. A.P. Vayda) New York,
        Natural History Press

LIENHARDT, GODFREY
1958   *Anuak Village Headmen* (Articles reprinted from
        Africa 29 for African International Institute.
        London, Oxford Univ. Press

LINDQUIST, LAWRENCE W.
1968   "The Civic Responsibility of Anthropologists to
        Public Education" *Hum. Organ.* 27 1-4

LINTON, R.
1936   *The Study of Man*. New York, D. Appleton-Century
            Co.,Inc.

LISPET, S.M. and A. SOLARI
1967   *Elites in Latin America*. New York, Oxford Univ.
            Press

LOEB, E.M.
1929   "Shaman and Seer" *Amer. Anth.* 31   80-84

LOEWEN, JACOB
1968 a   "From Tribal Society to National Church" *Prac.
            Anth.* 15   97-111

1968 b   "Socialization and Social Control: A Resume of
            Processes" *Prac. Anth.* 15   145-156

1968 c   "The Indigenous Church and Resocialization" *Prac.
            Anth.* 15   193-204

1969   "Socialization and Conversion in the Ongoing
            Church" *Pract. Anth.* 16   1-17

LUZBETAK, L.
1963   *The Church and Cultures: An Applied Anthropology
            for the Religious Worker*. Techny, Divine Word
            Publications

MAINE, SIR HENRY
1886   *Popular Government*. New York, Henry Holt & Co.

MAIR, L.
1964   *Primitive Government*. Baltimore, Penguin Books,
            Ltd.

MAYER, A.C.
1967   "Rural Leadership in Four Overseas Indian Com-
            munities" Freedman, 1967   167-188

MAYERS, M.K.
1966   "The Two-man Feud in the Guatemalan Church" *Prac.
            Anth.* 13   115-125

MEGGITT, J.J.
1967   "The Pattern of Leadership Among the Mae-Enga of
            New Guinea" *Anth. Forum*   2   20-35

MENDELSON, E.M.
1960   "Religion and Authority in Modern Burma" *World
            Today* 16   110-118

MIDDLETON, JOHN (ed.)
1970   *From Child to Adult: Studies in the Anthropology
            of Education.* Amer. Museum Sourcebook Symposium
            New York, Natural History Press

NADEL, S.F.
1958   *The Foundations of Social Anthropology.* London,
            Cohen & West

NIDA, E.A. and W.L. WONDERLY
1963   "Selection, Preparation and Function of Leaders in
            Indian Fields" *Prac. Anth.* 10   6-16

OLIVER, D.
1955   *A Solomon Island Society: Kinship & Leadership
            among the Siuai of Bougainville.* Cambridge,
            Harvard Univ. Press 9-14   335-448

OLMSTED, DONALD W.
1961   *Social Groups, Roles and Leadership.* E.Lansing,
            Mich. State Univ. Press

OPLER, M.E.
1946   "The Creative Role of Shamanism in Mescalero
            Apache Mythology" *J. Amer. Folklore* 59   268-281

1947   "Notes on Chircahua Apache Culture: Supernatural
            Power and the Shaman" *Man* 20   1-14

OTTENBERG, S. and P. (eds.)
1963   *Cultures and Societies of Africa* New York, Random
            House Press   Sec. 4 "Authority & Govt." 271-341

RADCLIFF-BROWN, A.R.
1924   "The Mother's Brother in Africa" *So. Afr. J. Sci.*
            21   1-15

RAMBO, DAVID L.
1968   "Training Competent Leaders for the C & M A
            Churches in the Philippines" M.A. Thesis in
            Missions, School of World Mission, Fuller Theo-
            logical Seminary, Pasadena

RETZLAFF, R.H.
1962   *Village Government in India: A Case Study.* London,
            Asia Publishing House

ROSALDO, R.I.,Jr.
1968   "Metaphors of Hierarchy in a Mayan Ritual" *Amer.
            Anth.* 70   524-536

SAHLINS, MARSHALL D.
    1963   "Poor Man, Rich Man, Big Man, Chief! Political
                Types in Melanesia and Polynesia" *Comparative
                Studies in Society and History* 5   285-303, also
                in Vayda's *Peoples and Cultures of the Pacific*
                157-176

SCHAPERA, I.
    1967   *Government and Politics in Tribal Societies*.
                New York, Schocken Books

SMUTKO, GREGORY
    1971   "Developing Indigenous Leadership in Miskito
                Evangelization" *Prac. Anth.* 18   55-63

SRINIVAS, M.N. (ed.)
    1960   *India's Villages*. New York, Asia Publishing House

SWARTZ, MARC J. (ed.)
    1968   *Local-Level Politics: Social and Cultural Perspec-
                tives*. Chicago, Aldine Publishing Co.   Symposium

TAKAMI, TOSHIHIRO
    1969   "Concepts of Leadership for the Growth of
                Christian Churches, with Special Reference to
                India" M.A. Thesis in Missions, School of World
                Mission, Fuller Theological Seminary, Pasadena

TANNER, R.E.S.
    1956   "The Sorcerer in Northern Sukumaland, Tanganyika"
                SW. Journ. Anth. 12   437-443

TAUFA, LOPETI
    1968   "Changes and Continuity in Oceania" M.A. Thesis
                in Missions, School of World Mission, Fuller Theo-
                logical Seminary, Pasadena (Has leadership as one
                of its themes)

TIPPETT, A.R.
    1967 a   *The Growth of an Indigenous Church*. Pasadena,
                School of World Mission and Institute of Church
                Growth   Multigraphed

    1967 b   *Solomon Islands Christianity*. New York, Friend-
                ship Press 8-9   119-146

TURNER, C.V.
    1968   "The Sinasina 'Big Man' Complex: A Central Theme"
                Prac. Anth. 15   16-23

TURNER, P.R.
1967 "Village Rank and Culture Change" *Prac. Anth.* 14
    209-213

VAN GENNEP, A.
1960 *The Rites of Passage.* Chicago, Univ. of Chicago
    Press

VAYDA, ANDREW P.
1961 "Maori Prisoners and Slaves in the 19th Century"
    Ethnohistory 8 144-155

VIDYARTHI, L.P.
1964 *Cultural Contours of Tribal Bihar.* Calcutta,
    Punthi Pustak 8 149-162

1967 *Leadership in India.* Bombay, Asia Publishing House

WATSON, JAMES B. and JULIAN SAMORA
1954 "Subordinate Leadership in a Bicultural Community:
    An Analysis" *Amer. Soc. Rev.* 19 413-421

WILLIAMS, F.E.
1951 *The Blending of Cultures: An Essay on the Aims of*
    Native Education. Port Moresby, Territory of
    Papua, Official Research Publication No. 1,
    Government Printer

WOODS, F.J.
1949 *Mexican Ethnic Leadership in San Antonio, Texas.*
    Washington, D.C., Catholic Univ. of America

YELD, E.R.
1960 "Islam and Social Stratification in Nigeria"
    Brit. J. of Sociology 11 112-128

ACCULTURATION, CULTURE CLASH, CULTURE CHANGE

Some items on Decision-making, (in that it effects Culture Change) are included here, but for Directed Change and Group Dynamics see "Applied Anthropology". Check also "Anthropology and the Missionary" and "Communication".

ACHEBE, CHINUA
  1958   *Things Fall Apart*. London, Heinemann Educational
              Books (African Writers Series) (Novel)

AIYAPPAN, A.
  1965   *Social Revolution in a Kerala Village: A Study in
              Culture Change*. New York, Asia Publishing House

BAEZ-CAMARGO, G.
  1956   "Church, State and Religious Liberty in Latin
              America" *World Dominion* 34   29-32

BARNETT, H.G.
  1942   "Invention and Cultural Change" *Amer. Anth.* 44
              14-30

BARTH, FREDERICK
  1967   "On the Study of Social Change" *Amer. Anth.* 69
              661-669

BEETHAM, T.A.
  1967   *Christianity and the New Africa*. New York, Fredk.
              A. Praeger

BENNETT, CLAUDE F.
  1969   "Diffusion within Dynamic Populations" *Human Org.*
              28   243-247

BENNETT, E.B.
  1955   "Discussion, Decision, Commitment and Consensus in
              'Group Decision' " *Human Relations* 8   251-273

BERTSCHE, JAMES E.
  1965   "Congo Rebellion" *Prac. Anth.* 12   210-226

BLASCHKE, ROBERT C.
1959   "A Franco-African Cross-Cultural Clash" *Prac.*
Anth. 6 193-197

BLUMSTOCK, ROBT. E.
1967   "Mission to the Jews: Reduction of Inter-Group
Tension" *Prac. Anth.* 14 37-43

BOCK, PHILIP K. (ed.)
1970   *Culture Shock: A Reader in Cultural Anthropology.*
New York, Alfred A. Knopf

BOHANNAN, PAUL & FRED PLOG (eds.)
1967   *Beyond the Frontier: Social Process and Culture*
Change. New York, The Natural History Press
(Symposium)

BOULDING, KENNETH E.
1964   "Where Are We Going: If Anywhere?" *Prac. Anth.*
11 14-24, 34

BRAMELD, THEODORE
1959   *The Remaking of a Culture: Life and Education in*
Puerto Rico. New York, John Wiley & Sons

BROWN, INA C.
1963   "Peoples in Transition" Ch. 10 of *Understanding*
Other Cultures. Englewood Cliffs, Prentice-Hall

BUSIA, K.A.
1959 a   "Africa in Transition: I. Before European Coloni-
zation" *Prac. Anth.* 6 117-123

1959 b   "Africa in Transition: II. Under European Coloni-
zation" *Prac. Anth.* 6 171-178

1959 c   "Africa in Transition: III. Technical Civilization" *Prac. Anth.* 6 223-230

BUSWELL, J.O. III
1968   "Cultural Ethos of Primitive Tribes: Yir Yiront,
Kaingang and Auca" *Prac. Anth.* 15 177-188

CLARKE, J.J.
1970   "On the Unity and Diversity of Cultures" *Amer.*
Anth.   72 545-554

COLEMAN, JAMES S.
1956   "Social Cleavage and Religious Conflict" *The*
Journ. of Social Issues 12 44-56

COMAS, J.
1961   " 'Scientific' Racism Again" *Curr. Anth.* 2 303-40

COSTHUIZAN, G.C.
1964   "The Church Among African Forces" *Prac. Anth.* 11
            161-178

DALTON, GEORGE (ed.)
1971   *Economic Development and Social Change: The Modern-
            ization of Village Communities.* New York, The
            Natural History Press (Symposium)(Pt.3 especially)

DELORIA, VINE, JR.
1969   *Custer Died for Your Sins: An Indian Manifesto.*
            New York, Avon Books

1970   *We Talk, You Listen: New Tribes, New Turf.*
            New York, The Macmillan Co.

DICKERSON, DORIS H.
1970   "Possible Conflicts as Karens Approach Integration"
            Prac. Anth. 17   1-9

DICKSON, K.A.
1971   "Christian and African Traditional Ceremonies"
            Prac. Anth. 18   64-71

DIKE, K.O.
1961   "Benin: A Great Forest Kingdom of Mediaeval
            Nigeria" *Prac. Anth.* 8   31-35

DUBBELDAM, L.F.B.
1964   "The Devaluation of the Kapauku Cowrie as a Factor
            of Social Disintegration" *Amer. Anth.* 66   293-
            303   (Special number on New Guinea)

EGGAN, FRED
1963   "Cultural Drift and Social Change" *Curr. Anth.*
            4   347-355

ELKIN, A.P.
1937   "The Reaction of Primitive Races to the White Man's
            Culture: A Study in Culture Contact" *Hibbert
            Journ.* 35   537-545

ENGLISH, PAUL WARD
1966   *City and Village in Iran: Settlement and Economy
            in the Kirman Basin.* Madison, Univ. of Wisconsin
            Press

FALLERS, LLOYD A.
1965   "Ideology and Culture in Uganda Nationalism"
            Prac. Anth. 12   227-236

FIRTH, RAYMOND
1957   *Social Change in Tikopia: Restudy of a Polynesian
            Community after a Generation.* London,Allen & Unwin

FRAZIER, E. FRANKLIN
1970   *Race and Culture Contacts in the Modern World.*
            Boston, Beacon Press

Freed, S.A.
1957   "Suggested Type Societies in Acculturation Studies"
            Amer. Anth. 59   55-68

FUETER, PAUL D.
1964   "The African Contribution to Christian Education"
            Prac. Anth. 11   1-13

GANGEL, KENNETH O.
1971   "The Amish of Jamesport, Missouri" *Prac. Anth.*
            18   156-166

GEERTZ, C.
1957   "Ritual and Social Change: A Javanese Example"
            Amer. Anth. 59   32-54

GLUCKMAN, MAX
1967   *Custom and Conflict in Africa.* New York, Barnes
            and Noble

GOLD, DELORES
1967   "Psychological Changes Associated with Accultur-
            ation of Saskatchewan Indians" *Journ. Soc. Psych.*
            71   177-184

GOLDSCHMIDT, W.
1965   Symposium on "Variation and Adaptability of
            Culture" *Amer. Anth.* 67   400-447

GOODENOUGH, W.H.
1966   *Cooperation in Change: An Anthropological Study to
            Community Development.* New York, John Willey &
            Sons   Science Edition Paperback

GOODY, J.
1957   "Anomie in Ashanti?" *Africa* 27   356-363

GRIMES, JOS. E. & BARBARA
1960   "Individualism in the Huichol Church" *Prac. Anth.*
            7   58-62

HALLOWELL, A.I.
  1945   "Sociopsychological Aspects of Acculturation"
            Linton 1945   171-200

  1963   "American Indians, White and Black: The Phenomenon
            of Transculturation" *Curr. Anth.* 4   519-531

HANSON, R.C. & O.G. SIMMONS
  1968   "The Role Path: A Concept and Procedure for Study-
            ing Migration to Urban Communities" *Human Organ.*
            27   152-158

HATCH, JOHN
  1961   *Africa Today - and Tomorrow: An Outline of Basic
            Facts and Major Problems.* New York, F.A. Praeger

HERSKOVITS, M.J.
  1938   *Acculturation: the Study of Culture Contact.*
            New York, Augustin

  1945   "The Processes of Culture Change" Linton 1945
            143-170

  1964   *Cultural Dynamics.* New York, Alfred A. Knopf

HILLERY, GEO. A. JR.
  1966   "Navajos and Eastern Kentuckians: A Comparative
            Study in the Cultural Consequences of the Demo-
            graphic Transition" *Amer. Anth.* 68   52-70

HOGBIN, H.I.
  1958   *Social Change.* London, C.A. Watts

HOLLINSTEINER, MARY R.
  1961   "A Lowland Philippine Municipality in Transition"
            Prac. Anth. 8   54-62

HOLMBERG, ALLAN R.
  1954   "Adventures in Culture Change" *Method and Per-
            spective in Anthropology.* R.F. Spencer, ed.
            Minneapolis, Univ. of Minnesota Press   103-113

HOWARD, JOHN R.
  1970   *Awakening Minorities: American Indians, Mexican
            Americans, Puerto Ricans,* Chicago, Aldine Pub. Co.

HUDDLESTON, TREVOR
  1957   *Naught for Your Comfort.* London, Collins (Fontana
            Book)

ILOGU, E.
1965   "Christianity and Ibo Traditional Religion"
            I. R. M. 54   335-342

ISAACS, HAROLD R.
1963   "Back to Africa" *Prac. Anth.* 10   71-88 (from
            New Yorker May 13, 1961)

KAUNDA, KENNETH
1966   *A Humanist in Africa: Letters to Colin Morris.*
            Nashville, Abingdon Press

KEESING, F.M.
1953   *Culture Change: an Analysis and Bibliography of
            Anthropological Sources to 1952.* Stanford,
            Stanford Univ. Press

LAWRENCE, P.
1963   "Religion: Help or Hindrance in Economic Develop-
            ment in Papua and New Guinea" *Mankind* 6   3-11

LEAKEY, L.S.B.
1953   *Mau Mau and the Kikuyu.* London, Methuen & Co.

LEWIS, OSCAR
1960   *Tepoztlan: Village in Mexico.* New York, Holt,
            Rinehart & Winston

1963   *Life in a Mexican Village: Tepoztlan Restudied.*
            Urbana, Univ. of Illinois Press (See Lewis 1960)

LINTON, R.
1940   *Acculturation in Seven American Tribes.* New York,
            Appleton-Century-Crofts

LURIE, N.O.
1961   "The Voice of the American Indian" (Conference
            Report) *Curr. Anth.* 2   478-491(See also Sol Tax)

MADDOX, GEO. L. & JOSEPH H. FICHTER
1966   "Religion and Social Change in the South" *Journ.
            Soc. Issues* 22   44-58

MALINOWSKI, BRONISLAW
1945   *The Dynamic of Culture Change: An Inquiry into
            Race Relations in Africa.* London, Oxford Univ.
            Press

MANDELBAUM, D.G.
1943   "Culture Change Among the Nilgiri Tribes" *Amer.
            Anth.* 43   19-26

MANDELBAUM, D.G.
1965   "Alcohol and Culture" *Curr. Anth.* 6 281-293

MANNERS, ROBERT A. (ed.)
1964   *Process and Pattern in Culture.* Chicago, Aldine
              Publishing Co. (Symposium)

MATHIESEN, THOMAS
1968   "A Functional Equivalent to Inmate Cohesion"
              Human Organ. 27   117-124

MAYERS, MARVIN K.
1966   "The Two-Man Feud in the Guatemalan Church" *Prac.
              Anth.* 13   115-125

McANDREWS, ROBT. L.
1967   "Liberian Village Trial and 'American Justice'"
              Prac. Anth. 14 103-112

MEAD, MARGARET
1953   *Growing Up in New Guinea.* New York, New American
              Library (Mentor Book, first issued 1930) (See
              Mead 1961)

1955   *Cultural Patterns and Technical Change.* New York,
              The New American Library (Mentor Book)

1961   *New Lives for Old: Cultural Transformation - Manus
              1928-1953.* New York, New Amer. Library (See 1953)

1963   "Socialization and Enculturation" *Curr. Anth.* 4
              184-188

1964 a   *Continuities in Cultural Evolution.* New Haven,
              Yale Univ. Press

1964 b   "The Application of Anthropological Techniques to
              Cross-National Communication" in *Anthropology: A
              Human Science.* New York, Van Nostrand Co. 105-125

1968   *The Mountain Arapesh.* Vols. 1-3. New York, The
              Natural History Press

MILLER, PAUL A.
1952   "The Process of Decision-making within the Context
              of Community Organization" *Rural Socio.* 17 153-61

NASH, MANNING
1962   "Race and the Ideology of Race" *Curr. Anth.* 3
              285-302

NASH, MANNING
1967   *Machine Age Maya: The Industrialization of a Guatemalan Community.* Chicago, Univ. of Chicago Press

1968   "The Market as Arena for Change in Kelantan, Malaysia" *Amer. Anth.* 70 944-949

NEUFELD, ELMER
1964   "The Unfinished Revolution" (Congo) *Prac. Anth.* 11 118-138

NIEHOFF, A.H. (ed.)
1966   *A Casebook of Social Change.* Chicago, Aldine Publishing Co.

NIELSEN, ERIK W.
1964   "Asian Nationalism" *Prac. Anth.* 11 211-226

NIXON, ROBERT E.
1965   "Growing Up in Today's World" *Prac. Anth.* 12 134-144

O'BRIEN, D. & A. PLORG
1964   "Acculturation Movements among the Western Dani" *Amer. Anth.* 66 281-292 (Spec. No. on New Guinea)

OLIVER, ROLAND
1952   *The Missionary Factor in East Africa.* London, Longmans, Green & Co.

OWENS, RAYMOND
1971   "Industrialization and the Indian Joint Family" *Ethnology* 10 223-250

PANDWE, MURRAY B.
1963   "An African Student Overseas" *Prac. Anth.* 10 230- 232

PASTERNAK, BURTON
1968   "Atrophy of Patrilineal Bonds in a Chinese Village in Historical Perspective" *Ethnohistory* 15 293-327

PATON, ALAN
1960   *Cry, The Beloved Country.* London, Penguin Books (Novel: first published 1944)

POGGIE, J.J. JR. & F.C. MILLER
1969   "Contact, Change and Industrialization in a Network of Mexican Villages" *Human. Organ.* 28 190-98

PRESTON, D.A.
  1969   "Rural Emigration in Andean America" *Human Organ.*
              28   279-286

RAO, MARK SUNDAR
  1968   "Indigenous Heritage and Foreign Influence"
              Stud. World 61   324-329   (Religion)

REDFIELD, ROBT.
  1953   *The Primitive World and Its Transformations.*
              Ithica, Cornell Univ. Press

  1962   *A Village that Chose Progress: Chan Kom Revisited.*
              Chicago, Univ. of Chicago Press (See Redfield and
              Rojas 1934)

REDFIELD, ROBT. & A.V. ROJAS
  1934   *Chan Kom: A Maya Village.* Washington, D.C.
              Carnegie Institution (Reissued 1962 by Univ. of
              Chicago Press, Chicago) (See Redfield 1962)

REYBURN, W.D.
  1958 a   "Motivations for Christianity: An African Con-
              version" *Prac. Anth.*   5   27-32

  1958 b   "Meaning and Reconstruction: A Cultural Process"
              Prac. Anth. 5 79-82

  1958 c   "The Missionary and Cultural Diffusion" Parts 1,
              11 and 111. *Prac. Anth.* 5   139-146,185-90,216-21

  1960   "Conflicts and Contradictions in African Christi-
              anity" *Prac. Anth.* Suppl. 53-57

  1964   "The Missionary Sense of Loss" *Prac. Anth.* 11
              277-282

RICH, JOHN A.
  1970   "Religious Acculturation in the Philippines"
              Prac. Anth.   17   193-196

RIGGS, FRED W.
  1962   "The Prevalence of Clects" *Amer. Behav. Sci.*   5
              15-18

RIVERS, W.H.R.
  1922   *Essays on the Depopulation of Melanesia.*
              Cambridge, The University Press

ROGERS, E.M.
  1962   *Diffusion of Innovations.* New York, Free Press of
              Glencoe

ROSENFELD, HENRY
1968   "Change, Barriers to Change and Contradictions in
            the Arab Village Family" *Amer. Anth.* 70 732-752

RYAN, JOHN
1969   *The Hot Land: Focus on New Guinea.* Melbourne,
            Macmillan

SAHAY, KESHARI N.
1968   "Impact of Christianity on the Uraon of the Chain-
            pur Belt in Chotanagpur: An Analysis of its
            Cultural Process" *Amer. Anth.* 70   923-942

SALISBURY, RICHARD F.
1970   *Vunamani: Economic Transformation in a Traditional
            Society.* Berkeley, Univ. of California Press
            (New Britain)

SAMARIN, WM. J.
1959   "Gbeya Pre-scientific Attitudes and Christianity"
            Prac. Anth. 6   179-182

SCHWARTZ, GARRY & D. MERTEN
1968   "Social Identity and Expressive Symbols; The Mean-
            ing of an Initiation Ritual" *Amer. Anth.* 70
            1117-1131

SHARMA, K.N.
1961   "Occupational Mobility of Castes in a North Indian
            Village" *SW. Journ. Anth.* 17   146-164

SHARP, LAURISTON
1952   "Steel Axes for Stone-age Australians" *Human
            Organ.* 11   17-22

SHEPARDSON, MARY & B. HAMMOND
1964   "Change and Persistence in an Isolated Navajo
            Community" *Amer. Anth.* 66   1029-1050

SHIVER, WAYMAN B., JR.
1965   "My Life Abroad: Changes in Fundamental Attitudes"
            Prac. Anth. 12   131-133

SIEGEL, M.
1941   "Religion in Western Guatemala: A Product of
            Acculturation" *Amer. Anth.* 43   62-76

SILVERMAN, M.G.
1962   "The Resettled Banaban (Ocean Is.) Community in
            Fiji: A Preliminary Report" *Curr. Anth.* 3   429-431

116

SINHA, D.P.
  1968   *Culture Change in an Intertribal Market (Hill Peoples of Chotapagpur)* New York, Asia Publish.Co.

SMALLEY, WM. A.
  1958   "Planting the Church in a Disintegrating Culture" *Prac. Anth.* 5   228-233 (Reply to Sorensen)

  1960   "The Gospel and Culture of Laos" *Prac. Anth.* Suppl. 63-39

SORENSEN, LOIS
  1958   "A People in Transition" *Prac. Anth.* 5   222-227 (See Smalley)

SPICER, E.H.
  1958   "Social Structure and the Acculturation Process (Yaqui Religious Acculturation)" *Amer. Anth.* 60 433-441

STEINER, STAN
  1968   *The New Indians.* New York, Dell Publishing Co.

STEWARD, J.H.
  1943   "Acculturation Studies in Latin America: Some Needs and Problems" *Amer. Anth.* 45   189-206

STOWE, DAVID M.
  1970   "Changing Patterns of Missionary Service in Today's World" *Prac. Anth.* 17   107-118

STUNTZ, H.
  1944   "Christian Missions and Social Cohesion" *Amer. Journ. Sociol.* 50   184-188

TAX, SOL
  1961   "What the Indians Want" (Conference Report) *Curr. Anth.* 2   492-500 (See also N.O. Lurie)

TIPPETT, A.R.
  1955   "Fijian Pilot Project in Community Development" *I. R. M.* 44   229-231

  1967 a   "Period of Rapid Acculturation" in *The Growth of an Indigenous Church.* Pasadena, Fuller Theological Seminary

  1967 b   "Religions, Group Conversion in Non-Western Society" Research-in-Progress Pamphlet Series 11 Pasadena, School of World Mission

TIPPETT, A.R.
  1967 c   *Solomon Islands Christianity: A Study in Growth
            and Obstruction.* London, Lutterworth Press (Parts
            4-6, 137-345, particularly)

  1968   *Fijian Material Culture: A Study of Culture Con-
            text, Function and Change.*   Honolulu, Bishop
            Museum Press (Bull. 232)

  1969   *Verdict Theology in Missionary Theory.* Lincoln,
            Lincoln Christian College Press (Pt. 3, 95-154
            concerns social change and Christian mission)

TRAGER, FRANK N.
  1962   "Some Comments on 'Transitional Societies in Asia'"
            Amer. Behav. Sci. 5   5-8

TURNER, GLEN D.
  1964   "Indian Assimilation and Bilingual Schools" *Prac.
            Anth.* 11   204-210

TURNER, JONATHAN
  1971   "Patterns of Value Change During Economic Develop-
            ment: An Empirical Study" *Human Organ.* 30 126-36

UCHENDU, VICTOR C.
  1964   "Missionary Problems in Nigerian Society" *Prac.
            Anth.* 11   105-117

ULRICH, D.U.
  1970   "The Introduction and Diffusion of Firearms in New
            Zealand, 1800-1840" *Journ. Polynesian Soc.* 79
            399-410

VANDERLYN, R.P.
  1969   "Comparative Funeral Practices" *Prac. Anth.* 16
            49-62

VISSER'T HOOFT, W.A.
  1967   "Accommodation - True and False" *SE. Asia Journ.
            of Theol.* 8   5-18

VOGT, EVON Z. & E.M. ALBERT (eds.)
  1966   *People of Rimrock: A Study of Values in Five
            Cultures.* Cambridge, Harvard Univ. Press

VON DER KROEF, J.
  1959   "Culture Contact and Culture Conflict in Western
            New Guinea" *Anth. Qr.* 32   134-160

WADLOW, RENÉ V.L.
　　1969　　　"An African Church and Social Change" *Prac. Anth.*
　　　　　　　16　264-273

WALLACE, ANTHONY F.C.
　　1956　　　"Revitalization Movements" *Amer. Anth.*　58 264-81

WANG, G.T. & J.A. FOWLER
　　1970　　　"Accomodation in an Iban Church Today" *Prac.
　　　　　　　Anth.*　17　220-234

WASHBURN, WILCOMB E.
　　1964　　　*The Indian and the White Man.*　New York, Doubleday
　　　　　　　& Co.　(Anchor Book)

WEBSTER, DOUGLAS
　　1964　　　"A 'Spiritual Church' " *Prac. Anth.*11　229-32,240

WIEBE, PAUL D.
　　1970　　　"Christianity and Social Change in South India"
　　　　　　　Prac. Anth.　17　128-136

WILSON, GODFREY & MONICA
　　1945　　　*The Analysis of Social Change, based on Observa-
　　　　　　　tions in Central Africa.*　Cambridge, The Universi-
　　　　　　　ty Press

WITTMER, JOE
　　1971　　　"Cultural Violence and Twentieth Century Progress"
　　　　　　　(Amish)　*Prac. Anth.*　18　146-155

WONDERLY, WM. L.
　　1960　　　"Urbanization: The Challenge of Latin America in
　　　　　　　Transition" *Prac. Anth.*　7　205-209

　　1967　　　"The Indigenous Background of Religion in Latin
　　　　　　　America" *Prac. Anth.*　14　241-248

WYLLIE, ROBT. W.
　　1968　　　"Ritual and Social Change: A Ghanian Example"
　　　　　　　Amer. Anth.　70　21-33

ACCULTURATION, CULTURE CHANGE

(SUPPLEMENTARY)

BASCOM, W.R. & M.J. HERSKOVITS
1959   *Continuity and Change in African Cultures.*
Chicago, Univ. of Chicago Press

BUREAU, M.R.
1965   "Influence de la Christianisation sur les institutions   traditionnelles des ethnies côtières du
Cameroun" Baëta 1968   165-181

CHAI, CH'U & WINGERG
1962   *The Changing Society of China.* New York, New
American Library (Mentor)

CHRISTIANSEN, J.B.
1959   "The Adaptive Functions of the Fanti Priesthood"
Bascom & Herskovits 1959   257-278

EBERHARD, WOLFRAM
1967.   *Settlement and Social Change in Asia.* Hong Kong,
Hong Kong Univ. Press

EISENSTADT, S.N.
1965   "Social Change and Modernization in African Societies South of the Sahara" Lewis 1965   223-237

FULLER, C.E.
1959   "Ethnohistory in the Study of Culture Change in
Southeast Africa" Bascom & Herskovits 1959
113-129

GELLNER, ERNEST
1965   "Tribalism and Social Change in North Africa"
Lewis 1965   107-118

HOLMES, LOWELL D.
1958   *TA'U: Stability and Change in a Samoan Village.*
Wellington, Polynesian Society (Reprint 7)

LERNER, DANIEL
1967   "Comparative Analysis of Processes of Moderni-
            zation" Miner 1967   21-38

LYSTAD, R.A.
1959   "Marriage and Kinship among the Ashanti and the
            Agni: A Study of Differential Acculturation"
            Bascom & Herskovits 1959   187-204

MESSENGER, J.C. JR.
1959   "Religious Acculturation among the Anang Ibibio"
            Bascom & Herskovits 1959   279-299

MINER, HORACE
1967   "The City and Modernization" Miner 1967   1-20

OTTENBERG, SIMON
1959   "Ibo Receptivity to Change" Bascom & Herskovits
            1959   130-143

SCHAPERA, I.
1958   "Christianity and the Tswana" *Journ. Roy. Anth.
            Inst.* 88   1-9 (Also in Ottenberg 1960   489-503)

SCHNEIDER, H.K.
1959   "Pakot Resistance to Change" Bascom & Herskovits
            1959   144-167

SILVERT, K.H. (ed.)
1963   *Expectant Peoples: Nationalism and Development.*
            New York, Vintage Books

SRINIVAS, M.N.
1966   *Social Change in Modern India.* Berkeley, Univ. of
            California Press

VILAKAZI, A.
1962   *Zulu Transformations: A Study of the Dynamics of
            Social Change.* Pietermaritzburg, Univ. of Natal
            Press

CULTURE AND PERSONALITY

ACKERKNECHT, E. H.
1943   "Psychopathology, Primitive Medicine and
            Primitive Culture" *Bull. of the History of
            Medicine*, 14, 30-67

ALEXANDER, FRANZ
1942   "Educative Influences of Personality Factors in
            the Environment" in Kluckhohn & Murray, 1969: 421-
            435

ARONOFF, JOEL
1967   *Psychological Needs and Cultural Systems*.
            Princeton, New Jersey, D. Van Nostrand Co.

BARNOUW, VICTOR
1950   "Acculturation and Personality among the Wisconsin
            Chippewa" *Amer. Anthropological Association Memoir*
            72, Menasha

1963   *Culture and Personality*. Homewood, Illinois,
            Dorsey Press

BECK, ROBT. J.
1967   "Some Proto-Psychotherapeutic Elements in the
            Practice of the Shaman" *Hist. of Relig.* 6,
            303-327

BENEDICT, RUTH
1934   "Anthropology and the Abnormal" *Journ. of Gen.
            Psych.* 10, 59-80   Also in Haring,1956: 183-201

1938   "Continuities and Discontinuities in Cultural
            Conditioning" *Psychiatry* 1, 161-167. Also in
            Kluckhohn & Murray, 1969: 522-531

BENEDICT, RUTH
1946   *The Chrysanthemum and the Sword; Patterns of Japanese Culture.* Boston, Houghton Mifflin Co.

1959   *Patterns of Culture.* Boston, Houghton Mifflin Co.

BERNE, ERIC
1959   "The Mythology of Dark and Fair: Psychiatric Use of Folklore" *J. Amer. Folklore* 72, 1-13

BETLEY, BRIAN J.
1971   "Otomi Juez: An Analysis of a Political Middleman" *Hum. Organ.* 30, 57-63

BIDNEY, DAVID
1953   *Theoretical Anthropology.* New York, Columbia University Press (especially chapters 3 and 11)

BISCHOF, LEDFORD J.
1964   *Interpreting Personality Theories.* New York, Harper & Row

BOURGUIGNON, ERIKA
1965   "The Self, the Behavioral Environment and the Theory of Spirit Possession" in Spiro's *Context and Meaning in Cultural Anthropology*

BRANDEURE, ERNEST
1971   "The Place of the Big Man in Traditional Hagen Society in the Central Highlands of New Guinea" *Ethnology* 10, 194-210

BRUNER, EDWARD M.
1964   "The Psychological Approach in Anthropology" in *Horizons of Anthropology*, ed. by Sol Tax. Chicago, Aldine Publishing Co. pp. 71-80

CENTLIVRES, M. & P. AND M. SLOBIN
1971   "A Muslim Shaman of Afghan Turkestan" *Ethnology* 10, 160-173

CHANCE, NORMAN A.
1965   "Acculturation, Self-Identification and Personality Adjustment" *Amer. Anth.* 67, 372-393

COHEN, YEHUDI A.
1961   *Social Structure and Personality.* New York, Holt, Rinehart and Winston

1966   "On Alternate Views of the Individual in Culture-and-Personality" *Amer. Anth.* 68, 355-361

D'ANDRADE, ROY G.
 1965   "Trait Psychology and Componential Analysis"
             Amer. Anth.   215-228

DE JESUS, CAROLINA MARIA
 1962   *Child of the Dark: The Diary of Carolina Maria
             de Jesus.* New York, The New American Library

DE VOS, GEORGE and WAGATSUMA, HIROSHI
 1967   *Japan's Invisible Race.* Berkeley, University of
             California Press

DOBKIN, MARLENE
 1969   "Fortune's Malice: Divination, Psychotherapy and
             Folk Medicine in Peru" *J. Amer. Folklore*, 82,
             132-141

DOBZHANSKY, THEODOSIUS
 1965   "Religion, Death and Evolutionary Adaptation" in
             Spiro, 1965

DOLLARD, JOHN
 1938   "The Life History in Community Studies" *Amer. Soc.
             Rev.* 3, 724-737. Also in Kluckhohn & Murray
             1969

 1949   *Criteria for the Life History, with analyses of
             Six Notable Documents,* New Haven, Yale University
             Press

DU BOIS, CORA
 1961   *The People of Alor: A Psychological Study of an
             East Indian Island.* Vols. 1-2. New York, Harper
             & Brs.

DYK, WALTER
 1938   *Son of Old Man Hat,* New York, Harcourt, Brace &
             Co. (Paperback edition, University of Nebraska
             Press, 1966)

EDGERTON, R.B.
 1966   "Conceptions of Psychosis in Four Eastern African
             Societies" *Amer. Anth.* 68, 408-425

 1970   "Method in Psychological Anthropology" Naroll &
             Cohen, 1970, 338-352

ERIKSON, ERIK H.
 1963   *Childhood and Society.* New York, W. W. Norton
             & Co.

FERGUSON, F.N.
1968   "Navaho Drinking: Some Tentative Hypotheses"
            Hum. Organ. 27,   159-167

FISCHER, J. L.
1963   "The Socio-psychological Analysis of Folktales",
            Cur. Anth. 4,   235-295

FISCHER, J.L. and M.J. SWARTZ
1960   "Socio-psychological Aspects of Some Trukese and
            Ponapean Love Songs" *J. Amer. Folklore* 73,
            218-224

FOSTER, GEO. M.
1961   "Interpersonal Relations in Peasant Society" *Hum.
            Organ.* 19,   174-84   Comments by Lewis and Pitt
            Rivers and rejoinder

1969   "Character and Personal Relationships Seen through
            Proverbs in Tzintzuntzan, Mexico" *J. Amer.
            Folklore*, 83,   304-317

FRANK, JEROME D.
1963   *Persuasion and Healing.* New York, Schocken Books

FREUD, SIGMUND
1961   *Civilization and its Discontents.* New York, W. W.
            Norton & Co.

GILLIN, JOHN
1948   *The Ways of Men: An Introduction to Anthropology.*
            New York, D. Appleton-Century Co., Inc.

GLADWIN, THOS.
1958   "Canoe Travel in the Truk Area: Technology and its
            Psychological Correlates" *Amer. Anth.* 60,   893-
            899

GOLDFRANK, ESTHER
1945   "Socialization, Personality and Structure of
            Pueblo Society" (Hopi and Zuni) *Amer. Anth.* 47,
            516-539. Also in Haring, 1956: 303-327

GOLDKIND, VICTOR
1970   "Anthropologists, Informants and the Achievement
            of Power in Chan Kom", *Sociologus*, 20,   17-41

GOODMAN, MARY ELLEN
1967   *The Individual and Culture.* Homewood, The Dorsey
            Press

GORER, G.
1950   "The Concept of National Character" *Science News*, 18,   105-122. Also in Kluckhohn & Murray 1969: 246-259

GRAVES, T.D.
1970   "The Personal Adjustment of Navaho Indian Migrants to Denver, Colorado" *Amer. Anth.* 72, 35-54

HAGEN, E.E. and M.E. SPIRO
1968   "Personality and Religion in Burma" *Amer. Anth.* 70,   357-363 (Exchange of letters)

HAGOPIAN, E.C.
1964   "The Status and Role of the Marabout in Pre-Protectorate Morroco" *Ethnology* 3,   42-52

HALL, CALVIN S. and GARDNER LINDZEY
1957   *Theories of Personality*. New York, Wiley & Sons

HALLOWELL, A. IRVING
1950   "Personality Structure and the Evolution of Man" *Amer. Anth.* 52,   159-173

1953   "Culture, Personality and Society" in Kroeber's *Anthropology Today* Chicago, University of Chicago Press. pp.587-620

1955   *Culture and Experience*. Philadelphia, University of Pennsylvania Press

1956   "The Structural and Functional Dimensions of a Human Existence" *Quar. Rev. of Biology* 31

HANS, DILBAR
1962   "The Rediscovery of the Tribal Personality in the New Context" *Religion & Society* 9,   5-14

HARING, DOUGLAS G. (ed.)
1956   *Personal Character and Cultural Milieu*. Syracuse, Syracuse University Press

HAY, THOMAS H.
1971   "The Windigo Psychosis: Psychodynamic Cultural and Social Factors in Aberrant Behavior" *Amer. Anth.* 73,   1-19

HIEBERT, PAUL G.
1969   "Caste and Personal Rank in an Indian Village: An Extension in Techniques" *Amer. Anth.* 71, 434-453

HILL, JAMES E.
1969   "Theological Education for the Church in Mission
            (Argentine)" M.A. thesis in Missions, SWM-ICG,
            Fuller Theological Seminary, Pasadena, especially
            pp. 88-93

HOLLAND, W.R. and R.G. THARP
1964   "Highland Maya Psychotherapy" *Amer. Anth.* 66,
            41-52

HOLMES, LOWELL D.
1964   "Leadership and Decision-Making in American Samoa"
            Cur. Anth. 5,   446-449

1965   *Anthropology: An Introduction.* New York, The
            Ronald Press Co.   pp. 299-321

HONIGMAN, J.J.
1953   "Toward a Distinction between Psychiatric and
            Social Abnormality" *Social Forces* 31,   274-277.
            Also in Haring, 1956: 439-445

1954   *Culture and Personality.* New York, Harper Bros.

1967   *Personality in Culture.* New York, Harper & Row

1968   "Interpersonal Relations in Atomistic Communities"
            Hum. Organ. 27,   220-229

HOPKINS, L.C.
1945   "The Shaman or Chinese Wu: His Inspired Dancing
            and Versatile Character" *J. Roy. Asiatic Soc.*
            3-16

HOTCHKISS, JOHN C.
1967   "Children and Conduct in a Ladino Community of
            Chiapas, Mexico" *Amer. Anth.* 69,   711-730

HOWEGAWA, C.
1963   "The Hongwanji Buddhist Minister in Hawaii: A
            Study of an Occupation" *Social Process* 26,
            73-79

HSU, FRANCIS L.K.
1967   *Under the Ancestors' Shadow.* Garden City, New York
            Doubleday

1971   "Psychosocial Homeostatis and Jen: Conceptual
            Tools for Advancing Psychological Anthropology"
            Amer. Anth. 73,   23-44

HSU, FRANCIS L.K. (ed.)
1967 *Psychological Anthropology: Approaches to Culture
and Personality.* Homewood, The Dorsey Press

HU, HSIEN-CHIN
1944 "The Chinese Concepts of 'Face'" *Amer. Anth.* 46,
45-64

HUNT, ROBERT (ed.)
1967 *Personalities and Cultures: Readings in
Psychological Anthropology.* New York, The Natural
History Press

JONES, J.A.
1971 "Operant Psychology and the Study of Culture"
Cur. Anth. 12, 171-190

KAEPPLER, A.L.
1971 "Rank in Tonga" *Ethnology* 10, 174-193

KAPLAN, BERT
1961 *Studying Personality Cross-Culturally.* New York,
Harper and Row Symposium

KARDINER, ABRAM
1939 *The Individual and His Society.* New York,
Columbia University Press

1945 "The Concept of Basic Personality Structure as an
Operational Tool in the Social Sciences" in
Linton's *The Science of Man in the World Crisis.*
New York, Columbia University Press, 107-122

KARDINER, ABRAM, et al.
1945 *The Psychological Frontiers of Society.* New York,
Columbia University Press

KEESING, FELIX M.
1963 *Cultural Anthropology: The Theory of Custom.*
New York, Holt, Rinehart & Winston, pp. 138-187

KIEFER, CHRISTIE WEBER
1968 "Personality and Social Change in a Japanese
Dauchi" Ph.D., Berkeley, University of
California

1970 "The Psychological Interdependence of the Family,
School and Bureaucracy in Japan" *Amer. Anth.*
72, 66-75

KIEV, A.
1964   "Psychotherapeutic Aspects of Pentacostal Sects
            Among West Indian Immigrants to England" *Brit. J.
            Sociol.* 15,   129-138

KLUCKHOHN, CLYDE
1960   "Patterning as Exemplified in Navaho Behavior" in
            Spier 1960

1962   *Culture and Behavior.* New York, Free Press of
            Glencoe

KLUCKHOHN, CLYDE and DOROTHEA LEIGHTON
1948   *Children of the People.* Cambridge, Harvard
            University Press

KLUCKHOHN, CLYDE and HENRY A. MURRAY (ed.)
1969   *Personality in Nature, Society and Culture.*
            New York, Alfred A. Knopf

KLUCKHOHN, FLORENCE
1969   "Dominant and Variant Value Orientations" in
            Kluckhohn & Murray 1969 edition, 342-357

KRECH, D.R.S. et al.
1962   *Individual in Society.* New York, McGraw-Hill

KROEBER, A.L.
1948   *Anthropology.* New York, Harcourt, Brace & Co.,
            pp. 572-621

1952   "A Southern Personality Type" in *The Nature of
            Culture.* Chicago, University of Chicago Press,
            323-326, Part IV, 297-326 is psychologically
            slanted

KUPER, ADAM
1970   "Gluckman's Village Headman" *Amer. Anth.* 72,
            355-358

LA BARRE, W.
1947   "Primitive Psychotherapy in Native American
            Cultures: Peyotism and Confession" *J. Abnorm.
            Soc. Psych.* 42,   294-309

LEWIS, OSCAR
1949   "Husbands and Wives in a Mexican Village: A Study
            of Role Conflict" *Amer. Anth.* 51,   602-610

LINTON, RALPH
1936   *The Study of Man.* New York, Appleton-Century-
            Crofts

LINTON, RALPH
1945   *The Cultural Background of Personality*. New York,
            D. Appleton-Century-Crofts

1956   *Culture and Mental Disorders*. Springfield,
            Charles C. Thomas

LOEWEN, J.A.
1969   "Confession, Catharsis and Healing" *Pract. Anth.*
            16   63-74

LOMMEL, ANDREAS
1970   Reviews and discussion of Shamanism: The Beginnings
            of Art, (New York, McGraw-Hill 1967) *Curr. Anth.*
            11

LOMNITZ, LARISSA
1969   "Patterns of Alcohol Consumption among the Mapuche"
            Human Organ. 28   287-296

MAFUD, JULIO
1959   *El Desarraigo Argentino.*

1965   *Psicologia de Viveza Criolla.*   Buenos Aires,
            Ed. Americalle

MANDELBAUM, DAVID G. (ed.)
1958   *Selected Writings of Edward Sapir in Language,
            Culture and Personality*. Berkeley, University of
            California Press. Part III "The Interplay of
            Culture and Personality" (An abridged paperback
            is available.)

MANNERS, ROBERT A. & DAVID KAPLAN (eds.)
1968   *Theory in Anthropology*. New York, Aldine Publish-
            ing Co. Part V "Culture & Personality",   301-364

MASLOW, A.H.
1970   *Motivation and Personality*. New York, Harper & Row

MASLOW, A.H. & J.J. HONIGMAN
1970   "Synergy: Some Notes of Ruth Benedict" *Amer.
            Anth.* 72   320-333

McGINN, N.F., E. HARBURG & G.P. GINSBURG
1965   "Responses to Interpersonal Conflict in Middle
            Class Males in Guadalajara and Michigan" *Amer.
            Anth.* 67   1483-1494

MEAD, MARGARET
1928   "The Role of the Individual in Samoan Culture"
            Journ. Roy. Anth. Inst. 58   181-495

MEAD, MARGARET
1940   "Social Change and Cultural Surrogates" *Journ. of Educ. Sociol.* 14 92-110 (Also in Kluckhohn & Murray 1969 651-662)

1953 a   "National Character" in Kroeber's *Anthropology Today*. Chicago, Univer. of Chicago Press 642-667

1953 b   *Growing Up in New Guinea: A Comparative Study of Primitive Education*. New York, The New American Library

1956 a   *New Lives for Old: Cultural Transformations - Manus 1928-33*. New York, William Morrow & Co.

1956 b   "The Implications of Culture Change for Personality Development" Haring 1956 623-636

1961   *Coming of Age in Samoa: A Psychological Study of Primitive Youth for Western Civilization*. New York, The New American Library

1964   "An Application of Anthropological Techniques to Cross-National Communication" pp. 105-125 in Mead's *Anthropology: A Human Science*. Princeton, D. Van Nostrand & Co.

MERRILL, FRANCIS E.
1958   *Society and Culture: An Introduction to Sociology*. Englewood Cliffs, Prentice-Hall, Inc. Part II "Culture and Personality 115-220

MILLER, DANIEL
1961   "Personality and Social Interaction" in Kaplan 1961 271-298

1970   "The Personality as a System" Naroll & Cohen 1970 509-526

MORTON-WILLIAMS, P.
1960   "Yoruba Responses to the Fear of Death" *Africa*. 30 34-40

MURRAY, H.A. & C. KLUCKHOHN
1969   "Outline of a Conception of Personality" in Kluckhohn & Murray 1969 3-49 (Updated edition)

NAROLL, RAOUL & RONALD COHEN
1970   *A Handbook of Method in Cultural Anthropology*. New York, The Natural History Press

NASH, JUNE
1967   "Death as a Way of Life: The Increasing Resort to
            Homicide in a Maya Indian Community" *Amer. Anth.*
            69   455-470

NEWMAN, PHILIP L.
1964   " 'Wild Man' Behavior in a New Guinea Highlands
            Community" *Amer. Anth.* 66   1-19

OPLER, MARVIN K. (ed.)
1959   *Culture and Mental Health: Cross Cultural Studies.*
            New York, The Macmillan Co.

OPLER, MORRIS
1946   "Themes as Dynamic Forces in Culture" *Amer. Journ.*
            of Sociology 51   198-206

1958   "Spirit Possession in a Rural Area of Northern
            India" in Lessa & Vogt 1958   (In 1958 edition
            only)

1964   "The Human Being in Culture Theory" *Amer. Anth.*
            66   507-528

PARRINDER, E.G.
1951   *West African Psychology: A Comparative Study of*
            Psychological and Religious Thought.   London,
            Lutterworth Press

PARSONS, TALCOTT
1961   "Social Structure and the Development of the
            Personality" in Kaplan 1961   165-199

PAZ, OCTAVIO
1961   *The Labyrinth of Solitude.*   New York, Grove Press
            Inc.

PHILLIPS, HERBERT P.
1966   *Thai Peasant Personality.*   Berkeley, University of
            California Press

POZAS, RICHARDO
1962   *Juan, the Chamula: An Ethnological Reconstruction*
            of the Life of a Mexican Indian.   Berkeley,
            University of California Press

PRICE-WILLIAMS, D.R. (ed.)
1969   *Cross-cultural Studies: Selected Readings.*
            Baltimore, Penguin Books

RABIN, ALBERT I.
1961   "Personality Study in Isireli Kibbutzim" in
            Kaplan 1961   519-529

RADIN, PAUL
1963   *The Autobiography of a Winnebago Indian.* New York,
            Dover Publications, Inc.

RAMOS, SAMUEL
1962   *Profile of Man and Culture in Mexico.* Austin,
            University of Texas Press

REYNOLDS, T.R., L. LAMPHERE & C.E. COOK
1967   "Time, Resources and Authority in a Navaho
            Community" *Amer. Anth.* 69,   188-199

RÓHEIM, GÉZA
1950   *Psychoanalysis and Anthropology; Culture, Person-
            ality and the Unconscious.* New York, Inter-
            national Universities Press

SAHLINS, MARSHALL D.
1963   "Poor Man, Rich Man, Big Man Chief: Political
            Types in Melanesia and Polynesia" *Compar. Stud.
            in Society & Hist.* 5,   285-303. Also in Vayda's
            Peoples and Cultures of the Pacific New York,
            Natural History Press 1968

SAPIR, EDWARD
1932   "Cultural Anthropology & Psychiatry" *Jr.Abnormal
            & Soc. Psych.* 27,   229-242

1934 (a)   "Personality" in *Encyc. of the Social Sciences*
            12,   85-87

1934 (b)   "The Emergence of the Concept of Personality in a
            Study of Cultures" *Jr. Soc. Psych.* 5,   408-415
            (See also Mandelbaum 1958)

SEWELL, W.H.
1949   "Field Techniques in Social Psychological Study in
            a Rural Community" *Amer. Soc. Rev.* 14,   718-726

SHANKER, A.H.
1959   "Some Aspects of Personality Structuring in
            Indian (Hindu) Social Organization" *J. Soc. Psych.*
            44,   155-163

SILBERMAN, BERNARD S.
1962   *Japanese Character and Culture.* Tucson,
            University of Arizona Press

SILVERMAN, S.F.
1966   "An Ethnographic Approach to Social Stratification:
            Prestige in a Central Italian Community" *Amer.
            Anth.* 68,   899-921

133

SIMMONS, LEO (ed.)
1942   *Sun Chief: Autobiography of a Hopi Indian*. New
            Haven, Yale University Press (Paperback edition
            1963) (Autobiography of Don C. Talayesva)

SINGER, MILTON
1961   "A Survey of Culture and Personality Theory and
            Research" in Kaplan, 1961: 9-90

SKINNER, B.F.
1962   *Walden Two*. Toronto, Macmillan

SPEILBERG, JOSEPH
1968   "Small Village Relations in Guatemala: A Case
            Study" *Hum. Organ* 27,   205-211

SPIER, L. et al. (ed.)
1960   *Language, Culture and Personality*. Salt Lake
            City, University of Utah Press   Symposium

SPIRO, MELFORD E.
1951   "Culture and Personality: The Natural History of a
            False Dichotomy" *Psychiatry* 14,   19-46

1961   "Social Systems, Personality and Functional
            Analysis" in Kaplan, 1961: 93-127

SPIRO, MELFORD E. (ed.)
1965   *Context and Meaning in Cultural Anthropology*.
            New York, The Free Press

SPINDLER, L. & G.
1961   "A Modal Personality Technique in the Study of
            Menomini Acculturation" in Kaplan, 1961:   479-491

SPRATT, P.
1966   *Hindu Culture and Personality: A Psychoanalytic
            Study*. Manaktalas, Review by R.W. Taylor in
            Religion & Society 15,   73-76, 1968

STARK, W.
1958   "Psychology and Social Messianism" *Social
            Research* 25,   145-157

SWANSON, CHANG-SU
1968   "Problems and Solutions: Korean Folktales and
            Personality" *J. Amer. Folklore* 81,   121-132

TURNER, C.V.
1968   "The Sinasina 'Big Man' Complex: A Central Theme"
            Prac. Anth. 15,   16-23

WALLACE, A.F.C.
1952   *Modal Personality of Tuscarora Indians.*
            Washington,D.C.,Bur. of Amer. Enthol.Bull. 10

1961   "The Psychic Unity of Human Groups" in Kaplan,
            1961: 129-163

1961   *Culture and Personality.* New York, Random House
            Press

WATSON, O.M. & T.D. GRAVES
1966   "Quantitative Research in Proxemic Behavior" *Amer.*
            Anth. 68,   971-986

WILBUR, G.B. & W. MUENSTERBERGER
1967   *Psychoanalysis & Culture.* New York, Science
            Editions, J. Wiley & Sons

WISSLER, CLARK
1923   *Man and Culture.* New York, Thomas Crowell

                        SUPPLEMENTARY

BIESHEUVEL, S.
1949   "Psychological Tests and Their Application to Non-
            European Peoples" in *Cross-Cultural Studies* (Ed.
            D. Price-Williams), Baltimore, Penguin Books

FRIJDA, N. & G.JAHODA
1966   "On the Scope and Methods of Cross-Cultural Res-
            earch" in *Cross-Cultural Studies* (Ed. D. Price-
            Williams) Baltimore, Penguin Books

MADDI, SALVATORE R.
1968   *Personality Theories: A Comparative Analysis.*
            Homewood, The Dorsey Press

MURPHY, GARDNER & LOIS
1968   *Asian Psychology.* New York, Basic Books

THOMAS, FRANKLIN
1929   *The Environmental Basis of Society.* New York,
            The Century Co (Johnson Reprint 1965)

APPLIED ANTHROPOLOGY

INCLUDING

DIRECTED CHANGE AND GROUP DECISION-MAKING

ARENSBERG, C.M. & A.H. NIEHOFF
1964   *Introducing Social Change.* Chicago, Aldine
            Publishing Co.

BALANDIER, GEORGES
1955   *L'anthropologie appliqué aux problèmes des pays
            sous-développés.* Paris, Cours de droit

BARNETT, H.G.
1953   *Innovation: The Basic of Cultural Change.* New
            York, McGraw-Hill Book Co.

1956   *Anthropology in Administration.* Evanston, Row,
            Peterson & Co.

BARNEY, G. LINWOOD
1960   "The Meo - An Incipient Church" *Prac. Anth.*
            Suppl. 41-52

BEE, ROBT. L.
1970   " 'Self-Help' at Fort Yuma: A Critique" *Human
            Organ.* 29   155-161

BEEKMAN, JOHN
1960   "Cultural Extensions in the Chol Church" *Prac.
            Anth.* 7   54-61

BENNETT, E.B.
1955   "Discussion, Decision, Commitment & Consensus in
            'Group Decision' " *Human Rel.* 8   251-273

BERGMANN, MICHAEL
1970   "Laymen Abroad as Agents of Social Change" *Prac.
            Anth.* 17   97-106

BROKENSHA, D. & M. PEARSALL
1969   *The Anthropologist of Development in Sub-Saharan
            Africa.* Lexington, Soc. for App. Anth. Mono.10

BUNKER, ROBERT & JOHN ADAIR
1958   *The First Look at Strangers*. New Brunswick,
            Rutgers Univ. Press

BURGER, HENRY G.
1969   " 'Ethnonics': Converting Spanish Speakers' Ethno-
            graphy for Directed Change" *Prac. Anth.* 16 241-51

1970   " 'Ethno-Janus': Utilizing Cultural Heritage to
            Plan for Future Employment" *Prac. Anth.* 17 241-52

CARTWRIGHT, DORWIN
1951   "Achieving Change in People: Some Application of
            Group Dynamics Theory" *Human Rel.* 4   381-392

CASAGRANDE, JOSEPH B. & THOS. GLADWIN
1954   *Some Uses of Anthropology: Theoretical and Applied.*
            Washington, D.C., Anthro. Society of Washington

CHAPPLE, ELIOT D.
1953   "Applied Anthropology in Industry" Kroeber 1953
            819-831

CLIFTON, JAMES A. (ed.)
1970   *Applied Anthropology: Readings in the Uses of the
            Science of Man.* Boston, Houghton, Mifflin

COLBY, BENJAMIN N.
1960   "Social Relations and Directed Change Among the
            Zinacantan" *Prac. Anth.* 7   241-250

COLSON, ELIZABETH
1967   "Competence and Incompetence in the Context of
            Independence" *Curr. Anth.* 8   92-111

DALE, JOHN T.
1966   "The Home as an Evangelizing Agent" *Prac. Anth.*
            13   122-137

DAVIS, A.K. & C.J. ERASMUS
1968   "Community Development: Science or Ideology"
            (Articles, Comments and Rejoiners) *Human Organ.*
            27   56-94

DOSHI, S.L.
1969   "Non-clustered Tribal Villages and Community
            Development" *Human Organ.* 28   297-302

DOZIER, E.P.
1951   "Resistance to Acculturation and Assimilation in
            an Indian Pueblo" *Amer. Anth.* 53   56-66

EISENSTADT, S.N.
  1961   "Anthropological Studies of Complex Societies"
              Curr. Anth. 2   201-222

EPSTEIN, A.L.
  1967   "Urbanization and Social Change in Africa" *Curr.
              Anth.* 8   275-295

ERASMUS, CHARLES J.
  1961   *Man Takes Control: Cultural Development and Ameri-
              can Aid.* Minneapolis, Univ. of Minnesota Press

FORDE, DARYLL
  1953   "Applied Anthropology in Government: British
              Africa" Kroeber 1953   841-866

FOSTER, G.M.
  1969   *Applied Anthropology.* Boston, Little,Brown & Co.

GABRIEL, A.O.
  1970   "Sociocultural Constraints on Urban Renewal Poli-
              cies in Emerging Nations: The Ibadan Case" *Human
              Organ.* 29   133-139

GALDSTON, IAGO (ed.)
  1959   *Medicine and Anthropology.* New York, Internation-
              al Universities Press

GJESSING, GUTORM
  1968   "The Responsibility of the Social Scientist"
              Curr. Anth. 9   397-402

GOODENOUGH, W.H.
  1963   *Cooperation in Change: An Anthropological Study to
              Community Development.* New York, John Willey &
              Sons

HAYDEN, HOWARD
  1954   *Moturiki: A Pilot Project in Community Development.*
              London, Oxford Univ. Press

HELD, G. JAN
  1953   "Applied Anthropology in Government: The Nether-
              lands" Kroeber 1953   866-879

HOULE, CARROL
  1969   "Socio-Economic Development in Tribal Life" *Prac.
              Anth.* 16   128-132

HYMAN, H.H., G.N. LEVINE & C.R. WRIGHT
  1967   *Inducing Social Change in Developing Countries.*
              Switzerland, U.N. Res. Inst. for Soc. Develop.

INNINGER, MERLIN W.
1963   "Mass Movements & Individual Conversion in
            Pakistan" *Prac. Anth.* 10   122-126

ISAAC, BARRY L.
1971   "Preliminary Note on an Agricultural Innovation in
            Mando Chiefdon, Sierra Leone" *Human Organ.* 30
            73-78

KEESING, FELIX M.
1953   "Cultural Dynamics and Administration" Auckland,
            Seventh Pacific Science Congress Proceedings

1963   "Applied Anthropology" Keesing 1963   419-422

KENNARD, A.E. & G. MacGREGOR
1953   "Applied Anthropology in Government: United States"
            Kroeber 1953   832-840

KIETZMAN, DALE W.
1958   "Conversion and Culture Change" *Prac. Anth.* 5
            203-209

KRAFT, CHARLES H.
1963   "Mission in a World of Rapid Social Change" *Prac.
            Anth.* 10   271-279

KROEBER, A.L.   (ed.)
1953   *Anthropology Today: An Encyclopedic Inventory.*
            Chicago, Univ. of Chicago Press

KUSHNER, GILBERT
1968   "Indians in Israel: Guided Change in a New   Immi-
            grant Village" *Human Organ.* 27   352-361

LEWIN, K.
1947   "Frontiers in Group Dynamics" *Human Rel.* 1 5-41,
            143-153

LEWIS, OSCAR
1970   *Anthropological Essays.*   New York, Random House

LINTON, RALPH
1945   *The Science of Man in the World Crisis.*   New York,
            Columbia Univ. Press

LOEWEN, JACOB A.
1966   "The Question of the Communication of the Gospel"
            Prac. Anth. 13   213-226

1968   "Socialization and Social Control: A Resume of
            Processes" *Prac. Anth.* 15   145-156
139

LOOMIS, CHARLES P.
1950   *Studies in Applied and Theoretical Social Science*
               at Michigan State College. East Lansing, Michigan
               State College Press

LUZBETAK, LOUIS J.
1961   "Toward an Applied Missionary Anthropology" *Anth.*
               Qr. 34   165-176

1963   "The Nature and Scope of Applied Missionary Anthro-
               pology" Ch. 2 in *The Church and Cultures*. Techny,
               Divine Word Publications

MAIR, LUCY
1961   *Studies in Applied Anthropology*. London, Univ. of
               London, The Althone Press

1963   *New Nations*. London, Weidenfeld and Nicholson

MAYER, PHILIP
1951   *Two Studies in Applied Anthropology in Kenya*.
               London, H.M. Stationery Office

MC GINNIES, ELLIOTT
1967 a   "Studies in Persuasion: 1. An attempt to induce
               both direct and generalized attitude change in
               Japanese students" *Journ. Soc. Psych.* 70 69-75

1967 b   "Studies in Persuasion: 11. Primary-recency
               effects with Japanese students" *Journ.Soc. Psych.*
               70   77-85

1967 c   "Studies in Persuasion: 111. Reactions of Japanese
               students to one-sided and two-sided conversations.
               Journ. Soc. Psych. 70   87-93

MEAD, MARGARET
1964   *Anthropology: A Human Science*. Princeton, D. Van
               Nostrand Co.

MEAD, MARGARET (ed.)
1955   *Cultural Patterns and Technical Change*. New York,
               The New American Library (World Federation for
               Mental Health Manual)

METRAUX, ALFRED
1953   "Applied Anthropology in Government: United
               Nations" Kroeber 1953   880-894

MILLER, D.C.
1958   "Decision-making Cliques in Community Power
               Structures" *Amer. Journ. Soc.* 64   299-310

MILLER, E.S.
1970   "The Christian Missionary: Agent of Secularization"
            Anth. Qr. 43   14-22

MILLER, PAUL A.
1952   "The Process of Decision-making within the Context
            of Community Organization" *Rural Sociology* 17
            153-161

MUKHERJI, P.N.
1970   "A Study in Induced Social Change: An Indian
            Experiment" *Human Organ.* 29   169-177

NEIHOFF, ARTHUR H. (ed.)
1966   *A Casebook of Social Change.*   Chicago, Aldine
            Publishing Co.

PARSONS, ANNE
1967   "The Pentecostal Immigrants: A Study of an Ethnic
            Central City Church" *Prac. Anth.* 14   249-268

PAUL, BENJAMIN DAVID (ed.)
1955   *Health, Culture and Community: Case Studies of
            Public Reactions to Health Programs.*   New York,
            Russell Sage Foundation

ROGERS, E.M.
1962   *Diffusion of Innovations.*   New York, Free Press of
            Glencoe

ROSSI, PETER H.
1957   "Community Decision Making" *Administrative Sci.*
            Qr. 1   415-443

SAUNDERS, LYLE
1954   *Cultural Difference and Medical Care: the Case of
            the Spanish-speaking People of the Southwest.*
            New York, Russell Sage Foundation

SCHACHTER, S.
1951   "Deviation, Rejection and Communication" *Journ.
            of Abnorm. & Soc. Psych.* 46   190-207

SHEARER, ROY E.
1968   "A Christian Functional Substitute for Ancestor
            Worship" *Church Growth Bulletin* 4,2   3-5 (Five
            Year Vol. 258-260)

SIBLEY, WILLIS E.
1969   "Social Organization, Economy and Directed
            Cultural Change in Two Philippine Barrios" *Human
            Organ.* 28 148-154

SMITH, DONALD K.
1971 a   "People Must Change" *Prac. Anth.* 18   49-54

1971 b   "The Refiner's Fire" *Prac. Anth.* 18   114-127

1971 c   "Changing People's Minds" *Prac. Anth.* 18 167-176

SMITH, EDWIN W.
1926   *The Golden Stool: Some Aspects of the Conflict of Cultures in Modern Africa.* London, Holborn Publishing House

SMITH, W.C.
1923   "Missionary Activities and the Acculturation of Backward Peoples" *Journ. Applied Soc.* 7 175-186

SPICER, EDWARD H.
1961   *Perspectives in American Indian Culture Change.* Chicago, Univ. of Chicago Press

1965   *Human Problems in Technological Change.* New York, Science Editions

SPINDLER, GEORGE D. (ed.)
1955   *Education and Anthropology.* Stanford, Stanford Univ. Press

TIPPETT, A.R.
1955   "Fijian Pilot Project in Community Development" *I. R. M.* 44   229-231 (1955) (Review of Hayden 1954)

1965   "Shifting Attitudes to Sex and Marriage in Fiji" *Prac. Anth.* 12   85-91

1966   "Church Growth or Else!" *World Vision Magazine,* Feb. 12-13, 28

1967   *Solomon Islands Christianity: A Study of Growth and Obstruction.* London, Lutterworth Press

1969   *Verdict Theology in Missionary Theory.* Lincoln, Lincoln Christian College Press (Part III, 95-154 deals with the missionary directing change)

TORRES, HENRY AND EUGENE NIDA
1964   "Cultural Independence and Response to the Message" *Prac. Anth.* 11   235-238

TURNER, JONATHAN
1971   "Patterns of Value Change During Economic Development: An Empirical Study" *Human Organ.* 30   126-136

VICEDOM, G.F.
  1962   "An Example of Group Conversion" *Prac. Anth.* 9
            123-128 from *Church and People in New Guinea.*

WARNSHUIS, A.L.
  1937   "Group Conversion" *I. R. M.* 26   345-352

WILLIAMS, F.E.
  1935   *The Blending of Cultures: an Essay on the Aims of
            Native Education.* Territory of Papua Anthropo-
            logical Reports 16. Repub. 1951 Port Moresby,
            Government Printer

WOLF, ERIC R.
  1956   "Aspects of Group Relations in a Complex Society:
            Mexico" *Amer. Anth.* 58   1065-1078

WOLSTENHOLME, G. & M. O'CONNOR (eds.)
  1965   *Man and Africa.* Boston, Little, Brown & Co.
            Symposium

WONDERLY, W.L. & EUGENE NIDA
  1963   "Cultural Differences and the Communication of
            Christian Values" *Prac. Anth.* 10   259-270

URBAN ANTHROPOLOGY

This unit covers the social structure, cultural
dynamics and social relationships of the ethnic
urban situation, and also any aspects of the
rural-urban migration or exchange. It does not
touch the Negro in the U.S., but does deal with
the smaller ethnic groups.

ADAMS, BERT N.
1968   *Kinship in an Urban Setting.* Chicago, Markham
            Publishing Co.

AGARWALA, S.N.
1970   *A Demographic Study of Six Urbanizing Villages.*
            (India) Bombay, Asia Publishing House

ALDOUS, JOAN
1962   "Urbanization, the Extended Family, and Kinship
            Ties in West Africa" *Social Forces* 41   6-12
            (Also in van den Berghe 1965   107-116)

ANDERSON, NELS (ed.)
1964   *Urbanism and Urbanization.* Leiden, E.J. Brill
            Symposium

BANTON, MICHAEL
1957   *West African City: A Study of Tribal Life in
            Freetown.*   London, Oxford Univ. Press

BANTON, MICHAEL (ed.)
1966   *The Social Anthropology of Complex Societies.*
            New York, F.A. Praeger

BASCOM, WILLIAM
1962   "Some Aspects of Yoruba Urbanism" *Amer. Anth.* 64
            699-709 (Also in van den Berghe 1965   369-380)

BEALS, R.L.
1951   "Urbanism, Urbanization and Acculturation" *Amer.
            Anth.*   53   1-10

BENET, F.
1964   "The Ideology of Islamic Urbanization" Anderson
            1964   211-226

BOSE, N.K.
1965   "Calcutta: A Premature Metropolis" *Scientific American* 213 90-102

BREESE, GERALD
1966   *Urbanization in Newly Developing Countries.* Englewood Cliffs, Prentice-Hall

CHURCH GROWTH BULLETIN
1970   "Urban Church Planting" *Church Growth Bulletin* 6 3 Special Number

DALTON, GEORGE (ed.)
1971   *Economic Development and Social Change: The Modernization of Village Communities.* New York, The Natural History Press

DAVIS, KINGSLEY
1965   "The Urbanization of the Human Population" *Scientific American* 213 40-53

DE RIDDER, J.C.
1961   *The Personality of an Urban African in South Africa: A Thematic Apperception Test Study.* London, Routledge & Regan Paul

DORE, R.P.
1958   *City Life in Japan: A Study of a Tokyo Ward.* Berkeley, Univ. of California Press

DOWLING, J.H.
1968   " A 'Rural' Indian Community in an Urban Setting" *Human Organ.* 27 236-240

ENGLISH, PAUL WARD
1966   *City and Village in Iran: Settlement and Economy in the Kirman Basin.* Madison, Univ. of Wisconsin Press

EPSTEIN, A.L.
1967   "Urbanization and Social Change in Africa" *Curr. Anth.* 8 275-295

FITCHER, JOSEPH H.
1954   *Social Relations in the Urban Parish.* Chicago, Univ. of Chicago Press

FUGMANN, GERNOT JOHANN CHRISTIAN
1969   "Church Growth and Urbanization in New Guinea: A Preliminary Study in an Area of Young Christianity" M.A. thesis, School of World Mission, Fuller Thelogical Seminary, Pasadena

GAMBLE, D.P.
1963   "The Temne Family in a Modern Town (Lunsar) in
        Sierra Leone" *Africa* 33   209-226

GANS, HERBERT J.
1962   *The Urban Villagers: Group and Class in the Life
        of Italian-Americans.* New York, The Free Press

GHURYE, G.S.
1963   *Anatomy of a Rururban Community.* Bombay, Popular
        Prakashan

GLAZER, N. & D.P. MOYNIHAN
1963   *Beyond the Melting Pot: The Negroes, Puerto Ricans,
        Jews, Italians and Irish of New York City.*
        Cambridge, The M.I.T. Press

GLUCKMAN, MAX
1960   "Tribalism in Modern British Central Africa"
        Cahiers d'Etudes Africaines 1-1   55-70 (Reprinted
        in van den Brughe 1965   346-360)

GUSSMAN, BORIS
1953   "Industrial Efficiency and the Urban African: A
        Study of Conditions in Southern Rhodesia" *Africa*
        23   135-144 (Also in van den Brughe 1965 396-408)

GUTKIND, PETER C.W. (ed.)
1970   *The Passing of Tribal Man in Africa.* Leiden, E.J.
        Brill   Symposium

HANCE, WM. A.
1960   "The Economic Location and Function of Tropical
        African Cities" *Human Organ.* 19   135-136

HANDLIN, OSCAR
1959   *The Newcomers: Negroes and Puerto Ricans in a
        Changing Metropolis.* Cambridge, Harvard Univ.Press

HANSON, R.C. & O.G. SIMMONS
1968   "The Role Path: A Concept and Procedure for Study-
        ing Migration to Urban Communities" *Human Organ.*
        27   152-158

HELLMANN, ELLEN
1935   "Life in a Johannesburg Slum Yard" *Africa* 8
        34-62 (Also in Ottenberg 1960   546-564)

KAHL, JOSEPH A.
1959   "Some SocialConcomitants of Industrialization and
        Urbanization" *Human Organ.* 18   53-74

KEMPER, ROBT. V.
1970   "The Anthropological Study of Migration to Latin
            American Cities" *Kroeber Anthropological Society
            Papers* 42   1-25

KOMAROVSKY, MIRRA
1946   "The Voluntary Associations of Urban Dwellers"
            Amer. Soc. Rev. 11   686-698

KOTTER, HERBERT
1964   "Changes in Urban-Rural Relationships in Industri-
            al Society" Anderson 1964   121-129

KRAPF-ASKARI, EVA
1969   *Yoruba Towns and Cities: An Enquiry into the
            Nature of Urban Social Phenomena.* Oxford, The
            Clarendon Press

LEE, ROBERT
1967   *Stranger in the Land: A Study of the Church in
            Japan.* New York, Friendship Press

LEWIS, OSCAR
1952   "Urbanization without Breakdown: A Case Study"
            Scientific Monthly 75   31-41 (Also in *Anthro-
            pological Essays* 1970   413-426)

1959   *Five Families: Mexican Case Studies in the Culture
            of Poverty.* New York, Basic Books

1965   *La Vida: A Puerto Rican Family in the Culture of
            Poverty: San Juan and New York.* New York, Random
            House

1966   "The Culture of Poverty" *Scientific American* 215
            19-25

1970   *Anthropological Essays.* New York, Random House

LITTLE, KENNETH
1957   "The Role of Voluntary Associations in West
            African Urbanization" *Amer. Anth.* 59   579-596
            (Also in van den Burghe 1965   325-345)

1959   "Urbanism in West Africa" *Sociol. Rev.* 7   5-13

1960   "The West African Town: Its Social Basis"
            Diogenes 29   16-31

1962 a   "The Urban Role of Tribal Associations in West
            Africa" *African Studies* 21   1-9

LITTLE, KENNETH
1962 b   "Some Traditionally Based Forms of Mutual Aid in West African Urbanization" *Ethnology* 1   197-211

1965   *West African Urbanization: A Study of Voluntary Associations in Social Change.* Cambridge, The University Press

1967   "Voluntary Associations in Urban Life: A Case Study of Differential Adaptation" Freedman 1967 153-165

LLOYD, P.C.
1959   "The Yoruba Town Today" *Sociol. Rev.* 7   45-63

MARRIS, PETER
1962   *Family and Social Change in an African City: A Study of Rehousing in Lagos.* Evanston, Northwestern Univ. Press

MAYER, PHILIP
1962   "Migrancy and the Study of Africans in Towns" *Amer. Anth.* 64   576-592 (Also in van den Berghe 1965   305-324)

1963   *Townsmen or Tribesmen: Conservatism and the Process of Urbanization in a South African City.* Cape Town, Oxford Univ. Press

MC CALL, DANIEL F.
1955   "Dynamics of Urbanization in Africa" *Annals of Amer. Acad. of Pol. & Soc. Sci.* 298   151-160 (Also in Ottenberg 1960   522-535)

MC GAVRAN, D.A.
1970   "Urban Church Planting" *Church Growth Bull.* 7 110

MINER, HORACE (ed.)
1967   *The City in Modern Africa.* New York, F.A. Praeger Symposium

MITCHELL, J. CLYDE
1963   "Theoretical Orientations in African Urban Studies" Banton 1966   37-68

MITCHELL, J. CLYDE & A.L. EPSTEIN
1959   "Occupational Presitge and Social Status among Urban Africans in Northern Rhodesia" *Africa* 29 22-39 (Also in van den Berghe 1965   198-220)

MORRILL, W.T.
1961   "Two Urban Cultures of Calabar, Nigeria" Ph.D. dissertation, Univ. of Chicago, Chicago

MUKHERJEE, RAMKRISHNA
1964 "Urbanization and Social Transformation in India"
    Anderson 1964 178-210

NASH, MANNING
1967 *Machine Age Maya, The Industrialization of a*
    Guatemalan Community. Chicago, Univ. of Chicago
    Press

NIJHOFF, MARTINUS (ed.)
1968 *Urbanization in Developing Countries.* The Hague,
    International Union of Local Authorities-Symposium

OWENS, RAYMOND
1971 "Industrialization and the Indian Joint Family"
    Ethnology 10 223-250

PARRINDER, GEOFFREY
1953 *Religion in an African City.* London, Oxford Univ.
    Press

PARSONS, ANNE
1967 "The Pentecostal Immigrants: A Study of an Ethnic
    Central City Church" *Prac. Anth.* 14 249-268

PLOTNICOV, LEONARD
1967 *Strangers to the City: Urban Man in Jos, Nigeria.*
    Pittsburgh, Univ. of Pennsylvania Press

POGGIE, J.J., JR. & F.C. MILLER
1969 "Contact, Change and Industrialization in a Net-
    work of Mexican Villages" *Human Organ.*28,190-198

PORTER, A.T.
1960 "The Development of the Creole Society in Freetown,
    Sierra Leone: A Study in Social Stratification and
    the Process of Social Mobility" Ph.D. thesis,
    Boston University, Boston

POWDERMAKER, HORTENSE
1962 *Copper Town: Changing Africa.* New York, Harper &
    Row

PRICE, JOHN A.
1968 "The Migration and Adaptation of American Indians
    to Los Angeles" *Human Organ.* 27 168-175

RAMU, G.N.
1971 "Migration, Acculturation and Social Mobility
    Among the Untouchable Gold Miners in South India:
    A Case Study" *Human Organ.* 30 170-178

RODWIN, LLOYD
1965   "Ciudad Guyana: A New City" (Venezuela) *Scientific American* 213   122-132

ROSEN, BERNARD C.
1971   "Industrialization, Personality and Social Mobility in Brazil" *Human Organ.* 30   137-148

SCHWAB, WM. B.
1954   "An Experiment in Methodology in a West African Urban Community" *Human Organ.* 13   13-19

SCIENTIFIC AMERICAN, THE
1963   *Technology and Economic Development. Scientific American* 209 Special Number

1965   *Cities. Scientific American* 213 Special Number

SCIENTIFIC AMERICAN, THE (eds.)
1965   *Cities.* New York, Alfred A. Knopf

SEXTON, PATRICIA C.
1965   *Spanish Harlem: Anatomy of Poverty.* New York, Harper & Row

SIMMS, RUTH P.
1965   *Urbanization in West Africa: A Review of Current Literature.* Evanston, Northwestern Univ. Press

SMITH, T. LYNN
1964   "Urbanization in Latin America" Anderson, 1964 227-242

SMYTH, H.H.
1960   "Urbanization in Nigeria" *Anth. Qr.* 33 143-148

SMYTH, H.H. & M.M.
1960   *The New Nigerian Elite.* Stanford, Stanford Univ. Press

SOCIOLOGICAL REVIEW, THE
1959   *Urbanism in West Africa. Sociol. Rev.* 7 1 Symposium

SOVANI, N.V.
1966   *Urbanization and Urban India.* New York, Asia Publishing House

ST CLAIR, DAVID (Translator)
1962   *Child of the Dark: The Diary of Carolina Maria de Jesus.* New York, The New American Library

TAYLOR, J.V. & D. LEHMANN
  1961   *Christians of the Copperbelt: The Growth of the
              Church in Northern Rhodesia.* London, S.C.M. Press

THIJSSE, J.P.
  1967   "The Process of Urbanization" Nijhoff 1968 67-71

THRASHER, F.M.
  1963   *The Gang: A Study of 1,313 Gangs in Chicago.*
              Chicago, Univ. of Chicago Press (Originally issued
              1927)

VERHAEGEN, P.
  1962   "Bibliographie de l'Urbanisation de l'Afrique
              Noire: Son cadre, ses causes et ses consequences
              economique, sociale et culturelles" Centre de
              Documentation Economique et Sociale Africaine,
              Enquetes Bibliographiques 9

VERSLUYS, J.D.N.
  1964   "Urbanization in Southeast Asia" Anderson 1964
              140-151

WARD, CONOR K.
  1961   *Priests and People: A Study in the Sociology of
              Religion.* Liverpool, Liverpool Univ. Press

WEST, MORRIS
  1957   *Children of the Sun: The Slum Dwellers of Naples.*
              London, Wm. Heinemann

WIRTH, LOUIS
  1938   "Urbanism as a Way of Life" *Amer. Journ of Soc.*
              44   1-24

WHYTE, WM. FOOTE
  1941   "Corner Boys: A Study in Clique Behavior" *Amer.
              Journ. of Soc.* 46   647-664

  1943   "Social Organization in the Slums" *Amer. Soc.
              Rev.* 8   34-39

  1965   *Street Corner Society: The Social Structure of an
              Italian Slum.* Chicago, Univ. of Chicago Press
              (Originally issued 1943)

WHYTE, WM. H.
  1956   *The Organization Man.* New York, Simon & Schuster

WOLFE, ERIC R.
  1963   "Kinship, Friendship and Patron-Client Relations
              in Complex Societies" Banton 1966   1-22

WONDERLY, WM. L.
    1960   "Urbanization: The Challenge of Latin America in
                Transition" *Prac. Anth.* 7   205-209

WONG, JAMES (ed.)
    1971   "Urbanization and Church Growth in Singapore"
                Singapore, Church Growth Study Group Graduates
                Christian Fellowship (Multigraphed Symposium)

ETHNOLINGUISTICS AND COMMUNICATION

This unit makes no attempt to include works
and articles on technical linguistics, but only
on those aspects of language that bear on culture
and communication.
For material on proverbs, riddles and myths,
see "The Philosophy of Animism". For items on
hymnology, see "Missionary Anthropology".

BANKS, DONALD
    1965   "Making Literature African" *E.M.Q.* 2   33-40

BARKER, GEORGE C.
    1945   "The Social Functions of Language" *A Rev. of Gen.
                Semantics* 2   228-234

BOAZ, FRANZ
    1940   *Race, Language and Culture*. New York, The Mac-
                millan Co.

BODMER, FREDERICK
    1944   *The Loom of Language*. New York, W.W. Norton & Co.

CAPELL, A.
    1969   "Names for 'God' in Oceanic Languages" *Bib.
                Trans.* 20   154-157

CARROLL, JOHN B. (ed.)
    1956   *Language, Thought and Reality: Selected Writings
                of Benjamin Lee Whorf*. New York, Technology Press
                of Massachusetts Institute of Technology and John
                Wiley & Sons

DOBLE, MARION
    1963   "Grace and Justification Linked in Kapauku" *Bib.
                Trans.* 14   37-38

DOUGLAS, WILFRED H.
    1961   "The Vernacular Approach to the Australian
                Aborigines" *Prac. Anth.* 8   63-70

DUNCAN, H.D.
1962   *Communication and the Social Order.* New York,
            Buckminster

EVANS-PRITCHARD, E.E.
1948   "Nuer Modes of Address" *The Uganda Journ.* 12
            166-171 (Also in Hymes 1964   221-227)

FEHDERAU, HAROLD W.
1960   "Approaching Language Learning" *Prac. Anth.* 7
            30-35

FERGUSON, CHARLES A.
1967   "On Sociolinguistically Oriented Language Surveys"
            Bib. Trans. 18   128-132

GIESEKKE, D.W.
1970   "Venda Names for God" *Bib. Trans.* 21   180-185

GLEASON, HENRY ALLAN, JR.
1962   "Linguistics in the Service of the Church" *Prac.
            Anth.* 9   205-219

GONDA, J.
1948   "The Javanese Vocabulary of Courtesy" *Lingua* I
            333-376

GRIMES, JOSEPH E.
1963   "Measuring 'Naturalness' in a Translation" *Bib.
            Trans.* 14   49-62

GUMPERY, JOHN J. (ed.)
1964   *The Ethnography of Communication.* *Amer. Anth.* 66
            (Special Publication)

HALL, EDWARD T.
1959   *The Silent Language.* New York, Doubleday & Co.

HAWKINS, ROBERT E.
1965   "A Recording Technique for Christian Literature"
            Prac. Anth. 12   38-39

HAYAKAWA, S.I.
1941   *Language in Action.* New York, Harcourt, Brace &
            Co.

1961   *Language in Thought and Action.* New York,
            Harcourt, Brace & World Inc.

HENLE, PAUL (ed.)
1965   *Language, Thought and Culture.* Ann Arbor, Univ.
            of Michigan Press

HICKMAN, J.M.
   1968   "Linguistic and Socio-cultural Barriers to
               Communication" *Prac. Anth.* 15   63-72

HOIJER, HARRY
   1954   *Language in Culture.* Amer. Anth. Assn. Memoir 73
               Chicago, Univ. of Chicago Press

HYMES, DELL
   1964   *Language in Culture and Society: A Reader in
               Linguistics and Anthropology.* New York, Harper &
               Row

KEY, MARY
   1964   "Gestures and Responses in Some Indian Tribes"
               Prac. Anth. 11   171-176

KIJNE, JOHN J. (ed.)
   1963   "Symposium of Honorifics" *Bib. Trans.* 14 145-200

KRAMERS, R.P.
   1963   "On Being Polite in Chinese" *Bib. Trans.* 14
               165-173

LANDAR, HERBERT
   1966   *Language and Culture.* New York, Oxford Univ.Press

LARSON, DONALD N.
   1966   "Cultural Static and Religious Communication"
               E.M.Q. 3   38-47

LAW, HOWARD W.
   1968   *Winning a Hearing: An Introduction to Missionary
               Anthropology.* Grand Rapids, Wm. B. Eerdmans
               Publishing Co.

LEWIS, M.M.
   1948   *Language in Society: The Linguistic Revolution and
               Social Change.* New York, Social Science Publishers

LOEWEN, JACOB A.
   1964   "Culture, Meaning and Translation" *Bib. Trans.*
               15   189-194

   1965   "Language: Vernacular, Trade or National" *Prac.
               Anth.* 12   97-106

   1968   "Why Minority Languages Persist or Die" *Prac.
               Anth.* 15   8-15

LOEWEN, J.A. & A.
1967   "Role, Self Image and Missionary Communication"
            Prac. Anth. 14   145-160

MANDELBAUM, DAVID G. (ed.)
1958   *Selected Writings of Edward Sapir in Language,
            Culture and Personality.* Berkeley, Univ. of
            California Press

MARRISON, G.E.
1964-5   "Tribal Languages and Christian Usage" *Bib. Trans.*
            15   181-188; 16   20-24

1965   "The Art of Translation and the Science of Mean-
            ing" *Bib. Trans.* 16   176-183

MBITI, JOHN
1965   "The Ways and Means of Communicating the Gospel"
            Baëta 1968   329-350

MILNER, G.B.
1961   "The Samoan Vocabulary of Respect" *Journ. Roy.
            Anth. Inst.* 91   296-317

MOHRLAND, R.
1968   "How Anthropological Study Aided Language Learning"
            Prac. Anth. 15   245-248

MOORE, B.R.
1964   "Second Thoughts on Measuring 'Naturalness' "
            Bib. Trans. 15   83-86

MOULTON, H.K.
1962   "The Names and Attributes of God" *Bib. Trans.* 13
            71-80

NIDA, EUGENE
1960   "The Role of Language in Contemporary Africa"
            Prac. Anth. Supp. 30-38

1960   *Message & Mission: The Communication of the
            Christian Faith.* New York, Harper & Bros.

1961   "Do Tribal Languages have a Future?" *Bib. Trans.*
            11   116-122

NIDA, EUGENE A. & WM. L. WONDERLY
1971   "Communication Roles of Languages in Multilingual
            Societies" *Bib. Trans.* 22   19-37

NOORDUYN, J.
1963   "Categories of Courtesy in Sudanese" *Bib. Trans.*
               14   186-191

NOSS, PHILIP A.
1967   "Wanto and Crocodile: The Story of Joseph" *Prac.*
               Anth.   14   222-227

OSGOOD, C.E. & T.A. SEBEOK (eds.)
1954   *Psycholinguistics: A Survey of Theory and Research*
               Problems. Baltimore, Waverly Press

REYBURN, WM. D.
1969-70   "Cultural Equivalents and Non-equivalents in Trans-
               lation" *Bib. Trans.* 20   158-167; 21   26-35

RICHERT, ERNEST L.
1965   "How the GUHU-SAMANE Cult of 'Poro' Affects Trans-
               lation" *Bib. Trans.* 16   81-87

ROBINS, R.H.
1959   "Linguistics and Anthropology" *Man* 59-175-178

SAMARIN, WM. J.
1965   "Language of Silence" *Prac. Anth.* 12   115-119

SAPIR, EDWARD
1949   *Language.* New York, Harcourt, Brace & Co.
               (Originally published 1921)

1970   "Language in Resocialization" *Prac. Anth.*   17
               269-279

SCHNEIDER, T.
1970   "The Divine Names in the Tsonga Bible" *Bib.*
               Trans. 21   89-99

SCOTT, WM. HENRY
1961   "The Apo-Dios Concept in North Luzon" *Prac. Anth.*
               8   207-216

SIERTSEMA, B.
1969   "Language and World View" *Bib. Trans.* 20   3-20,55

SMALLEY, WM. A.
1959   "Vocabulary and Preaching the Gospel" *Prac. Anth.*
               6   182-185

1960   "Religious Systems and Allegiance to Christ"
               Prac. Anth. 7   223-236

SNAITH, N.H.
1965   "The Meaning of a Word" *Bib. Trans.* 16   44-52

STEWART, W.
1962 a   "Church" *Bib. Trans.* 13   124-127

1962 b   "Ministry" *Bib. Trans.* 13   128-131

SWELLENGREBEL, J.L.
1963   "Politeness and Translation in Balinese" *Bib. Trans.* 14   158-164

TAKAHASHI, M.
1963   "The Use of Honorific in Japanese" *Bib. Trans.* 14   174-177

TIPPETT, A.R.
1958   "The Integrating Gospel: An Ethnological and Ethnolinguistic Study in the Communication of the Gospel in the Fiji Islands" Davuilevu, Fiji Bound manuscript at School of World Missions, Fuller Theological Seminary, Pasadena

1968   "The Missionary Problem of Meaning" *Church Growth Bulletin* 4,3   7-9 (Five Year Volume 273-275)

VINCENT, S.V.
1963   "The Use of Honorifics in Burmese" *Bib. Trans.* 14   196-197

WILS, JOHN
1964   "The Mission and Linguistics" *Bib. Trans.* 15 3-10

WONDERLY, WM.
1966   "At Home in a Second Language" *Prac. Anth.* 13   97-102

WONDERLY, WM. L. & E.A. NIDA
1964   "Linguistics and Christian Missions" *Bib. Trans.* 15   51-69, 107-116, 154-166

YOUNG, ROSEMARY
1968   "Words Under a Bushell" *Prac. Anth.* 15   213-216

MISSIONARY ANTHROPOLOGY

This unit includes such themes as the value of anthropology to
the missionary, his problems of cross-cultural adjustment, aids
and obstructions to his participation in culture patterns with
different values from his own.   A number of items on Ethno-
musicology have also been included. See also the sections on
Culture Change and Culture Shock, Applied Anthropology and
Communication.

ADAMS, DON
  1962   "Cultural Pitfalls of a Foreign Educational
              Advisor" *Prac. Anth.* 9   179-184

ALMQUIST, L.A.
  1968 a   "Medicine and Religion: A Missionary Perspective"
              Prac. Anth. 15   217-228

  1968 b   "Whitey, Your Time is Running Out" *Prac. Anth.* 15
              24-28

ANONYMOUS (D.A. McGAVRAN)
  1965   "Should Christianity Help Tribes Maintain Their
              Identity?" *Church Growth Bulletin* 1,6   11-14

APPASAMY, A.J.
  1961   "Christian Ashrams" *Frontier* 4   281-285

BACDAYN, ALBERT S.
  1970   "Religious Conversion and Social Change: A Northern
              Luzon Case" *Prac. Anth.* 17   119-127

BAËTA, C.G. (ed.)
  1968   *Christianity in Tropical Africa.* London, Oxford
              Univ. Press

BAREH, HAMLET
  1962   "Christian Conversion and Transformation in the
              Hill Areas of Assam" *Relig. and Soc.* 9   57-64

BARRETT, DAVID
   1969   "The Expansion of Christianity in Africa in the
                 Twentieth Century" *Church Growth Bulletin* 5,5
                 71-75

BEALS, R.L.
   1959   "On the Study of Missionary Policies" *Amer. Anth.*
                 61   298-301

BERNDT, C.H.
   1958   "Anthropology and Mission Activity" *South Pacific*
                 10   38-43

BOMBART, JEAN PIERRE
   1969   "Les cultes Protestants dans une favela de Rio de
                 Janeiro" *América Latina* 12   137-139

BRANDENFELS, FRED
   1963   "Some Sociological Factors in Group Conversion to
                 Christianity" M.A. thesis, Hartford Theological
                 Seminary, Hartford

BROKENSHA, DAVID
   1963   "Suggestions to Visitors in Africa" *Prac. Anth.*
                 10   32-34

BROWN, INA C.
   1946   "The Anthropological Approach" *Christian World
                 Mission* 183-192 Nashville, Commission on
                 Ministerial Training, Anderson (ed.)

BROWN, KENNETH I.
   1966   "Worshipping with the Church of the Lord (Aladura)"
                 Prac. Anth. 13   59-84

BROWN, WESLEY H.
   1963   "Teaching Congolese to Preach" *Prac. Anth.* 10
                 135-136

BUKER, RAYMOND B. Sr.
   1964   "Missionary Encounter with Culture" *E.M.Q.* 1 9-18

BUSWELL, JAMES O.,III
   1961 a   "Anthropology in Action" *Prac. Anth.* 8   111-124

   1961 b   "Anthropology & Administrator"*Prac.Anth.* 8 157-167

CHARTBURT, MAITREE
   1963   "A Frank Talk to Missionaries" *Prac.Anth.*10 280-82

CHENOWETH, V. & D. BEE
   1968   "On Ethnic Music" *Prac. Anth.* 15   205-212

CHURCH GROWTH BULLETIN
1969   "Polygamy and Church Growth" *Church Growth Bulletin* 5, No. 4 (Feedback 6,1 6-8 & 6,5 70-72) Symposium

CHURCH GROWTH BULLETIN
1971   "Without Crossing Barriers" *Church Growth Bulletin* 7 (wrongly numbered 8) No. 5   Symposium

CRAWFORD, JOHN R.
1967   "Some Problems in Missionary Stewardship" *Prac. Anth.* 14   118-123

CULSHAW, WESLEY J.
1965   "The Christian Mission Among Tribal Minorities in India" *Prac. Anth.* 12   152-157

CUTHBERT, M.
1965   "Anthropology in Mission Training" *Prac. Anth.* 12   119-122

DALBEY, E.G., Jr.
1968   "The Technicolored Christian" *Prac. Anth.* 15 86-90

DAVIS, JOHN R.
1966   "Cross-Cultural Church Discipline" *Prac. Anth.* 13 193-198

DAVIS, J.Y. & M. WHITNEY;K. & I. OVERTON, W. REYBURN
1964   "Negro Missionary Reaction to Africa" *Prac. Anth.* 11   61-70

DENTON, CHAS. F.
1971   "Protestantism and the Latin American Middle Class" *Prac. Anth.* 18   24-28

DODGE, R.E.
1944   "Missions and Anthropology" Ph.D. dissertation, Hartford Theological Seminary, Hartford

EASTERFIELD, T.E.
1958   "Missions and Anthropology in the Solomons" *Frontier* 121-125 (also in *Prac. Anth.* abbr.)

EBERT, DANIEL J., III
1963   "Establishing Indigenous Churches Among Aboriginal People" *Prac. Anth.* 10   34-38

ELLENBERGER, JOHN D.
1964   "Multi-Individual Conversion in West Irian" *E.M.Q.* 1   31-34

EMERY, JAMES
1963   "The Preparation of Leaders in Ladino-Indian
            Church" *Prac. Anth.* 10   127-134

1967   "The Pith Helmet Attitude" *Prac. Anth.* 14 186-189

FARGHAR, BRIAN
1966   "Their Answer to Our Problem" *Prac. Anth.* 13
            140-143

FEHDERAU, HAROLD W.
1961   "Missionary Endeavour and Anthropology" *Prac.
            Anth.* 8   221-223

FICHTER, JOSEPH H.
1953   "The Marginal Catholic: An Institutional Approach"
            Social Forces   167-173

FOULKES, RD. T.
1966   "The Cost of Identification" *E.M.Q.* 2   157-162

FOUNTAIN, O.
1966   "Religion and Economy in Mission Station - Village
            Relationships" *Prac. Anth.* 13   49-58

GALLIN, BERNARD
1959   "A Case for Intervention in the Field" H.O. Fall,
            reprinted in *Prac. Anth.* 10   57-65 (1963)

GAXIOLA, MANUEL
1969   "The Beginnings of a People Movement?" *Church
            Growth Bulletin* 6,2   29-30

GLENN, EDMUND S.
1967   "Across the Cultural Barrier" *Prac. Anth.* 14
            84-91

GRIMES, JOS. E.
1959   "Ethnographic Questions for Christian Missionaries"
            Prac. Anth. 6   275-276

GUNSON, NIEL
1969   "The Theology of Imperialism and Missionary Histo-
            ry of the Pacific" (Rev. Article) *Journ. Relig.
            Hist.* 5   254-265

HALL, EDWARD T. & W.F. WHYTE
1960   "Intercultural Communication: A Guide to Men of
            Action" *Human Organ.* 19 Reprinted *Prac. Anth.* 10
            216-229, 232 (1963)

HAMILTON, KEITH E.
1964   "Consultation on Andean Indian Work" *Prac. Anth.*
            11   55-60

HARKNESS, GEORGIA
1967   "Toward a Theology of Social Change" *Relig. in
            Life* 36   563-573

HENRY, JULES
1960   "A Cross-Cultural Outline of Education" *Curr.
            Anth.* 1   267-305. Comment: *Curr. Anth.* 2 255-
            264   1961

HICKMAN, JOHN M.
1965   "Vicos and Tama: Implications for Community De-
            velopment & Missionary Research" *Prac. Anth.* 12
            241-249

1971   "The Church and Community Development in the
            Bolivian Jungle" *Prac. Anth.* 18   72-81

HOSTETTER, RICHARD
1970   "Livingstone: Innovator of Indigenous Ideas"
            Church Growth Bulletin 7,1   95-97

JAMES, DOROTHY
1969   "Toward an Ethnic Hymnody" *Prac. Anth.* 16   34-38

KELLER, JEAN
1963   "The Churches of Equatorial Africa" *Prac. Anth.*
            10   27-31

KEYFITZ, NATHAN
1963   "Western Perspectives and Asian Problems" *Prac.
            Anth.* 10   160-166

KIETZMAN, DALE W. & WM. A. SMALLEY
1960   "The Missionary Role in Culture Change" *Prac.
            Anth.* Supp. 7   85-90

KOPER, H.
1946   "The Swazi Reaction to Missions" *African Studies*
            5   177-188

KOYAMA, KOSUKE
1967   "Aristotolian Pepper and Buddhist Salt" *Prac.
            Anth.* 14   97-102

KRAFT, CHARLES H.
1963   "Christian Conversion or Cultural Conversion"
            Prac. Anth. 10   179-187

KRASS, A.C.
1967   "A Case Study in Effective Evangelism in West
            Africa" *Church Growth Bulletin* 4,1   1-7, with
            comment by D.A.McGavran & "West African Muslims"
            4,2   8-9

KURATH, G.P.
1960   "Panorama of Dance and Ethnography" *Curr. Anth.*
            1   233-254

LAKE, H. MILLER
1960   "The Missionary and Government Authority" *Prac.
            Anth.* 7   79-81

LARSON, DONALD J.
1966   "That's My Business" *Prac. Anth.* 13   138-139

LASKOWSKI, W.T.
1968   "Music and Maximum Participation" *Prac. Anth.* 15
            37-39

LEWIS, ELAINE T., JAMES M. RICCITELLI & WM. A. SMALLEY
1964   "More about Developing Non-Western Hymnody" *Prac.
            Anth.* 11   35-46 (Also see Correspondence in
            Prac. Anth. 10   287-288; 12   96)

LOEWEN, JACOB A.
1963   "The Church Among the Choco of Panama" *Prac.
            Anth.* 10   97-108

1964 a   "Reciprocity in Identification" *Prac. Anth.*   11
            145-160

1964 b   "Sponsorship: The Difference between Good News and
            Propaganda" *Prac. Anth.* 11   193-203

1964 c   "The Church: Indigenous and Ecumenical" *Prac.
            Anth.* 11   241-258

1965 a   "Field, Term and Timing in Missionary Method"
            Prac. Anth. 12   1-21

1965 b   "Self-Exposure: Bridge to Fellowship" *Prac.
            Anth.* 12   49-62

1965 c   "Literacy: Bridge to Choco Evangelism" *Prac.
            Anth.* 12   76-84

1965 d   "Missionaries and Anthropologist Co-operate in
            Research" *Prac. Anth.* 12   158-190

LOEWEN, JACOB A.
1967   "Religion, Drives and the Place where it Itches"
            Prac. Anth. 14   48-72

1968 a   "Mission to Smaller Tribes: Challenge, Problems
            and Responsibility" *Prac. Anth.* 15   49-62

1968 b   "From Tribal Society to National Church" *Prac.
            Anth.* 15   97-111

1969 a   "Socialization and Conversion in the Ongoing
            Church" *Prac. Anth.* 16   1-17

1969 b   "Confessions in the Indigenous Church" *Prac.
            Anth.* 114-127

1970 a   "A Message for Missionaries from Mopass" *Prac.
            Anth.* 17   16-27

1970 b   "The Social Context of Guilt and Forgiveness"
            Prac. Anth. 17   80-96

1970 c   "Four Kinds of Forgiveness" *Prac. Anth.* 17
            153-168

LOEWEN, J.A. & A.
1967 a   "The Missionary 'Role' " *Prac. Anth.* 14   193-208

1967 b   "Role, Self Image and Missionary Communication"
            Prac. Anth. 14   145-160

LUZBETAK, LOUIS J.
1963 a   "Towards an Applied Missionary Anthropology"
            Prac. Anth. 10   199-208

1963 b   *The Church and Cultures: An Applied Anthropology
            for Religious Workers.* Techny, Divine Word Pub-
            lications

MAHON, DENNIS
1966   "Cultural Anthropology" *Prac. Anth.* 13   277

MERRIMAN, ALAN P.
1966   "The Anthropology of Music" *Curr. Anth.* 7 217-
            230   Book discussion

MOASOSANG, P.
1962   "Social and Cultural Changes in the Tribal Com-
            munities Today and the Responsibility of the
            Churches" *Rel. & Soc.* 9   40-45

MOBLEY, HARRIS W.
1970   *The Ghanian's Image of the Missionary: An Analysis
            of the Published Critiques of Christian Mission-
            aries by Ghanians.* 1897-1965, Leiden, E.J. Brill

MULLER-KRUGER, T.H.
1965   "The Cultural Orientation of Theological Educa-
            tion" *SE Asia Journ. Theol.* 6   59-73

NEWELL, WM. H.
1966   "Anthropology and Missionary Strategy" *SE Asia
            Journ. Theol.* 7   67-75

NIDA, EUGENE A.
1954   *Customs & Cultures: Anthropology for Christian
            Missions.* New York, Harper & Row

1959   "The Role of Cultural Anthropology in Christian
            Mission" *Prac. Anth.* 6   110-116

1960   *Message and Mission.* New York, Harper & Bros.

1963   "The Church and its Ministries" *Prac. Anth.* 10
            233-236

1966   "Missionaries and Anthropologists" *Prac. Anth.* 13
            273-276

1967   "Readjustment - An Even Greater Problem" *Prac.
            Anth.* 14   114-117

NIDA, EUGENE A. & WM. L. WONDERLY
1963   "Selection, Preparation and Function of Leaders in
            Indian Fields" *Prac. Anth.* 10   6-16

NOBLE, LOWELL L.
1961   "Can St. Paul's Methods be Ours?" *Prac. Anth.* 8
            180-185

NOSS, PHILIP A.
1970   "The Danger of Courtesy" *Prac. Anth.* 17   241-252

OGBERG, KALERVO
1960   "Cultural Shock: Adjustments to New Cultural
            Environments" *Prac. Anth.* 7   177-182

PARSONS, R.T.
1956   "The Missionary and the Cultures of Man" *I.R.M.*
            45   161-168

PAUL, BENJAMIN D.
1960   "Respect for Cultural Differences" *Prac. Anth.*
            7   210-216

PEEL, JOYCE M.
1966   "Village Drama in South India" *Prac. Anth.*   13
            227-232

PETERS, GEO. W.
1965   "Training Missionaries for Today's World" *E.M.Q.*
            2   19-28

PRACTICAL ANTHROPOLOGY
            Vol. 9 was a Symposium, *Developing Hymnody in New
            Churches* (Smalley & Nida, eds.)   It contained the
            following articles:
ELLENBERGER, JOHN D.
            "The Beginnings of Hymnody in a New Guinea Church"
KEY, MARY   "Hymn Writing with Indigenous Tunes"
KING, LOUIS L.
            "Indigenous Hymnody of the Ivory Coast"
RICCITELLI, JAMES M.
            "Developing Non-Western Hymnody"
SMALLEY, WM. A.
            "Music, Church and Ethnocentricism"
WALLACE, W.J.
            "Hymns in Ethiopia"

QUICK, JOHN B.
1967   "Breaking the Culture Barrier" *Prac. Anth.* 14
            44-48

RAWSON, D.P.
1968 a   "Church and Society in Africa" *E.M.Q.* 4   168-177

1968 b   "Africa's Social and Political Demands on the
            Church" *E.M.Q.*   4   193-203 (Also in *Prac. Anth.*
            16   75-83, 1969)

RELIGION IN LIFE
1964-5   Symposium "The Younger Churches" *Relig. in Life*
            33   498-539 and "The Younger Churchmen Reply"
            Relig. in Life 34   8-41

REYBURN, WM. D.
1960   "Identification in the Missionary Task" *Prac.
            Anth.* 7   1-15

1966   "Between the Embryo and the Elephant" *Prac. Anth.*
            13   1-12

REYBURN, WM. D.
1968   "Crossing Cultural Frontiers" *Prac. Anth.* 15
            249-257

1970   "The Helping Relationship in Missionary Work"
            Prac. Anth. 17   49-59

RELIGION AND SOCIETY
1966   Symposium "Religious Conversion" *Relig. & Soc.*
            13 No. 4

RICE, DELBERT
1971   "Developing an Indigenous Hymnology" *Prac. Anth.*
            18   97-113

ROSENSTIEL, ANNETTE
1959   "Anthropology and the Missionary" *Journ. Roy.*
            Anth. Inst. 89   107-115 (Also in *Prac. Anth.*   8
            15-24 1961)

SCHUSKY, ERNEST
1963   "Mission and Government Policy in Dakota Indian
            Communities" *Prac. Anth.* 10   109-144

SCOTT, W.H.
1968   "Some Contrasts in Missionary Patterns" *Prac.*
            Anth. 15   269-278

SHIRLEY, J. & P.R. TURNER
1968   "Folklore and the Missionary" *Prac. Anth.* 15
            73-78

SHROPSHIRE, D.W.T.
1938   *The Church and Primitive Peoples.*   London,S.P.C.K.

SINHA, SURAJIT
1967   "Religion in an Affluent Society" *Prac. Anth.* 14
            124-140 (Indian view of U.S. Society)

SMALLEY, WM. A.
1960 a   "Anthropological Study and Missionary Scholarship"
            Prac. Anth. 7   113-123

1960 b   "Making and Keeping Anthropological Field Notes"
            Prac. Anth. 7   145-152

1963   "Culture Shock, Language Shock and Shock of Self-
            Discovery" *Prac. Anth.* 10   49-56

1966   "Emotional Storm Signals: The Shocks of Culture,
            Language, Self-Discovery" *E.M.Q.* 2   146-157

SMALLEY, WM. A. (ed.)
1967   *Readings in Missionary Anthropology*. Tarrytown
            (from *Prac. Anth.*)

SMITH, EDWIN W.
1926   *The Golden Stool: Some Aspects of the Conflict of
            Cultures in Modern Africa*. London,   Holborn
            Publishing House

SRINAWK, K.
1968   "A Thai View of the American" *Prac. Anth.* 15
            278-282

STEINMETZ, PAUL P.
1970   "The Relationship Between Plains Indian Religion
            and Christianity" *Plains Anth.*   15   83-86

STROUP, H.
1960   "Theological Implications in Anthropology"
            Encounter 21   464-468

SUMNER, MARGARET
1963   "Mexican-Indian Minority Churches, U.S.A." *Prac.
            Anth.* 10   115-121

TABER, C.R.
1967   "The Training of Missionaries" *Prac. Anth.* 14
            267-274

1970   "The Missionary: Wrecker, Builder or Catalyst?"
            Prac. Anth. 17   145-152

TAYLOR, ROBERT B.
1967   "Training Facilities in Anthropology" *Prac. Anth.*
            14   73-83

TIPPETT, A.R.
1955   "Anthropological Research and the Fijian People"
            I.R.M. 44   212-219

1960   "Probing Missionary Inadequacies at the Popular
            Level" *I.R.M.* 49   411-419

1967   "Religious Group-Conversion in Non-Western Society"
            Research in Progress Pamphlet 11. School of World
            Mission, Fuller Theological Seminary, Pasadena

1968 a   "Anthropology: Luxury or Necessity for Missions?"
            E.M.Q. 5   7-19

1968 b   "Membership Shrinkage" *Church Growth Bulletin* 4,
            4   5-7 (Five Year Vol. 284-286)

TIPPETT, A.R.
 1969 a   "Polygamy as a Missionary Problem: The Anthro-
           pological Issues" *Church Growth Bulletin*
           (Also in *Prac. Anth.* 17   75-79   1970)

 1969 b   "The Components of Missionary Theory" *Church
           Growth Bulletin* 6   1-3

 1970   "From Awareness to Decision-Making" Research in
           Progress Pamphlet 12. School of World Mission,
           Fuller Theological Seminary, Pasadena

TOLIVER, RALPH
 1969   "Folk Art Sparks 'People Movement' " *Church
           Growth Bulletin* 6,2   19-20

TROBISCH, WALTER A.
 1966   "Congregational Responsibility for the Christian
           Individual" *Prac. Anth.* 13   199-212

TROUTMAN, CHAS. H.
 1970   "Evangelicals and the Middle Classes in Latin
           America" *E.M.Q.* 7   79-91, 154-163

TURNBULL, SANDY
 1969   "Dual Citizenship" *Prac. Anth.* 16   28-33

TURNER, CHARLES V.
 1964   "The Grease Complex of New Guinea" *Prac. Anth.* 11
           233-234

WAMBUTDA, DANIEL N.
 1970   "An African Christian looks at Christian Missions
           in Africa" *Prac. Anth.* 17   169-176

WINTER, RALPH D.
 1967   " 'Cultural Overhang' and the Training of Pastors"
           Church Growth Bulletin 4,2   5-6

 1969   "Polygamy: Rules and Principles" *Church Growth
           Bulletin* 5,4   63-65

WONDERLY, WM. L.
 1959   "Social Anthropology, Christian Missions and the
           Indians of Latin America" *Prac. Anth.* 6   55-64

WONDERLY, WM. L. & JORGE LARA-BRAUD
 1967   "Some Convictions of a Young Church" *Prac. Anth.*
           14   1-14

Religious Dimensions

GENERAL WORKS ON ANIMISTIC RELIGION

BASIC CONCEPTS: THE PHILOSOPHY OF ANIMISM

ANIMISTIC PRACTITIONERS AND SYSTEMS

Religious Systems, Structures and Rituals
Magic, Sorcery, Witchcraft & Divination
Shamanism and Curing
Spiritism, Possession, Glossolalia, Voodoo
Syncretism

ORGANIZED NATIVISTIC MOVEMENTS

ANIMISTIC BASES OF THE GREAT RELIGIONS

CHRISTIAN MISSION IN THE ANIMIST WORLD

GENERAL WORKS

ON

ANIMISTIC RELIGION

ANESAKE, MASAHARU
1961   *Religious Life of the Japanese People*. Tokyo,
          The Society for International Cultural Relations

BANTON, MICHAEL (ed.)
1966   *Anthropological Approaches to the Study of
          Religion*. New York, Fredk. A. Praeger

BENEDICT, RUTH
1938   "Religion" in Boas 1938   627-665

BUCK, PETER H.
1939   *Anthropology and Religion*.   New Haven, Yale Univ.
          Press

CALVERTON, V.F.
1931   *The Making of Man: An Outline of Anthropology*.
          New York, Random House   (Symposium in The
          Modern Library)

CARPENTER, EDWARD
1914   *Intermediate Types Among Primitive Folk*.   London,
          George Allen & Co.

CLARK, C.A.
1961   *Religions of Old Korea*.   Seoul, Christian Litera-
          ture Society of Korea

COURLANDER, H. & R. BASTIEN
1966   *Religion and Politics in Haiti*.   Washington, D.C.,
          Institute for Cross-Cultural Research

DESCHAMPS, HUBERT
1965   *Les Religions de l'Afrique Noire*.   Paris, Presses
          Universitaires de France

DURKHEIM, EMILE
1961   *The Elementary Forms of Religious Life.* New York,
            Collier Books   Paperback AS26

ELIADE, MIRCEA
n/d   *Patterns in Comparative Religion.* London, Sheed &
            Ward

1966-7   "Australian Religions" *Hist. of Relig.* 6 108-134,
            208-235; 7   61-90, 159-183, 244-268

EVANS-PRITCHARD, E.E.
1954   "Religion" in *The Institutions of Primitive
            Society.* Oxford, Blackwell   1-11

1956   *Nuer Religion.* Oxford, Clarendon Press

1965   *Theories of Primitive Religion.* Oxford, Clarendon
            Press

FIELD, M.J.
1937   *Religion and Magic of the Gã People.* London,
            Oxford University Press

FORTUNE, R.F.
1931   "Manus Religion" *Oceania* 2   74-108

1934   *Manus Religion: An Ethnological Study of the Manus
            Natives of the Admiralty Islands.* Lincoln, Univ.
            of Nebraska Press   Bison paperback BB303

GEERTZ, CLIFFORD
1965   "Religion as a Cultural System" Lessa & Vogt1965
            (2nd Ed.)   204-216

1965   *The Religion of Java.* Glencoe, Free Press of
            Glencoe (paperback)

GELFAND, MICHAEL
1962   *Shona Religion.* Cape Town, Juta & Co.

GOLDENWEISER, ALEXANDER
1946   "Magic, Religion and Ritual" in Goldenweiser 1946:
            pt. 2,Sec.3   208-295

GOODE, WILLIAM J.
1964   *Religion Among the Primitives.* Glencoe, Free
            Press of Glencoe (paperback)

GUIART, JEAN
    1956   *Un siècle et demi de Contacts Culturels à Tanna,*
              Nouvelles-Hebrides. Paris, Sociéte des Océanists,
              Musée de l'Homme

    1962   *Les Religions de l'Océanie.* Paris, Presses
              Universitaires de France

HARPER, EDWARD B. (ed.)
    1964   *Religion in South East Asia.* Seattle, Univ. of
              Washington Press

HENRY, JULES
    1964   *Jungle People:A Kaingang Tribe of the Highlands of*
              Brazil. New York, Vintage books   paperback V.521

HERSKOVITS, M.J. & F.S.
    1933   "An Outline of Dahomean Religious Beliefs" *Amer.*
              Anth. Assn. Memoir 41

HOGBIN, H.I.
    1947   "Pagan Religion in a New Guinea Village" *Oceania*
              18   120-145

HORI, ICHIRO
    1968   *Folk Religion in Japan: Continuity & Change.*
              Chicago, Univ. of Chicago Press

HOWELLS, WILLIAM
    1962   *The Heathens: Primitive Man and His Religion.*
              New York, Doubleday & Co.   paperback Anchor

HULTKRANTZ, AKE
    1966-67 "North American Indian Religion in the History of
              Research" *Hist. of Relig.* 6   91-107, 183-207;
              7   13-34

HUXLEY, FRANCIS
    1966   *Affable Savages: An Anthropologist among the Urubu*
              Indians of Brazil. New York, Capricorn Books
              paperback Cap. 129

JEVONS, F.B.
    1927   *An Introduction to the History of Religion.*
              London, Methuen & Co.

JUNOD, HENRI
    1963   *The Life of a South African Tribe.* (Thonga) Vol.2:
              Mental Life   New York, University Books

LANDES, RUTH
1968   *Ojibwa Religion and the Midewiwin.* Madison, Univ.
            of Wisconsin Press

LAWRENCE, P. & M.J. LEGGITT (eds.)
1965   *Gods, Ghosts and Men in Melanesia.* Melbourne,
            Oxford University Press

LEBRA, WM. P.
1966   *Okinawan Religion: Belief, Ritual and Social
            Structure.* Honolulu, Univ. of Hawaii Press

LESSA, WM. A. & EVON Z. VOGT (eds.)
1958   *Reader in Comparative Religions: An Anthropologi-
            cal Approach.* Evanston, Row, Peterson & Co.

1965   *Reader in Comparative Religions: An Anthropologi-
            cal Approach.* Second Edition: New York, Harper &
            Row

LEINHARDT, GODFREY
1961   *Divinity and Experience: The Religion of the Dinka*
            Oxford, Clarendon Press

LISSNER, IVAR
1961   *Man, God and Magic.* New York, G.P. Putnam's Sons

LOWIE, ROBT. H.
1952   *Primitive Religion.* London, Peter Owen Ltd.

MALEFIJT, A. de WAAL
1968   *Religion and Culture.* New York, Macmillan

MEAD, MARGARET & N. CALAS
1953   *Primitive Heritage.* New York, Random House

MIDDLETON, JOHN
1960   *Lugbara Religion: Ritual and Authority among East
            African People.* London, Oxford Univ. Press for
            International African Institute

NIDA, EUGENE & WM. A. SMALLEY
1959   *Introducing Animism.* New York, Friendship Press

NILLES, J.
1950   "The Kuman of the Chimbu Region, Central Highlands,
            New Guinea" *Oceania* 21   64-65

NORBECK, E.
1961   *Religion in Primitive Society.* New York, Harper &
            Bros.

176

PALMER, SPENCER J. (ed.)
1967   *The New Religions of Korea*. Trans. Korean Branch,
              Royal Asiatic Society   v.xliii

PARRATT, J.K.
1969   "Religious Change in Yoruba Society: A Test Case"
              Journ. of Relig. in Afr.   2   113-128

PARRINDER, E.G.
1949   *West African Religion*. London, Epworth Press

1951   *West African Psychology: A Comparative Study of
              Psychological and Religious Thought*. London,
              Lutterworth Press

1954   *African Traditional Religion*. London,
              Hutchinson's University Library

1969   *Religion in Africa*. New York, Praeger Publishers

PAUW, B.A.
1964   *Religion in a Tswana Chiefdom*. London, Oxford
              Univ. Press, for International African Institute

POLYNESIAN SOCIETY, THE
1941   *Polynesian Anthropological Studies, Memoir 17*.
              Wellington, Polynesian Society

RADIN, PAUL
1953   *The World of Primitive Man*. New York, Abelard
              Schuman

1957 a   *Primitive Man as a Philosopher*. New York, Dover
              Publications   paperback T392

1957 b   *Primitive Religion*. New York, Dover Publications
              paperback T393

REICHARD, G.A.
1950   *Navaho Religion: A Study of Symbolism*. 2 Vols.
              New York, Pantheon Books

SCHMIDT, W.
1931   *The Origin and Growth of Religion*. London,
              Methuen & Co.

1939   *Primitive Revelation*. St. Louis, Herder Book Co.

1939   *Primitive Religion*. St. Louis, Herder Book Co.

SWANSON, GUY E.
1960   *The Birth of the Gods: The Origin of Primitive
            Belief.* Ann Arbor, Univ. of Michigan

TANNER, RALPH E.S.
1967   *Transitions in African Beliefs: Sukumland, Tan-
            zania.* New York, Maryknoll Publications

TAYLOR, JOHN V.
1963   *The Primal Vision.* London, S.C.M. (in The
            Christian Presence Series)

UNDERHILL, RUTH
1965   *Red Man's America.* Chicago, Univ. of Chicago
            Press

1969   *Papago Indian Religion.* New York, AMS Press
            (originally printed 1946)

VETTER, GEO. B.
1958   *Magic and Religion: Their Philosophical Nature,
            Origin and Function.* New York, Philosophical
            Library

WALLACE, A.F.C.
1966   *Religion: An Anthropological View.* New York,
            Random House

WALLIS, WILSON D.
1939   *Religion in Primitive Society.* New York, F.C.
            Crofts & Co.

WHITEHEAD, HENRY
1921   *The Village Gods of Southern India.* Calcutta,
            Association Press

BASIC CONCEPTS

-

THE PHILOSOPHY OF ANIMISM

AKESSON, S.K.
1965   "The Akan Conception of the Soul" *African Affairs*
            64   280-291

ANDERSEN, JOHANNES
1941   "Maori Religion" Wellington, *Memoir Polynesian
            Society* 17   219-261

ANSTELS, R.T.
1963   "Christianity and Bantu Philosophy: Observations
            on the Thought and Work of Placide Tempels"
            I.R.M. 52   316-322

BEIDELMAN, T.O.
1963   "Kaguru Omens: An East African People's Concept of
            the Unusual, Unnatural and Supernormal"   *Anth.
            Quar.* 36   43-59

BENEDICT, RUTH
1923   *The Concept of the Guardian Spirit in North
            America.* American Anthropological Society Memoir
            29

BERNDT, R.M.
1966   "The Ghost Husband: Society and the Individual in
            New Guinea Myth" *Journ. Amer. Folklore* 79
            244-277

BOAS, FRANZ
1940   "The Concept of Soul among the Vandau" in *Race,
            Language and Culture.* New York, Macmillan

BODENSTEIN, W. & O.F. RAUM
1960   "A Present Day Zulu Philosopher" *Africa* 30
            166-181

BROWN, KENNETH I.
1966   "Worshipping with the African Church of the Lord
            (Aladura)" *Prac. Anth.* 13.1   59-84

BURRIDGE, K.O.
1956   "Social Implications of Some Tangul Myths" *SW.
            Journ. Anth.* 12   415-431

BUSIA, K.A.
1959   "Ancestor Worship" *Prac. Anth.* 6   23-26

CARNEIRO, R.L.
1964   "The Amahuaca and the Spirit World" *Ethnology* 3
            6-11

CHADWICK, N.K.
1930   "Notes on Polynesian Mythology" *Jr. Roy. Anth.
            Inst.* 60   425-446

CODRINGTON, R.H.
1958   "Mana" Lessa & Vogt 1958   206-207

DEVEREAUX, G.
1937   "Mohave Soul Concepts" *Amer. Anth.* 39   417-422

DOUGLAS, MARY
1966   *Purity and Danger: An Analysis of Concepts of
            Pollution and Taboo.* New York, Frederick A.
            Praeger

DU TOIT, B.M.
1960   "Some Aspects of the Soul-Concept Among the Bantu-
            Speaking Nguni Tribes of South Africa" *Anth. Qr.*
            33   134-142

EGGAN, R. & A. PACYAYA
1962   "The Sapilada Religion: Reformation and Accomoda-
            tion Among the Igorots of N. Luzon" *SW. Journ.
            Anth.* 18   95-113

ELIADE, MERCIA
1961   *The Sacred and the Profane.* New York, Harper &
            Row   Torchbook paperback TB 81H

ELKINS, R.
1964   "The Anit Taboo: A Menobo Cultural Unit" *Prac.
            Anth.* 185-192

ELLIS, W.
1839-42   "Tabu" Lessa & Vogt 1958 213-216

EVANS-PRITCHARD, E.E.
1953   "The Nuer Concept of Spirit in its Relation to the
            Social Order" *Amer. Anth.* 55 201-214

FARON, L.C.
1961   "On Ancestor Propitiation Among the Mapuche of
            Central Chili" *Amer. Anth.* 63 824-830

FILBECK, DAVID
1964   "Concepts of Sin and Atonement among the Thin"
            Prac. Anth. 11 181-184

FINNEY, BEN R.
1964   "Bond-Friendship in Tahiti" *Jr. Polynesian Soc.*
            73 431-435

FIRTH, RAYMOND
1941   "The Analysis of Mana: An Empirical Approach"
            Wellington, *Polynesian Soc. Memoir* 17   189-218

FLANNERY, REGINA
1952   "Two Concepts of Power" in Sol Tax (ed.) *Selected
            Papers of Fifth International Congress of
            Americanists.* Chicago, Univ. of Chicago Press

FORTES, M. & G. DIETERLEN (eds.)
1965   *African Systems of Thought.* London, Oxford Univ.
            Press   Symposium

FRAZER, J.G.
1913   *Belief in Immorality and the Worship of the Dead.*
            London, Macmillan & Co. (Reprinted 1968)

1931   "Magic & Religion" Calverton 1931 693-713

GABA, C.R.
1969   "The Idea of a Supreme Being among the Anlo People
            of Ghana" *Jr. Relig. in Afr.* 2 64-79

GEORGES, ROBT. A.
1968   *Studies on Mythology.* Homewood, The Dorsey Press

GREENWAY, JOHN (ed.)
1965   *The Primitive Reader.* Hatboro, Folklore Associ-
            ates   (Anthropology of Mythology)

GREGERSON, M.B.
1969   "Rengao Myths: A Window on a Culture" *Prac. Anth.*
            16 216-227

GREY, GEORGE
1946   "The Creation According to the Maori" Kroeber &
            Waterman 1946 444-458

HALLOWELL, A. IRVING
1940   "Spirits of the Dead in Salteaux Life and Thought"
            J. Roy. Anth. Inst. 70   29-52; also in *Culture
            & Experience* 7   Philadelphia, Univ. of
            Pennsylvania Press

HANDY, E.S.C.
1941   "Perspectives in Polynesian Religion" Wellington,
            Polynesian Society Memoir 17   121-142

1958   "Mana in Polynesia" Lessa & Vogt 1958   208-218

HARNER, MICHAEL J.
1962   "Jivaro Souls" *Amer. Anth.* 64   258-272

HARNEY, W.E.
1943   *Taboo*. Sydney, Australasian Publishing Co.

HENNIG, ED. W.
1964   "Two Studies in Animism" *Prac. Anth.* 11   47-48

HEWITT, J.N.B.
1902   "Orenda and a Definition of Religion" *Amer. Anth.*
            4   33-46; also in *Selected Papers from the Amer.
            Anth. 1888-1920*. Evanston, Row, Peterson & Co.
            1960

HOBLEY, C.W.
1967   *Bantu Beliefs and Magic ....Kikiyu and Kamba
            Tribes of Kenya...*   London, Frank Cass & Co.
            First edition 1922

HOMANS, G.C.
1941   "Anxiety and Ritual: Theories of Malinowski and
            Radcliffe-Brown" *Amer. Anth.* 43   164-172

HOOKE, S.H.
1955   "Omens - Ancient and Modern" *Folklore* 66   330-
            339

HORTON, R.
1962   "The Kalabari World View" An Outline and Interpre-
            tation" *Africa* 32   197-220

IDOWU, E. BOLAJI
1962   *Olodumare: God in Yoruba Belief*. London, Longmans

JAHN, JANHEINZ
1961   *Muntu: the new African Culture*. New York, Grove
            Press Inc.

KENNEDY, JOHN G.
1967   "Mushahara: A Nubian Concept of Supernatural
            Danger and the Theory of Taboo" *Amer. Anth.* 69
            685-702

KLUCKHOHN, C.
1958   "Myths and Rituals" Lessa & Vogt 1958   135-151

KROEBER, A.L.
1931   "The Growth of a Primitive Religion"   Calverton
            1931   714-744

1958   "Totem and Taboo in Retrospect" Lessa & Vogt 1958
            57-66

KURATH, G.P.
1960   "Calling the Rain Gods" *Journ. Amer. Folklore* 73
            312-316

LA BARRE, WESTON
1966   "The Aymara: History and World View" *Journ. Amer.
            Folklore* 79   130-144

LEACOCK, S.
1964   "Fun-Loving Deities in an Afro-Brazilian Cult"
            Anth. Qr. 37   94-110

LEVIN, S.S.
1968   "The Overthrow of the Kapu System in Hawaii"
            Journ. Polynesian Soc. 77   402-430

LEVY-BRUHL, LUCIEN
1925   *How Natives Think*. New York, Alfred A. Knopf

LIVINGSTONE, DAVID
1960   "Dialogue Showing Rain-maker's Arguments" in
            Livingstone's Private Journals 1851-53. ed.
            Shapera 239-243. Berkeley, Univ. of Calif. Press

LOEWEN, JACOB A.
1964 a   "Bible Stories: Message and Matrix" *Prac. Anth.*
            11   49-54, 60

1964 b   "The Choco and Their Spirit World" *Prac. Anth.* 11
            97-104

1966   "Lengua Indians and their 'Innermost'" *Prac. Anth.*
            13   252-272

LOEWEN, JACOB A.
  1969 a   "Confession, Catharsis and Healing" *Prac. Anth.*
              16.2   63-74

  1969 b   "Confession in the Indigenous Church" *Prac. Anth.*
              16.3   114-127

LONG, CHAS. H.
  1964   "The West African High God: History and Religious
              Experience" *Hist. of Relig.*   3   328-342

LOWIE, ROBT.H.
  1966   "Religion in Human Life" *Prac. Anth.*   13   34-46

MALINOWSKI, BRONISLAW
  1948   *Magic, Science and Religion.*   New York, Doubleday
              & Co.   paperback Anchor 23

MANDELBAUM, D.G.
  1966   "Transcendental and Economic Aspects of Religion"
              Amer. Anth.   68   1174-1191

MARRETT, R.R.
  1929   *The Threshold of Religion.*   London, Metheun & Co.

  1932   *Faith, Hope and Charity in Primitive Religion.*
              New York, The Macmillan Co.

MBITI, JOHN M.
  1969   *African Religions and Philosophy.*   London,
              Heinemann

  1970   *Concepts of God in Africa.*   London, S.P.C.K.

McGREGOR, DON E.
  1969   "Learning from Wape Mythology" *Prac. Anth.*   16
              201-215

MESSENGER, J.
  1962   "A Critical Re-examination of the Concept of
              Spirits: With Special Reference to Traditional
              Folklore and Contemporary Irish Folk Culture"
              Amer. Anth.   62   367-373

MIDDLETON, JOHN (ed.)
  1967   *Myth and Cosmos: Readings in Mythology and
              Symbolism.*   New York, The Natural History Press

MONBERG, TORBEN
  1966   *The Religion of Bellona Island: The Concepts of
              Supernaturals.*   Copenhagen, National Museum of
              Denmark
184

MOSS, ROSALIND
1925   *The Life and Death in Oceania and the Malay Archipelago*. London, Oxford Univ. Press

O'CONNELL, J.
1962   "The Withdrawl of the High God in West African Religion: An Essay in Interpretation" *Man* 62 67-69 Comment by R. Horton 137-140

OLIVER-SMITH, ANTHONY
1969   "The Pishtaco: Institutionalized Fear in Highland Peru" *Journ. Amer. Folklore* 82   363-368

OOSTHUIZEN, G.C.
1968   "Isaiah Shembe and the Zulu World View" *Hist. of Relig.* 8   1-30

OPLER, MORRIS
1960   "Myth and Practice in Jisarilla Apache Eschatology" *Journ. Amer. Folklore* 73   133-153

PAUW, B.A.
1963   "African Christians and their Ancestors" Hayward, 1963 33-46
PRACTICAL ANTHROPOLOGY
1969   Reviews on books about Myths. *Prac. Anth.* 16 228-240

RADCLIFFE-BROWN, A.R.
1958   "Taboo" Lessa & Vogt 1958   99-111

REYBURN, W.D.
1969   "African Myths" *Prac. Anth.* 16   193-200

ROSE, RONALD
1956   *Living Magic*. New York, Rand McNally (Australian Aborigines)

1959   *South Seas Magic*. London, Robt. Hale Ld. (Samoa)

RUBINGH, EUGENE
1962   "The Fall of a World View" *The Reformed Jour.* Feb.

SCHMIDT, W.
1958   "The Nature, Atrributes and Worship of the Primitive High God" Lessa & Vogt 1958   24-39

SIMMONDS, JOHN W.
1963   "How the Banyarwands Understand Man" *Prac. Anth.* 10   17-20
SHELTON, A.J.
1968   "Causality in African Thought: Igbo & Others" *Prac. Anth.* 15   157-169

SMITH, EDWIN W.
1923   *The Religion of the Lower Races - as illustrated
            by the African Bantu.* New York, Macmillan Co.

SMITH, EDWIN W. (ed.)
1950   *African Ideas of God.* London, Edinburgh House
            Press

SMITH, ROBERTSON
1958   "Sacrifice Among the Semites" Lessa & Vogt 1958
            47-56

SONG, CHOAN-SENG
1964   "Culture and Incarnation" (Indigenous theology)
            Prac. Anth. 11   138-141

SPIRO, M. & R.G. D'AANDRADE
1958   "A Cross-cultural Study of Some Super-Natural
            Beliefs" *Amer. Anth.* 60   456-466

STANKIEWICZ, EDWARD
1958   "Slavic Kinship Terms and the Perils of the Soul"
            Journ. Amer. Folklore 71   115-122

STANNER, W.E.H.
1958   "The Dreaming" (Australian) Lessa & Vogt 1958
            513-523
1966   "On Aboriginal Religion" Sydney, Univ. of Sydney
            (Oceania Monograph 11)

1967   "Reflections on Durkheim & Aboriginal Religion"
            Freedman 1967   217-240

STEFANISZN, B.
1954   "African Reincarnation   Re-examined" *African
            Studies* 13   130-146

STEINER, FRANZ
1967   *Taboo.* Baltimore, Penguin Books

TANNER, R.E.S.
1956   "An Introduction to the Spirit Beings of the
            Northern Basukuma" *Anth. Qr.* 29   69-81

TEMPELS, R.P. PLACIDE
1961   *La Philosophie Bantoue.* Paris, Présence Africaine

THOMAS, L.V.
1960   "Brève esquisse sur le pensée cosmologique du
            Diola" Fortes & Dieterlen 1965   366-381

TIDANI, A. SERPOS
1950   "Rituels" *Le Monde Noire, Présence Africaine*
            8-9   297-305

TIPPETT, A.R.
1955   "Mana" *The Writer* 3-7

1965   "Primitive Man's Capacity for Receiving the Gospel"
            Tippett 1967a   13-18

1967 a   "The Gods Must Die" Tippett 1967 a   4-8

1967 b   "Pre-Christian Religion" Ch. 1 in *Solomon Islands
            Christianity*. London, Lutterworth Press

TSCHOPIK, H.J.
1951   *The Aymara of Chucuito, Peru, Pt. 1, Magic*.
            New York, Anthropological Papers, American Museum
            of Natural History,   44   137-308

TUTU, D.M.B.
1970   "African Ideas of Salvation" *Ministry* 10   119-
            123

TYLOR, EDWARD B.
1958   "Animism" Lessa & Vogt   1958   11-23; also
            Calverton 1931   635-659

VAUGHAN, J.H.,Jr.
1964   "The Religion and the World View of the Marghi"
            Ethnology 3   389-397

WALES, H.G.O.
1959   "The Cosmological Aspect of Indonesian Religion"
            Journ. Roy. Asiatic Soc. 3   100-139

WALLACE, A.F.C.
1958   "Dreams and Wishes of the Soul...." (Iroquois)
            Amer. Anth. 60   234-248

WARREN, MAX
1958   "Great Pan is Not Dead" *Prac. Anth.* 5   66-78

WEBB, M.C.
1965   "The Abolition of the Taboo System in Hawaii"
            Journ. Polynesian Soc.   74   21-39

WELBOURN, F.B.
1963   "The Importance of Ghosts"   Hayward 1963 15-26

WELTON, MICHAEL R.
  1971   "Themes in African Traditional Belief and Ritual"
              Prac. Anth. 18   1-18

WILLOUGHBY, W.C.
  1928   *The Soul of the Bantu: A Sympathetic Study of the
              Magico-religious Practices and Beliefs of the
              Bantu Tribes of Africa.* New York, Doubleday,
              Doran & Co.

WOLF, ERIC R.
  1958   "The Virgin of Guadelupe: A Mexican National
              Symbol" *Journ. Amer. Folklore* 71   34-39

WRIGHT, MICHAEL A.
  1968   "Some Observations on Thai Animism" *Prac. Anth.*
              15.1   1-7

ANIMISTIC PRACTITIONERS
AND SYSTEMS

RELIGIOUS SYSTEMS, STRUCTURES AND RITUALS

ALLEN, M.R.
  1967   *Male Cults and Secret Initiations in Melanesia.*
            Melbourne, Melbourne Univ. Press

ARINZE, FRANCIS A.
  1970   *Sacrifice in Ibo Religion.*   Ibadan, Ibadan Univ.
            Press

BLAU, HAROLD
  1964   "The Iroquois White Dog Sacrifice: Its Evolution
            and Symbolism" *Ethnohistory* 11   97-119

BRIFFAULT, R.
  1930   "Birth Customs" *Encyclopedia of Social Sciences*
            vol. 2   565-568

BUNZEL, RUTH
  1932   "Introduction to Zuñi Ceremonialism" *Bur. Amer.
            Eth.*   47

CALLAWAY, HENRY
  1870   *The Religious System of the Amazulu.*   London,
            Trubner & Co.

  1870   "The Religion of the Amazulu of South Africa as
            told by Themselves" Kroeber & Waterman 1946
            420-429

CARTER, WM.E.
  1968   "Secular Reinforcement in Aymara Death Ritual"
            Amer. Anth. 70   238-263

CODRINGTON, R.H.
  1946   "Melanesian Religion" Kroeber & Waterman   1946
            412-420

COLSON, E.
1958   "Ancestral Spirits and Social Structure Among the
        Plateau Tonga" Lessa & Vogt 1958   395-400

ELKIN, A.P.
1958   "Australian Totemism" Lessa & Vogt 1958 232-241

FERREIRA, JOHN V.
1965   *Totemism in India.* London, Oxford Univ. Press

FIRTH, R.W.
1930   "Totemism in Polynesia" *Oceania* 1 291-321

1967   *Tikopia Ritual and Belief.* Boston, Beacon Press

FORDE, DARYLL
1949   "Integrative Aspects of the Yako First Fruits
        Ritual" *Journ. Roy. Anth. Inst.* 79 1-10

FORTES, M.
1936   "Ritual Festivals and Social Cohesion in the
        Hinderland of the Gold Coast" *Amer. Anth.* 38
        590-604

1960   "Some Reflections on Ancestor Worship in Africa"
        Fortes & Dieterlen 1965 122-143

FREED, R.S. & S.A.
1966   "Unity in Diversity in the Celebration of Cattle-
        curing Rites in a North Indian Village: A Study in
        the Resolution of Conflict" *Amer. Anth.* 68
        673-692

GOLDENWEISER, A.
1958   "Totemism" Lessa & Vogt 1958 222-232

GOODWIN, G.A.
1945   "Comparison of Navaho & White Mountain Apache
        Ceremonial Forms and Categories" *SW. Journ Anth.*
        1 498-506

GUNSON, NIEL
1964   "Great Women and Friendship Contract Rites in Pre-
        Christian Tahiti" *Journ. Polynesian Soc.* 73
        53-69

HAHM, PYONG CHOM
1969   *Religion and Law in Korea.* Berkeley, Kroeber Soc.
        Anthropological Paper, 41

HAMMOND-TOOKE, W.D.
1960   "Some Bhaca Religious Categories" *Afr. Stud.* 19
        1-13

HANDY, E.S.C.
1927   *Polynesian Religion*. Honolulu, Bishop Museum
            Sections on Priest, Tohunga, Divine Chief, etc.

HOGG, GARRY
1966   *Cannibalism and Human Sacrifice*. New York, The
            Citadel Press

JENSON, ADOLF E.
1965   "Myth and Cult Among Primitive Peoples" *Curr.
            Anth.* 6   199-215   Book Discussion

JUNOD, HENRI
1962   *The Life of a South African Tribe*. New York,
            University Books   Part 6, Vol. 2   301-608
            (Originally published 1912)

KILSON, MARION
1969   "Libation in Ga Ritual" *Jour. of Relig. in Africa*
            2   161-178

1970   "Taxonomy & Form in Ga Ritual" *Jour. of Relig. in
            Africa* 3   45-66

KNUTSSON, KARL ERIC
1967   *Authority and Change: A Study of the Kallu Insti-
            tution Among the Macha Galla of Ethiopia*.
            Göteborg, Ethnografiska Museet

KRADER, L.
1954   "Buryat Religion and Society" *SW. Journ. Anth.*
            10   322-351

LÉVI-STRAUSS, CLAUDE
1962   *Le Totémisme Aujourd'hui*. Paris, Presses
            Universitares de France

LIEN-HWA, CHOW
1964   "The Problems of Funeral Rites" *Prac. Anth.*   11
            226-228

MAQUET, J.J.
1958   "Religion of the Kingdom of Ruanda" Lessa & Vogt
            1958   523-532

MATTHEWS, WASHINGTON
1946   "Navaho Songs and Prayers" Kroeber & Waterman
            1946   442-444

MIDDLETON, JOHN
1970   "The Religious System" Naroll & Cohen   1970
            500-508

MIDDLETON, JOHN (ed.)
1967   *Gods and Rituals*. American Museum Sourcebook Q6
            New York, The Natural History Press

NEWMAN, PHILIP L.
1964   "Religious Belief and Ritual in a New Guinea
            Society" *Amer. Anth.* 66   257-272 (Special
            number devoted to New Guinea)

NYUAK, L.
1906   "Religious Rites and Customs of the Iban or Dyaks
            of Sarawak" *Anthropos*. 1   11-23,165-184,403-425

OTTENBERG, S.
1958   "Ibo Oracles and Intergroup Relations" *SW. Journ.*
            Anth. 14   295-317

REICHARD, G.A.
1945   "Distinctive Features of the Navaho Religion" *SW.*
            Journ. Anth.   1   199-220

RENSHAW, PARKE
1966   "A New Religion for Brazilians" *Prac. Anth*.   13
            126-132

ROWE, J.H.
1958   "Inca Religion" Lessa & Vogt   1958   540-553

SAHAGUN, B. de
1958   "Aztec Sacrifice" Lessa & Vogt   1958   442-445

STONOR. G.R.
1957   "Notes on Religion and Ritual Among the Daffa
            Tribes of the Assam Himalayas" *Anthropos*. 52 1-23

THOMPSON, J.E.S.
1958   "A Maya Priest in Action" Lessa & Vogt 1958
            445-452

THURNWALD, R.D.
1946   "Banaro Society" Kroeber & Waterman   1946   284-96

TIPPETT, A.R.
1968   *Fijian Material Culture: A Study of Cultural Con-*
            text, Function and Change. Honolulu, Bishop
            Museum Press (Contains much on ceremonials and
            rites associated with craftsmanship and the use of
            artifacts in social life.)

1970   "The First Fruit of the Corn Harvest" (Tishena)
            Tippett 1970   89-95

TITIEV, M.
1958   "Religion of the Hopi Indians" Lessa & Vogt   1958
            532-539

TOKAREV, S.A.
1966   "The Problem of Totemism as Seen by Soviet Scholars"
            Curr. Anth.   7   185-188

TURNER, VICTOR
1960   "Ritual Symbolism, Morality & Social Structure
            among the Ndembu" Fortes & Dieterlen   1965   79-91

1967   *The Forest of Symbols: Aspects of Ndembu Ritual.*
            Ithica, Cornell Univ. Press

VAN GENNEP, ARNOLD
1960   *The Rites of Passage.* (Translated)   Chicago, Univ.
            of Chicago Press   Phoenix paperback P64

VOGT, E.
1965   "Ceremonial Organization in Zinacantan"   *Ethnology*
            4   39-52

WATERMAN, T.T.
1946   "Aztec Rituals"   Kroeber & Waterman   1946   437-440

WEDGEWOOD, CAMILLA H.
1930   "The Nature and Functions of Secret Societies"
            Oceania   1   129-145

WESCOTT, J   & P. MORTON-WILLIAMS
1962   "The Symbolism and Ritual Content of the Yoruba
            Laba Shango" *Journ. Roy. Anth. Inst.*   92   23-37

WILLEMS, E.
1949   "Acculturative Aspects of the Feast of the Holy
            Ghost in Brazil" *Amer. Anth.*   51   400-408

WILLIAMS, F.E.
1940   *The Drama of Orokolo: Social and Ceremonial Life
            of the Elema"*   Oxford, Clarendon Press

WILSON, MONICA
1954   "Nyakusa Ritual & Symbolism" *Amer. Anth.*   56
            228-241
WISSLER, CLARK & H.J. SPINDEN
1916   "The Pawnee Human Sacrifice to the Morningstar"
            Amer. Museum Jour.   16   49-55

WORSLEY, P.M.
1955   "Totemism in a Changing Society" *Amer. Anth.*   57
            851-861

MAGIC, SORCERY, WITCHCRAFT AND DIVINATION

AMES, D.
  1959   "Belief in 'Witches' Among the Rural Wolof of the
                Gambia" *Africa* 29   263-273

BASCOM, WILLIAM
  1969   *Ifa Divination: Communication between Gods and Men
                in West Africa.* Bloomington, Indiana Univ. Press

BOHANNAN, LAURA
  1956   "Miching Mallecho: that means Witchcraft" From
                the Third Programme, J. Morris (ed.) London,
                Nonesuch Press

BUCK, PETER H.
  1936   *Regional Diversity in the Elaboration of Sorcery
                in Polynesia.* New Haven, Yale Univ. Press

CRAWFORD, J.R.
  1967   *Witchcraft and Sorcery in Rhodesia.* London,
                Oxford Univ. Press

DAVIES, T.W.
  1969   *Magic, Divination & Demonology among the Hebrews &
                Their Neighbours.* New York, KTAV Publishing House

DEBRUNNER, H.
  1961   *Witchcraft in Ghana.* Accra, Presbyterian Bk.Depot

EHNMARK, E.
  1956   "Religion & Magic: Frazer, Söderblom and
                Häagerström" *Ethnos.* 21   1-10

EKVALL, R.B.
  1963   "Some Aspects of Divination in Tibetan Society"
                Ethnology 2   31-39

EVANS-PRITCHARD, E.E.
  1929   "The Morphology and Function of Magic: a Compara-
                tive Study of Trobriand and Zande Rituals and
                Spells" *Amer. Anth.* 31   619-641

  1932-3   "The Zande Corporation of Witchdoctors" *Journ.
                Roy. Anth. Inst.* 62   291-336; 63   63-100

  1935   "Witchcraft" *Africa* 8   419-422

  1937   *Witchcraft, Oracles and Magic Among the Azande.*
                Oxford, Clarendon Press

EVANS-PRITCHARD, E.E.
  1958   "Consulting the Poison Oracle Among the Azande"
              Lessa & Vogt 1958   304-314

EVERS, H.D.
  1965   "Magic and Religion in Sinhalese Society" *Amer.*
              Anth. 67   97-99

FISHER, W.S.
  1949   "Black Magic Feuds" *African Studies* 8   20-72

FORDE, D.
  1958   "Spirits, Witches and Sorcerers in the Super-
              natural Economy of the Yako" *Journ. Roy. Anth.*
              Inst. 88   165-178

FORTUNE, R.F.
  1963   *Sorcerers of Dobu.* New York, E.P. Dutton & Co.
              paperback

FREELAND, L.S.
  1923   "Pomo Doctors and Poisoners" *UCPAAE*   20   57-73

GLUCKMAN, MAX
  1944   "The Logic of African Science and Witchcraft: An
              Appreciation of Evans-Pritchard's 'Witchcraft,
              Oracles & Magic among the Azande' of the Sudan"
              Rhodes-Livingstone Inst. Jour. June 61-71

GODDARD, P.E.
  1946   "Magical Formulas of the Hupa" Kroeber & Waterman
              1946   440-442

HOCART, A.M.
  1925   "Medicine and Witchcraft in Eddystone of the
              Solomons" *Journ. Roy. Anth. Inst.* 55   221-270

HSU, FRANCIS L.K.
  1960   "A Neglected Aspect of Witchcraft Studies" *Journ.*
              Amer. Folklore 73   35-38

HUGHES, PENNETHORN
  1952   *Witchcraft.* London, Longmans, Green & Co.

KLUCKHOHN, CLYDE
  1962   *Navaho Witchcraft.* Boston, Beacon Press

KRIGE, J.D.
  1958   "The Social Function of Witchcraft" Lessa & Vogt
              1958   282-291 (1st Edition only)

LIEBAN, RICHARD W.
  1967   *Cebuana Sorcery: Malign Magic in the Philippines*.
              Berkeley, Univ. of California Press

MAIR, LUCY
  1969   *Witchcraft*. New York, McGraw-Hill

MARWICK, M.G.
  1952   "The Social Context of Cewa Witchcraft Beliefs"
              Africa 22   120-135, 215-233

  1964   *Sorcery in its Social Setting: A Study of the
              Northern Rhodesian Cewa*. Manchester, Manchester
              Univ. Press

MARWICK, MAX (ed.)
  1970   *Witchcraft and Sorcery*. (Selected Readings)
              Baltimore, Penguin Books

MIDDLETON, J.
  1955   "The Concept of 'Bewitching' in Lugbara" *Africa*
              25   252-260

  1967   *Magic, Witchcraft and Curing*. American Museum
              Sourcebook Q7 New York, The Natural History Press

MIDDLETON, JOHN & E.H. WINTER (eds.)
  1963   *Witchcraft and Sorcery in East Africa*. London,
              Routledge & Paul

MULLEN, PATRICK B.
  1969   "The Function of Magic Folk Beliefs among Texas
              Coastal Fishermen" *Journ. Amer. Folklore* 82
              214-225

NADEL, S.F.
  1952   "Witchcraft in Four African Societies: An Essay
              in Comparison" *Amer. Anth.* 54   18-29

  1958   "Two Nuba Religions: An Essay in Comparison"
              Amer. Anth. 57   661-679

PARRINDER, G.
  1954   *Witchcraft*. London, Penguin Books A409 or
              Witchcraft: European and African. New York,
              Barnes & Noble 1963

  1956   "African Ideas of Witchcraft" *Folk Lore* (London)
              67   142-150

REYNOLDS, BARRIE
1963   *Magic, Divination and Witchcraft among the Barotse of Northern Rhodesia.* Berkeley, Univ. of Calif. Press

RICHARDS, A.I.
1935   "A Modern Movement of Witchfinders" *Africa* 8 448-461

ROBERTS, R.G.
1954   "Mind over Matter - Magical Performances in the Gilbert Islands" *Journ. Polynesian Soc.* 63 17-25

ROSE, B.W.
1964   "African and European Magic: A First Comparative Study of Beliefs and Practices" *African Studies* 23 1-9

SALER, B.
1964   "Nagual, Witch and Sorcerer in a Quiche Village" *Ethnology* 3 305-328

SHELTON, AUSTIN J.
1965   "The Meaning and Method of Afa Divination among the Northern Nsukka Ibo" *Amer. Anth.* 67 1441-56

SIMPSON, G.E.
1954   "Magical Practices in Northern Haiti" *Journ. Amer. Folklore* 67 395-403

SKEAT, W.W.
1900   *Malay Magic.* London, Macmillan & Co.

TANNER, R.E.S.
1956   "The Sorcerer in Northern Sukumaland, Tanganyika" *SW. Journ. Anth.* 12 437-443

THOMPSON, D.F. et al
1961   "Medicineman and Sorcerer in Arnham Land" *Man* 61 97-102

TIPPETT, A.R.
1967   *Solomon Islands Christianity.* London, Lutterworth Press 10-16 343-345

1970   *Peoples of Southwest Ethiopia.* South Pasadena, William Carey Library 152-225

WALLACE, W.J. & E.S. TAYLOR
1950   "Hupa Sorcery" *SW. Journ. Anth.* 6 188-196

WAX, MURRAY & ROSALIE
    1963   "The Notion of Magic" *Curr. Anth.* 4 495-518

WEBSTER, HUTTON
    1948   *Magic: A Sociological Study.* Stanford, Stanford
                Univ. Press

WEIMERS, W.E.
    1949   "Secret Medicines, Magic and Rites of the Kpelle
                Tribe in Liberia" *SW. Journ. Anth.* 5 208-243

WHITE, C.M.N.
    1948   "Witchcraft, Divination and Magic Among the
                Balovale Tribes" *Africa* 18 81-104

WILLIAMS, F.E.
    1928   *Orokaiva Magic.* London, Oxford Univ. Press

WILSON, MONICA
    1951   "Witch Beliefs and Social Structures" *Amer. Journ.
                of Sociol.* 56 307-313

WINANS, E.V. & R.B. EGERTON
    1964   "Hehe Magical Justice" *Amer. Anth.* 66 745-764

SHAMANISM AND CURING

ACKERNECHT, E.H.
    1958   "Problems of Primitive Medicine" Lessa & Vogt
                1958 343-353

BECK, ROBT. J.
    1967   "Some Proto-Psychotherapeutic Elements in the
                Practice of the Shaman" *Hist. of Relig.* 6 303-27

BRYANT, A.T.
    1970   *Zulu Medicine and Medicine Men.* Cape Town,
                C. Struik

CENTLIVRES, M. & P., & M. SLOBIN
    1971   "A Muslim Shaman of Afghan Turkestan" *Ethnology*
                10   160-173

CHADWICK, N.K.
    1936   "Shamanism Among the Tartars of Central Asia"
                Journ. Roy. Anth. Inst. 66 75-112

COE, M.
    1955   "Shamanism in the Bunun Tribe, Central Formosa"
                Ethnos 20   181-198

DIXON, R.B.
1908   "Some Aspects of the American Shaman" *Journ. Amer. Folklore* 21   1-12

DOBKIN, MARLENE
1969   "Fortune's Malice: Divination, Psychotherapy and Folk Medicine in Peru" *Journ. Amer. Folklore* 82   132-141

ELIADE, M.
1961   "Recent Works on Shamanism: A Review Article" *Hist. of Relig.* 1   152-186

1964   *Shamanism: Archaic Techniques of Ecstasy.* New York, Pantheon Books

FISCHER, J.L., A. & F. MAHONY
1959   "Totemism and Allergy" *Int'l. Journ. of Soc. Psychiatry* 5   33-40

FRAKE, C.O.
1961   "The Diagnosis of Disease among the Subanun of Mindanao" *Amer. Anth.* 63   113-132

GAYTON, A.H.
1930   "Yokuts-Nono Chiefs and Shamans" *UCPAAE* 24   361-420

GELFAND, MICHAEL
1956   *Medicine and Magic of the Mashona.*   Capetown, Juta & Co.

GILLIN, JOHN
1958   "Magical Fright" Lessa & Vogt   1958   352-362

GREEN, L.C. & M.W. BECKWITH
1926   "Hawaiian Customs and Beliefs Relating to Sickness and Death" *Amer. Anth.* 28   176-208

HAEBERLIN, H.
1918   "Sbetetda'q: A Shamanistic Performance of the Coast Salish" *Amer. Anth.* 20 249-257

HANDY, E.S.C., M.K. PUKUI & K. LIVERMORE
1934   *Outline of Hawaiian Physical Therapeutics*: Honolulu, Bishop Museum   Bulletin 126

HARLEY, G.W.
1941   *Native African Medicine, with Special Reference to its Practice in the Mano Tribe of Liberia.* Cambridge, Harvard Univ. Press

HONIGMANN, J.J.
   1949   "Parallels in the Development of Shamanism Among
                the Northern and Southern Athabaskans" *Amer. Anth.*
                51   512-514

HOPKINS, L.C.
   1945   "The Shaman or Chinese Wu: His Inspired Dancing and
                Versatile Character" *Journ. Roy. Asiatic Soc.*
                3-16

HOWITT, A.W.
   1887   "On Australian Medicine Men" *Journ. Roy. Anth*
                Inst. 16 23-59

INGHAM, JOHN M.
   1970   "On Mexican Folk Medicine" *Amer. Anth.* 72   76-87

LEIGHTON, A. & D.
   1967   "Therapeutic Values in Navaho Religion" *Arizona*
                Highways 43   2-13

LIBERTY, MARGOT P.
   1970   "Priest and Shaman on the Plains: A False
                Dichotomy?" *Plains Anthropologist* 15   73-79

LOEB, E.M.
   1929   "Shaman and Seer" *Amer. Anth.* 31   80-84

LOEWEN, J.A., A. BUCKWATER & J. KRATZ
   1965   "Shamanism, Illness and Power in the Toba Church"
                Prac. Anth. 12   250-280

LOMMEL, ANDREAS
   1970   Reviews and Discussion of *Shamanism: The Beginnings*
                of Art (McGraw-Hill, New York 1967) *Curr. Anth.*
                11 39-48

MADSEN, WM.
   1955   "Shamanism in Mexico" *SW. Journ. Anth.* 11   48-57

METZGER, DUANE & GERALD WILLIAMS
   1965   "Tenejapa Medicine 1: The Curer" Lessa & Vogt
                1965 (2nd Edition only) 593-602

MINER, HORACE
   1956   "Body Ritual Among the Nacrima" *Amer. Anth.* 58
                503-507

MORGAN, WM.
   1931   "Navaho Treatment of Sickness: Diognosticians"
                Amer. Anth. 33   390-402

MORRIS, H.S.
   1967   "Shamanism among the Oya Melanan" (Sarawak)
                Freedman 1967   189-216

MURDOCK, G.P.
  1965   "Tenino Shamanism" *Ethnology* 4   165-171

NADEL, S.F.
  1946   "A Study of Shamanism in the Nuba Mountains"
                Journ. Roy. Anth. Inst. 76   25-37

OPLER, M.E.
  1946   "The Creative Role of Shamanism in Mescalero
                Apache Mythology" *Journ. Amer. Folklore* 59 268-81

  1947   "Notes on Chirchahua Apache Culture: Supernatural
                Power and the Shaman" *Man* 20   1-14

RAHMANN, R.
  1959   "Shamanistic and Related Phenomena in Northern and
                Middle India" *Anthropos* 54   681-760

RASMUSSEN, K.
  1958 a   "An Eskimo Shaman Purifies a Sick Person" Lessa &
                Vogt 1958 362-367

  1958 b   "A Shaman's Journey to the Sea Spirit" Lessa &
                Vogt 1958   420-424

REICHARD, G.A.
  1939   *Navaho Medicine Man.* New York, J.J. Augustan

ROCK, J.F.
  1959   "Contributions to the Shamanism of the Tibetan
                Chinese Borderland" *Anthropos* 54   796-818

ROMANO, O.I. (V)
  1965   "Charismatic Medicine Folk-Healing and Folk-Saint-
                hood" *Amer. Anth.* 67   1151-1173

SILVERMAN, JULIAN
  1967   "Shamans and Acute Schizophrenia" *Amer. Anth.* 69
                21-31

TEXTOR, R.B.
  1962   "A Statistical Method for the Study of Shamanism:
                A Case Study from Field Work in Thailand" *Human
                Organ.* 21   56-60

THALBITZER, W.
  1946   "Shamans of the East Greenland Eskimo" Kroeber &
                Waterman 1946   430-436

TIPPETT, A.R.
  1970   "The Theory of Sickness and Religious Belief"
                (Ethiopia) Tippett 1970   199-225

WELBOURN, F.B.
  1963   "The Importance of Ghosts" Hayward 1963   15-26

BASTIDE, ROGER
1958   *Le Candomble de Bahia*. Paris, Mouton & Co.

BEATTIE, JOHN & JOHN MIDDLETON (eds.)
1969   *Spirit Mediumship & Society in Africa*. New York,
            Africana Publishing Corporation (Symposium)

BEYNON, E.D.
1938   "The Voodoo Cult Among Negro Migrants in Detroit"
            Amer. Journ. Sociol. 43   894-907

BOURGUIGNON, ERIKA
1965   "The Self, the Behavioral Environment and the
            Theory of Possession" Spiro 1965   39-60

CANNON, W.B.
1958   "Voodoo Death" Lessa & Vogt   1958   270-277

DAMBORIENA, PRUDENCIO
1969   *Tongues as of Fire: Pentecostalism in Contemporary
            Christianity*. Washington, D.C., Corpus Books
            101-120

ELLIOT, A.J.A.
1955   *Chinese Spirit-Medium Cults in Singapore*. London,
            London School of Economics & Political Science,
            Dept. of Anthropology

EVANS, MELVIN O.
1971   "Spirit Possession among Certain Southern Bantu
            Tribes in Relation to the Bible and Church Growth"
            M.A. thesis, School of World Mission, Fuller Theo-
            logical Seminary, Pasadena

FRAZER, JAMES G.
1935   "The Omnipresence of Demons" and "The Expulsion of
            Evils" *The Golden Bough, Pt. IV The Scapegoat*.
            New York, The Macmillan Co.   72-223

HARRIS, G.
1957   "Possession 'Hysteria' in a Kenya Tribe" *Amer.
            Anth.* 59   1046-1066

JOHNSON, HARMON A.
1969   "Authority Over the Spirits: Brazilian Spiritism &
            Evangelical Church Growth" M.A. thesis, School of
            World Mission, Fuller Theological Seminary,
            Pasadena

LANGTON, E.
1959   *Essentials of Demonology*.   London, Epworth Press

LOEDERER, RD. A.
1935   *Voodoo Fire in Haiti*.   New York, Doubleday, Doran
            & Co.

MAY, L. CARLYLE
1956   "A Survey of Glossolalia and Related Phenomena in
            Non-Christian Religions" *Amer. Anth.* 58   75-92

McGREGOR, PEDRO
1966   *The Moon & Two Mountains: The Myths, Ritual and
            Magic of Brazilian Spiritism*.   London, Souvenir
            Press

1967   *Jesus of the Spirits*.   New York, Stein & Day

NEVIUS, JOHN L.
1894   *Demon Possession and Allied Themes*.   Chicago,
            Fleming H. Revell Co.

NOBLE, D.S.
1961   "Demoniacal Possession Among the Giryama" *Man* 61
            50-52

OESTERREICH, T.K.
1966   *Possession: Demoniacal & Other, Among Primitive
            Races in Antiquity, the Middle Ages and Modern
            Times*.   New York, University Books

OPLER, MORRIS E.
1958   "Spirit Possession in a Rural Area of Northern
            India" Lessa & Vogt 1958 (1st Ed. only)   553-566

PEARSON, A.C.
1920   "Possession" (Classical) *Encyclopedia of Religion
            & Ethics*   10   127-130

SHORTER, AYLWARD
1970   "The Migawo: Peripheral Spirit Possession and
            Christian Prejudice" *Anthropos* 65   110-126

SIMPSON, E.G.
1940   "The Vodun Service in Northern Haiti" *Amer. Anth.*
            42   236-255

SONGER, HAROLD H.
1967   "Demonic Possession and Mental Illness" *Rel. in
            Life* 36   119-127

STAGG, F., E.G. HINSON & W.E. OATES
  1967   *Glossolalia: Tongue Speaking in Biblical, Histori-
            cal and Psychological Perspective.* Nashville,
            Abingdon Press

STEWART, K.M.
  1946   "Spirit Possession in Native America" *SW. Journ.
            Anth.* 2 323-339

TALLANT, ROBT.
  1962   *Voodoo in New Orleans.* New York, Collier Books

TIPPETT, A.R.
  1970   *Peoples of Southwest Ethiopia.* South Pasadena,
            William Carey Library, "Among the Ghimeera" 184-93

WALTENBERG, H.
  1962   "The Demoniacs of Manda" *The National Lutheran*

WERBNER, R.P.
  1964   "Atonement Ritual and Guardian Spirit Possession
            Among Kalanga" *Africa* 34 206-223

WESLEY, JOHN
  1944   "The Nature of Enthusiasm" *Forty-Four Sermons*
            London, Epworth Press 416-429. (This sermon
            first appeared in Wesley's *Sermons, Vol. III,*1750)

WHITE, HUGH W.
  1922   *Demonism Verified and Analysed.* Shanghai,
            Presbyterian Mission Press

SYNCRETISM

BEEKMAN, JOHN
  1959   "Minimizing Religious Syncretism Among the Chols"
            Prac. Anth. 6 241-250

DUNCAN, HALL F.
  1966   "African Art and the Church" *Prac. Anth.* 13
            107-114

FERNANDEZ, JAMES W.
  1964   "The Idea and Symbol of the Saviour in a Gabon
            Syncretistic Cult" *I.R.M.* 53 281-289

GUSTAFSON, JAS. W.
  1970   "Syncretistic Rural Thai Buddhism" M.A. thesis,
            School of World Mission, Fuller Theological
            Seminary, Pasadena

HERSKOVITS, MELVILLE J.
1958   "African Gods and Catholic Saints in New World
            Belief" Lessa & Vogt 1958 492-498

HOOGSHAGEN, SEARLE
1964   "The Mixe Supernatural and Christianity" *Prac.
            Anth.* 11 25-34

ISHIDA, YOSHIRA
1963   "Mukyokai: Indigenous Movement in Japan" *Prac.
            Anth.* 10 21-26

KRAEMER, HENDRICK
1938   *The Christian Message in a Non-Christian World.*
            London, I.M.C. Council

1956   *Religion and the Christian Faith.* London,
            Lutterworth   Chapters 24 & 25

1961   "Syncretism as a Theological Problem for Missions"
            in G.H. Anderson (ed.) *The Theology of Christian
            Mission.* New York, McGraw-Hill Book Co.   179-182

LINDSELL, HAROLD
1967   "Attack Syncretism with Dialogue" *E.M.Q.* 3 203-8

LUZBETAK, LOUIS J.
1966   "Christopaganism" *Prac. Anth.* 13   115-121

MADSEN, WILLIAM
1957   *Christo-Paganism: A Study of Mexican Religious
            Syncretism.* New Orleans, Middle Amer. Res. Inst.

MOORE, JOSEPH G.
1965   "Religious Syncretism in Jamaica" *Pract. Anth.* 12
            63-70

NIDA, EUGENE A.
1960   "Mariology in Latin America" *Prac. Anth.Supp.*7-15

1961   "Christopaganism" *Prac. Anth.* 8   1-15

1966   "African Influence in the Religious Life of Latin
            America" *Prac. Anth.* 13   133-138

NORMAN, W.H.H.
1957   "Non-Church Christianity in Japan" *I.R.M.* 46
            380-393

205

PARRATT, J.K. & A.R.I. DOI
1969 a   "Syncretism in Yorubaland: a religious or socio-
            logical phenomenon?" *Prac. Anth.*   16.3   109-113

1969 b   "Some Further Aspects of Yoruba Syncretism" *Prac.
            Anth.* 16   252-256

PRICE, WM. J.
1964   "Time is of the Gods" *Prac. Anth.* 11   266-272

SHEPHERD, JACK F.
1966   "Mission and Syncretism" Wheaton Conference *Study
            Papers* S1-14

STEENBERGHEN, PERE ROMBAUT
1959   "Neo-Paganism in Africa" *Frontier* 2   266-288

TIPPETT, A.R.
1969   "The Apostle and the Encounter of Communions" in
            Verdict Theology in Missionary Theory. Lincoln,
            Lincoln Christian College Press 25-33; 149-151

TOLIVER, RALPH
1970   "Syncretism: A Specter Among Philippine Protes-
            tants" *Prac. Anth.* 17   210-219

TURNER, CHARLES V.
1964   "The Socio-Religious Significance of Baptism
            Sinasina" *Prac. Anth.* 11   179-180

TURNER, H.W.
1961   "Searching and Syncretism: A West African
            Documentation" *Prac. Anth.* 8   106-110

1965   "Pagan Features in West African Churches" *Prac.
            Anth.* 12   145-151

VISSER'T HOOFT, W.A.
1963   *No Other Name.* London, S.C.M. Press

WANG, G.T. & J. ANDREW FOWLER
1970   "Accomodation in an Iban Church Today" *Prac.Anth.*
            17   220-234

WOLF, ERIC
1965   "The Virgin and Guadalupe: A Mexican National Sym-
            bol" Lessa & Vogt 1965 (2nd Ed. only) 226-230

WONDERLY, WM. L.
1958   "Pagan and Christian Concepts in a Mexican Indian
            Culture" *Prac. Anth.* 5   197-202

ORGANIZED NATIVISTIC MOVEMENTS

This unit covers all kinds of prophetic and nativistic movements, cargo cults, folk churches and unclassified sects.

ABERLE, DAVID
1965   "A Note on Relative Deprivation Theory as applied to Millenarian and Other Cult Movements" Lessa & Vogt (2nd Ed. only) 1965 537-541

1966   *The Peyote Religion Among the Navaho.* Chicago, Aldine Publishing Co.

BAËTA, C.G.
1962   *Prophetism in Ghana: A Study of Some 'Spiritual' Churches.* London, S.C.M. Press

BARBER, BERNARD
1958   "Acculturation and Messianic Movements" Lessa & **Vogt** 1958 474-478

BARRETT, DAVID B.
1968   *Schism and Renewal in Africa.* Nairobi, Oxford University Press

BEATTIE, J.M.
1964   "The Ghost Cult in Bunyoro" *Ethnology* 3 127-151

BECKEN, H.J.
1967   "On the Holy Mountain: New Year Festival of the Nazaretha Church..." *Jr.Relig. in Afr.* 1 138-149

BELSHAW, CYRIL S.
1958   "The Significance of Modern Cults in Melanesian Development" Lessa & Vogt 1958 486-492

BERNDT, R.M.
1952-3   "A Cargo Movement in the Eastern Central Highlands of New Guinea" *Oceania* 23 40-65, 137-58, 202-34

BERTSCHE, JAMES E.
1966   "Kimganguism: A Challenge of Missionary Statesmen"
            Prac. Anth. 13   13-33

BLAKNEY, CHARLES P.
1969   "Chipunha, A Rhodesian Cult" *Prac. Anth.* 16.3
            98-108

BURRIDGE, K.O.
1954   "Cargo Activity in Tangu" *Oceania* 24   241-254

CATO, A.C.
1947   "A New Religious Cult in Fiji" *Oceania* 18 146-156

CHINNERY, E.W.F. & A.C. HADDON
1917   "Five New Religious Cults in British New Guinea"
            Hibbert Journal 15   458-460

COLLIER, J.
1952   "The Peyote Cult" *Science* 115   503-504

COLLINS, J.M.
1950   "The Indian Shaker Church: A Study of Continuity
            and Change in Religion" *SW. Journ. Anth.* 6 399-411

CRANSWICK, G.H. & I.W.A. SHEVILL
1949   "The Church and the Strange New Cults" *New Deal
            for Papua.* Ch. 9. Melbourne, F.W. Cheshire

DE BRUYN, J.V.
1949   "The Masren Cult of Baik" *South Pacific* 5   1-10

DE CRAEMER, W.
1968   "The Jamaa Movement in the Katanga & Kasai Regions
            of the Congo" *Rev. Rel. Research* 10   11-23

DITTMANN, A.T. & H.C. MOORE
1957   "Disturbance in Dreams as Related to Peyotism
            among the Navaho" *Amer. Anth.* 59   642-649

DOUTRELOUX, M.A.
1960   "Propétisme e Culture" Fortes & Dieterlen 1965
            224-237

EMMET, D.
1956   "Prophets and Their Societies" *Jr. Roy. Anth.
            Inst.* 86   13-24

EWERS, J.C.
1956   "The Assiniboin Horse Medicine Cult" *Anth. Quar.*
            29   57-68

FERACCA, S.E.
1961   "The Yuwipi Cult of the Oglala and Sicangu Teton
        Sioux" *Plains Anth.* 6   155-163

FEHDERAU, HAROLD W.
1962   "Kimbanguism: Prophetic Christianity in Congo"
        Prac. Anth. 9   157-178

FERNANDEZ, JAMES W.
1965   "Politics and Prophecy: African Religious Move-
        ments" *Prac. Anth.* 12   71-75

1965 a "African Religious Movements" *Jr. Mod. Afr. Stud.*
        3   418-446

1965 b "Symbolic Consensus in a Fang Reformative Cult"
        Amer. Anth. 67   902-929

FRAKE, CHARLES O.
1965   "A Structural Description of Subanun 'Religious
        Behavior' " Lessa & Vogt 1965 (2nd Ed. only)
        582-593

FUCHS, STEPHEN
1965   *Rebellious Prophets: A Study of Messianic Move-
        ments in Indian Religions.* New York, Asia
        Publishing House

GALANG, P.P.
        The Huk Movement in the Philippines: Its Signifi-
        cance for Grass-Root Christianity" *Background
        Information*   18-22

GELFAND, M.
1960   "The Mhondoro Cult of the Shona-speaking People of
        Southern Rhodesia" Fortes & Dieterlin 1965 341-47

GUIART, JEAN
1951   " 'Cargo Cults' and Political Evolution in Mela-
        nesia" *South Pacific* 5   128-129

1952 a "The Co-operative Called 'Malekula Native Co.': A
        Border-line Type of Cargo Cult" *South Pacific* 6
        429-433

1952 b "John Frum Movement in Tanna" *Oceania* 22 165-177

1956   "Culture Contact and the 'John Frum' Movements on
        Tanna, New Hebrides" *SW. Journ. Anth.* 12 105-116

GUNSON, N.
1962   "An Account of the Mamaia or Visionary Heresy of
            Tahiti, 1826-41" *Journ. Polynesian Soc.* 71
            209-243

HAMMER, R.J.
1962   "Japan's New Religions" *Frontier* 5   356-361

HANNEMAN, E.L.
1948   "Le culte de cargo en Nouvelle-Guinee" *Le Monde
            Non-Chrétien* 8   937-962

HENDERSON, J. McLEOD
1963   *Ratana, The Origins and Story of the Movement.*
            Wellington, Polynesian Society

HERSKOVITS, J.J.
1958   "African Gods and Catholic Saints in the New World
            Belief" Lessa & Vogt 1958   492-498

HEUSTIS, E.
1963   "Bororo Spiritism as Revitalization" *Prac. Anth.*
            10   187-189

HILL, W.
1944   "The Navaho Religion & the Ghost Dance of 1890"
            Amer. Anth. 46   523

HOEBEL, E.A.
1941   "The Comanche Sun Dance and Messianic Outbreak of
            1873" *Amer. Anth.* 43   301-302

HOLT, JOHN B.
` 1957   "Holiness Religions: Cultural Shock and Social
            Reorganization" in Yinger's *Religion, Society and
            the Individual*   463-470

HONG, SUHN-KYOUNG
1968   "Tonghak in the Context of Korean Modernization"
            Rev. Relig. Research 10   43-51

HOWARD, J.H.
1957   "The Mescal-Bean Cult of the Central Southern
            Plains: An Ancestor of the Peyote Cult" *Amer.
            Anth.* 59   75-87

INGLIS, J.
1957   "Cargo Cults: The Problem of Explanation" *Oceania*
            27   249-263

INSELMANN, RUDOLPH
    1944   "Letub, the Cult of Secret Wealth" M.A. thesis,
                  Kennedy School of Missions, Hartford

    1946   " 'Cargo Cult' Not Caused by Missions" *Pac. Isl.*
                  Monthly 16   44-45

ISHIDA, Y.
    1963   "Mukyokai: Indigenous Movement in Japan" *Prac.*
                  Anth. 10   21-26

KAMMA, F.C.
    1952   "Messianic Movements in Western New Guinea"
                  I.R.M. 41   148-160

KAUFMANN, ROBERT
    1964   *Millénarisme et Acculturation.* Bruxelles,Institut
                  de Sociologie de l'Universite Libre de Bruxelles

LA BARRE, WESTON
    1959   *The Peyote Cult.*   Hamden, The Shoestring Press
                  (enlarged paperback edition, New York, Schocken
                  Books)

    1960   "Twenty Years of Peyote Studies" *Curr. Anth.* 1
                  45-60

    1962   *They Shall Take Up Serpents: Psychology of the*
                  Southern Snake-Handling Cult. Minneapolis, Univ.
                  of Minnesota Press

LATERNARI, V.
    1962   "Messianism: Its Historical Origin and Morphology"
                  Hist of Relig. 2   52-72

    1963   *The Religions of the Oppressed: A Study in Modern*
                  Messianic Cults. New York,Mentor Books paperback
                  MT608

    1965   "The Religions of the Oppressed: A Study of Modern
                  Messianic Cults" (Book Discussion) *Curr. Anth.*
                  6   447-465

LEESON, IDA
    1952   *Bibliography of Cargo Cults and Ohter Nativistic*
                  Movements in the South Pacific. Noumea, South
                  Pacific Commission Technical Paper 30

LOEWEN, JACOB A.
    1966   "Aureliano: Profile of a Prophet" *Prac. Anth.* 13
                  97-114

LOFLAND, JOHN
1966   *Doomsday Cult: A Study of Conversion, Proselytiza-
            tion and Maintenance of Faith.* Englewood Cliffs,
            Prentice-Hall

LINTON, RALPH
1958   "Nativistic Movements" Lessa & Vogt 1958 466-474

M.L. (M. LENORMAND)
1949   "Le 'cargo cult' à Bougainville"   *Etudes
            Melanésiennes* 4   82-83

MC FARLAND, H. NEILL
1967   *The Rush Hour of the Gods: A Study of New
            Religious Movements in Japan.* New York, The
            Macmillan Co.

MÉTRAUX, ALFRED
1942   "A Quechua Messiah in Eastern Peru" *Amer. Anth.*
            44   721-725

MIDDLETON, JOHN
1958   "The Yakan Cult Among the Lugbara" *Man* 58 112

1963   "The Yankanor Allah Water Cult Among the Lugbara"
            Jr. Roy. Anth. Inst. 93   80-108

MILNES, DAVID
1960   "Let My People Go!" *Frontier* 3   214-216

MISCHEL, F.
1957   "African 'Powers' in Trinidad: The Shango Cult"
            Anth. Qr. 30   45-49

MITCHELL, R.C.
1964   "African Prophet Movements" *Christian Century* 81
            1427-1429

MOONEY, JAMES
1965   *The Ghost-dance Religion and the Sioux Outbreak of
            1890.* Chicago, Univ. of Chicago Press

MOOS, F.
1964   "Some Aspects of Park Chang No Kyo - a Korean
            Revitalization Movement" *Anth. Qr.* 37   110-121

MORTON-WILLIAMS, P.
1960   "The Yoruba Ogboni Cult in Oyo" *Africa* 30 362-374

1964   "An Outline of the Cosmology and Cult Organi-
            zations of the Oyo Yoruba" *Africa* 34   243-261

NORMAN, W.H.H.
1957   "Non-Church Christianity in Japan" *I.R.M.*   47
            380-393

NUNEZ, THERON A., JR.
1958   "Creek Nativism and the Creek War of 1813-1814"
            Ethnohistory 5   1-47; 131-175; 292-301

OOSTERWAL, G.
1963   "A Cargo Cult in the Mamberamo Area" *Ethnology*   2
            1-14

O'REILLY, P.
1949   "Prophétisme aux Nouvelles-Hébrides: le mouvement
            Jonfrum à Tanna (1940-1947)" *Le Monde Non-
            Chrétien* 10   192-208

OSBORNE, K.B.
1970   "A Christian Graveyard Cult in the New Guinea
            Highlands" *Prac. Anth.*   17   10-15

PEREIRA DA QUEIROZ, MARIA ISAURA
1958 a   "L'influence du Milieu Social Interne sur les
            mouvements messianiques brésiliens" *Archives de
            Sociologie des Religions*   3-30

1958 b   "Classifications des Messianismes brésiliens"
            Archives de Sociologie des Religions   111-120

POIRIER, JEAN
1949   "Les mouvements de libération mythique aux
            Nouvelles-Hébrides" *Journal de la Société des
            Océanistes* 5   97-103

READ, K.A.
1958   "A 'Cargo' Situation in the Markham Valley, New
            Guinea" *SW. Journ. Anth.*   14   273-294

SCHWARTZ, THEODORE
1958   "The Palian Movement in the Admiralty Islands,
            1946-54" Ph.D. dissertation, University of
            Pennsylvania

SHONLE, R.
1925   "Peyote: The Giver of Visions" *Amer. Anth.*   27
            53-57

SIMPSON, G.E.
1957   "The Ras Tafari Movement in Jamaica" in Yinger's
            Religion, Society & the Individual.   507-514

SIMPSON, G.E.
1962   "The Shango Cult in Nigeria and Trinidad" *Amer.
             Anth.* 64   1204-1219

SLOTKIN, J.S.
1955   "Peyotism, 1521-1891" *Amer. Anth.* 57   202-230

STANNER, W.E.H.
1958   "On the Interpretation of Cargo Cults" *Oceania*
             29   1-25

STOEVESANDT, G.
1934   "The Sect of the Second Adam" *Africa* 7   479-482

SUNDKLER, BENGT
1960 a   "Bantu Messiah and White Christ" *Prac. Anth.* 7
             170-176

1960 b   "Chief and Prophet in Zululand and Swaziland"
             Fortes & Dieterlen 1965   276-287

1961   *Bantu Prophets in South Africa.* (updated ed.)
             London, Oxford Univ. Press

THOMSEN, HARRY
1963   *The New Religions of Japan.* Rutland, Charles
             Tuttle Co.

TIPPETT, A.R.
1967   "Comparative Analysis of Nativistic Movements"
             Ch. 14 and "The Western Solomons Schism" Part V in
             Solomon Islands Christianity. London, Lutterworth
             Press

TURNER, C.V.
1970   "The Sinasina Stone Bowl Cult" *Prac. Anth.* 17
             28-32

TURNER, H.W.
1967   "A Typology for African Religious Movements"
             Jr. Relig. in Africa 1   1-34

VAN SICARD, H.
1946   "The Free Cult in the Zimbawe Culture" *African
             Stud.* 5   257-267

WALKER, DEWARD E.,JR.
1969   "New Light on the Prophet Dance Controversy"
             Ethnohistory 16   245-256

WALLACE, A.F.C.
    1952   "Handsome Lake and the Great Revival in the West"
              Amer. Qr. 4 149-165

    1956   "Revitalization Movements" *Amer. Anth.* 58 264-81

    1958   "The Dekanawideh Myth Analysed as the Record of a
              Revitalization Movement" *Ethnohistory* 5 118-130

    1959   "Towards a Classification of Cult Movements: Some
              Future Considerations" *Man* 59 25-28

    1961   "The Cultural Composition of Handsome Lake
              Religion" *Bull. Bur. Amer. Eth.* 180   143-151

    1966   *Religion: An Anthropological View.* New York,
              Random House   30-51, 209-215

WALLIS, WILSON D.
    1918   *Messiahs: Christian and Pagan.* Boston, The Gorham
              Press

    1943   *Messiahs: Their Role in Civilization.* Washington,
              D.C., Amer. Council on Public Affairs

WARD, B.E.
    1956   "Some Observations on Religious Cults in Ashanti"
              Africa 26   47-61

WEEMS, BENJAMIN B.
    1964   *Reform, Rebellion and the Heavenly Way.* Tucson,
              Univ. of Arizona Press

WELBOURN, F.B.
    1961   *East African Rebels: A Study of Some Independent
              Churches.* London, S.C.M. Press

WELTON, MICHAEL R.
    1969   "The Holy Arousa: Religious Conservatism in a
              Changing Society" *Prac. Anth.* 16.1 18-27

WILLIAMS, F.E.
    1923   *The Vailala Madness and the Destruction of Native
              Ceremonies in the Gulf Division.* Port Moresby,
              Papuan Anthropology Reports, 4

    1928   *Orokaiva Magic.* London, Oxford Univ. Press

    1934   "Vailala Madness in Retrospect" in *Essays Pre-
              sented to C.G. Seligman.* London, Kegan Paul

WILSON, ORMOND
1965   "Papahurihia, First Maori Prophet" *Journ. Polynesian Soc.* 74 473-483

WORSLEY, PETER
1957   *The Trumpet Shall Sound: A study of Cargo Cults in Melanesia.* London, Macgibbon & Kee

1957   "Millenarian Movements in Melanesia" *Rhodes-Livingstone Institute XXI*

1959   "Cargo Cults" *Scientific American* 200 117-128

THE GREAT RELIGIONS

This unit is slanted to the cultural dimension
and that of the animistic bases of the great
religions. A limited number of general works
have been included but not those concerned with
the philosophical superstructures, for which a
separate bibliography is required under 'Theology
and Philosophy'.

ADDISON, JAMES T.
   1925   *Chinese Ancestor Worship: A Study of its Meaning
             and Relations with Christianity.* Chung Hua Sheng
             Kung Hui, Church Literature Committee

AMES, MICHAEL M.
   1964   "Buddha and the Dancing Goblins" *Amer. Anth.* 66
             75-82

ANASAKI, MASAHARU
   1961   *Religious Life of the Japanese People.*
             (Kishimoto's revision of a 1938 original) Tokyo,
             Society for International Cultural Relations

ANDERSON, J.N.D. (ed.)
   1950   *The World's Religions.* Grand Rapids,
             Wm. Eerdmanns Publishing Co.

ARIGA, TETSUTARO
   1958   "Christian Mission in Japan as a Theological
             Problem" *Religion in Life* 27   372-380

BEYERHAUS, PETER
   1966   "The Christian Approach to Ancestor Worship"
             Ministry 6   137-145

BHATNAGER, I.M.L.
   1965   "Tree Symbol Worship in Punjab" *Folklore* 6
             105-108

BHATT, G.S.
   1968   "Brahmo-Samaj, Arya Samaj, and the Church-Sect
             Typology" *Rev. Relig. Res.* 10   23-32

217

BOAS, M.I.
1961   *God, Christ and Pagan.* New York, Frederick Fell

CARPENTER, EDWARD
1920   *Pagan and Christian Creeds: Their Origin and Mean-
            ing.* New York, Harcourt, Brace & Co.

CENTLIVRES, M. & P. and M. SLOTKIN
1971   "A Muslim Shaman of Afghan Turkestan" *Ethnology*
            10   160-173

CH'IU, MING-CHANG
1970   "Two Types of Folk Piety: A Comparative Study of
            Two Folk Religions of Formosa" Ph.D. dissertation,
            Univ. of Chicago

CLOTHEY, FRED
1969   "Skanda-Sastti: A Festival in Tamil India" *Hist.
            of Rel.* 8   236-259

COMMITTEE COMMEMORATING HANAYAMA'S 65th BIRTHDAY
1960   *Bibliography on Buddhism.* Tokyo, Hokuseido

COOLEY, JOHN K.
1965   *Baal, Christ and Muhammed: Religion and Revolution
            in North Africa.* New York, Holt, Rinehart &
            Winston

CRAGG, KENNETH
1959   *Sandals at the Mosque.* New York, Oxford Univ.
            Press

1964   *The Call of the Minaret.* New York, Oxford Univ.
            Press

DANIELOU, A.
1964   *Hindu Polytheism.*   New York, Bollengen Foundation

DANIELOU, JEAN
1964   *Introduction to the Great Religions.* Notre Dame,
            Fides Publishers

de GROOT, J.S.M.
1892-1910 *The Religious Systems of China.* Leiden, E.J.Brill

DEVANANDAN, PAUL D.
1958   "The Contemporary Hindu Attitude to Conversion"
            Religion in Life 27   381-392

1961   *A Bibliography on Hinduism.* Bangalore, Christian
            Institute for the Study of Religion and Society

218

DODS, MARCUS
1905   *Muhammed, Buddha and Christ: Four Lectures on
            Natural and Revealed Religion.* London, Hodder and
            Stoughton

DOI, A.R.I.
1970   "A Muslim-Christian-Traditional Saint in Yoruba-
            land" *Pract. Anth.* 17   261-268

DRUMMOND, R.H.
1964   "Japan's New Religions and the Christian Community"
            Christian Century 81   1521-1523

DUBOIS, J.A. & H.K. BEAUCHAMP
1906   *Hindu Manners, Customs and Ceremonies.* Oxford,
            Clarendon Press

ELIADE, MIRCEA
1958   *Patterns in Comparative Religion.* Translated from
            French by R. Sheed. London, Sheed & Ward

n/d   *Shamanism: Archaic Techniques of Ecstasy.* Trans-
            lated from French by W.R. Trask. New York,
            Pantheon Books   (See also Bibliography on
            Shamanism)

ELIOT, CHARLES
1921   *Hinduism and Buddhism: An Historical Sketch.*
            London, Longmans, Green & Co.

1935   *Japanese Buddhism.* London, Longmans, Green & Co.

ELLINGWOOD, F.F.
1892   *Oriental Religions and Christianity.* New York,
            C. Scribner's Sons

ELLIOTT, ALAN J.A.
1955   *Chinese Spirit-Medium Cults in Singapore.* London,
            Dept. of Anthropology, London School of Economics

ESSLEMONT, J.E.
1923   *Baha'u'llah and the New Era.* (Bahai) London,
            George Allen & Unwin

FORMAN, CHAS. W.
1958   "The Challenge to Christian Exclusiveness"
            Religion in Life 27   352-361

GEERTZ, C.
1968   *Islam Observed: Religious Development in Morocco
            and Indonesia.* New Haven, Yale Univ. Press

GIBB, HAMILTON A.R.
 1962 *Studies on the Civilization of Islam.* (Especially
      pp. 187-196 and 177-187) London, Routledge and
      Kegan Paul

GOUGH, E.K.
 1958 "Cults of the Dead Among the Nayars" *J. Amer.*
      Folklore 71 446-478

GRAHAM, D.C.
 1961 *Folk Religion in Southwest China.* (Especially the
      section on ancestor worship) Washington, D.C.,
      Smithsonian Institution

GUSTAFSON, JAMES W.
 1970 "Syncretistic Rural Thai Buddhism" M.A. Thesis,
      School of World Mission, Fuller Theological
      Seminary, Pasadena

HALL, H. FIELDING
 1905 *The Soul of a People.* (Buddhism) London,
      Macmillan

HAMMER, RAYMOND
 1962 *Japan's Religious Ferment.* New York, Oxford
      University Press

HARPER, E.B.
 1957 "Shamanism in South India" *SW. Journ. Anth.* 13
      267-287

 1959 "A Hindu Village Pantheon" *SW. Journ. Anth.* 15
      227-234

HARPER, E.B. (ed.)
 1964 *Religion in South Asia.* Seattle, Univ. of
      Washington Press

HASTINGS, J. (ed.)
 1951 *Encyclopedia of Religion and Ethics.* New York,
      Scribners

HEIN, NORVIN
 1958 "The Ram Lila" *J. Amer. Folklore* 71 280-304

HESSELGRAVE, DAVID J.
 1967 "Soka Gakkai's Inner Thrust" *E. M. Q.* 3 129-137

HODOUS, LEWIS
 1929 *Folkways in China.* London, Arthur Probsthain

HOPKINS, E.W.
   1923   *The History of Religions*. New York, The
             Macmillan Co.

HORI, ICHIRO (eds. Kitagawa & Miller)
   1968   *Folk Religion in Japan: Continuity and Change*.
             Chicago, Univ. of Chicago Press

HOROWITZ, M.M.
   1963   "The Worship of South Indian Deities in
             Martinique" *Ethnology* 2   339-346

HOWES, J.F.
   1964   "New Writings on Japan's Religions: A Review
             Article" *Pacific Affairs* 37   166-178

HUGHES, K.
   1964   "Christianity and Islam in West Africa" *Christian
             Century* 81   264-267, 298-302

HUMPHRIES, CHRISTMAS
   1970   *The Buddhist Way of Life*. New York, Schocken
             Books

HUTTON, J.H.
   1963   *Caste in India: Its Nature, Functions and Origins*.
             (Especially pp. 223-262) London, Oxford Univ.
             Press

INGERSOLL, JOSEPH
   1964   "The Priest and the Path" Ph.D. dissertation,
             Cornell University

INTERNATIONAL MISSIONARY COUNCIL
   1910   *Non-Christian Religions*. Vol. 4 of the Edinburgh
             Conference Reports, I.M.C.

JAMES, E.O.
   1956   *History of Religions*. London, English Universities
             Press

JEFFERY, A.
   1943   "Present-day Movements in Islam" *Moslem World*
             33   165-186

JENNINGS, GEO. J.
   1971   "Islamic Culture and Christian Missions" *Pract.
             Anth*. 18   128-144

JONES, JOHN P.
   1903   *Indian's Problem: Krishna or Christ*. New York,
             Fleming H. Revell Co.

JONES, REX L.
1968   "Shamanism in South Asia: A Preliminary Survey"
            Hist. of Relig. 7 330-337

KABIRAJ, S.
1965   "Fertility Cult and Trees" *Folklore* 6   162-169

KANG, WI JO
1968   "Belief and Political Behavior in Ch'ondogyo"
            Rev. of Rel. Res. 10   39-43

KEENE, J. CALVIN
1958   "Christianity's New Challenge and Opportunity"
            Rel. in Life 27   393-400

LATOURETTE, K.S.
1956   *Introducing Buddhism.* New York, Friendship Press

LESLIE, CHARLES (ed.)
1960   *The Anthropology of Folk Religion* New York,
            Vintage Books

LEVY, RUBEN
1957   *The Social Structure of Islam.* London, Cambridge
            Univ. Press (especially ch. 10, pp. 458-505)

LEOHLIN, C. H.
1962   "Sikhs and Christians in the Punjab" *I.R.M.* 51
            451-460

MacCREERY, R.
1946   "Moslems and Pagans of the Anglo-Egyptian Sudan",
            Moslem World 36   252-260

MAJUMDAR, D.N.
1958   *Caste and Communication in an Indian Religion*,
            Bombay, Asia Publishing House

MALEFIJT, A. de W.
1964   "Animism and Islam Among the Japanese in Surinam"
            Anthrop. Qr. 37   149-155

MATHER, R.
1955   "The Conflict of Buddhism with Native Chinese
            Ideologies" *Rev. of Relig.* 20   25-37

MAY, L.C.
1954   "The Dancing Religion: A Japanese Messianic Sect"
            SW. Journ. Anth. 10   119-137

McFARLAND, H. NEILL
1967   *The Rush Hour of the Gods: A Study of New Religious Movements in Japan.* New York, Macmillan Co.

MIZUNO, K.
1969   *Primitive Buddhism.* Ono-ku Ube City, Yamaguchi-ken, Japan, The Karenbunko Oyama

MOORE, JAMES R.
1970   "Some Weakensses in Fundamental Buddhism" *E.M.Q.* 7 24-34

MOORE, G.F.
1914   *History of Religions.* New York, Chas. Scribner's Sons 2 vols.

MORIOKA, K. and W.H. NEWELL
1969   *The Sociology of Japanese Religion.* Leiden, E.J. Brill

MOZOOMDAR, P.C.
1894   *The Spirit of God.* New York, Geo. H. Ellis

NIDA, EUGENE
1968   *Religion Across Cultures: A Study in the Communication of the Christian Faith.* New York, Harper & Row

NAIR, P.T.
1965   "Tree Symbol Worship Among the Nairs" *Folklore* 6 114-124

NAKAMURA, H. (ed. N. Wiener)
1964   *Ways of Thinking of Eastern Peoples.* Honolulu, East West Center Press

NILES, D.T.
1967   *Buddhism and the Claims of Christ.* Richmond, Va., John Knox Press

OPLER, M.K.
1950   "Two Japanese Religious Sects" *SW. Journ. Anth.* 6 69-78

PARRINDER, GEOFFREY
1961   *Worship in the World's Religions.* London, Faber and Faber

1964   *The Christian Debate: Light from the East.* London, Victor Gollancz

PAUL, H.G.B.
1956   "A Prehistoric Cult still Practiced in Muslim
            Darfur" *J. Roy. Anth. Inst.*, 86   77-86

PEETERS, HERMES
1941   *The Religions of China: Confucianism, Daoism,
            Buddhism; Popular Belief.* Peking, College of
            Chinese Studies

PITT, MALCOLM
1955   *Introducing Hinduism.* New York, Friendship Press

PLATH, DAVID W.
1964   "Where the Family of God is the Family: The Role
            of the Dead in Japanese Households" (Ancestor
            Worship) *Amer. Anth.* 66   300-317

PRESLER, H.H.
1966   "The Ingredients of Popular Hinduism" *India
            Cultures Qr.* 24   18-32

1968   "The Mid-India Region: The Religious Veneration of
            Humans" *India Cultures Qr.* 25   10-23

PRICE, MORRIS T.
1924   *Christian Missions and Oriental Civilizations: A
            Study in Culture Contact.* Shanghai, Privately
            printed

REICHELT, K.L.
1951   *Religion in a Chinese Garment.* London, Lutterworth
            Press   (Translated from German by J. Tetlie)

REIK, THEODORE
1964   *Pagan Rites in Judaism.* New York, Farrer Straus

RELIGION AND SOCIETY
1961   Symposium of Seminar on "Village Religion" (India)
            Religion and Society 8

1964   "Sikhism and Christianity in the Punjab"
            Symposium *Religion and Society* 11

RELIGION IN LIFE
1956   Symposium on "Non-Christian Religions in the
            Contemporary World" *Religion in Life* 25 483-548

1957   Symposium on "Protestantism in Latin America"
            Religion in Life 27   5-53

1959   Symposium on "Asian Missions to America" *Religion
            in Life* 28   322-412

RÉVILLE, ALBERT
  1884   *Prolegomena of History of Religions*. London,
              Williams & Norgate (Translated from French by
              A. S. Squire)

RICHTER, JULIUS
  1908   *A History of Missions in India*. Edinburgh,
              Oliphant Anderson & Ferrier (Especially ch. IV)

ROBBINS, R.H.
  1959   *The Encyclopedia of Witchcraft and Demonology*.
              New York, Crown Publishers

SARKISYANZ, MANUEL
  1968   "Messianic Folk-Buddhism as Ideology of Peasant
              Revolts in 19th and early 20th Century Burma" *Rev.
              of Relig. Res.* 10   32-38

SCHOEPS, HANS-JOACHIM
  1968   *The Religions of Mankind*. New York, Doubleday &
              Do., Anchor paperback

SEU GUPTA, et al
  1965   "Tree Symbol Worship in India" *Folklore* 6   219-
              275

SHIPP, HORACE
  1946   *Faiths that Moved the World: Dreams and Dramas in
              the Search for God*. London, Evans Bros.

SKINNER, E.P.
  1958   "Christianity and Islam Among the Mossi" *Amer.
              Anth.* 60   1102-1119

SPAE, JOSEPH
  1967   *Christian Corridors to Japan*. Tokyo, Oriens
              Institute for Religious Research

  1968   *Christianity Encounters Japan*. Tokyo, Oriens
              Institute for Religious Research

TAMBIAH, S.J.
  1970   *Buddhism and the Spirit Cults in Northeast Thai-
              land*. London, Cambridge Univ. Press

TEXTOR, R.B.
  1960   "An Inventory of Non-Buddhist Supernatural Objects
              in a Central Thai Village", Ph.D. dissertation
              Cornell University

THOMPSON, LAURENCE G.
1969   *Chinese Religion: An Introduction.* California
            Dickenson Publishing Co.

THOMSEN, HARRY
1959   "Japan's New Religions" *I.R.M.* 48 283-293

1963   *The New Religions of Japan.* Rutland, Chas. E.
            Tuttle

TRIMINGHAM, J.S.
1955   *The Christian Church and Islam in West Africa.*
            London, S.C.M. Press

TUTTLE, HUDSON
1869   *The Career of the God-Idea in History.* Boston,
            Adams & Co.

VAN NIEUWENHUIJZE, C.A.O.
1958   *Aspect of Islam in Post-Colonial Indonesia.* The
            Hague, W. van Hoeve

von GRUNEBAUM, G.E.
1963   *Modern Islam: A Search for Cultural Identity.*
            New York, Random House

von GRUNEBAUM, G.E. (ed.)
1955   *Unity and Variety in Muslim Civilization* (more
            particularly pp. 231-310) Chicago, Univ. of
            Chicago Press

WARNECK, JOH.
1954   *The Living Christ and Dying Heathenism.* Grand
            Rapids, Baker Book House

WAYMAN, A..
1961   "Totemic Beliefs in the Buddhist Tantras" *Hist.
            of Relig.* 1 81-94

WEBER, MAX
1951   *The Religion of China: Confucianism and Taoism.*
            Glencoe, Free Press (Translated from the German
            by H.H. Gerth)

1958   *The Religion of India: The Sociology of Hinduism
            and Buddhism.* Glencoe, Free Press (Translated
            from German by H.H. Gerth & D. Martindale)

WEBSTER, WARREN
1965   "A Selected Bibliography on Islam and the Christ-
            ian Mission to the Muslims", typescript, School of
            World Mission, Pasadena

WELCH, HOLMES
1957   *Taoism: The Parting of the Way.* Boston, Beacon
            Press

WELLS, KENNETH
1960   *Thai Buddhism: Its Rites and Activities.* Bangkok,
            Christian Book Store

WHITEHEAD, HENRY
1921   *The Village Gods of South India.* Calcutta,
            Association Press

Williams, John A. (ed.)
1963   *Islam.* New York, Washington Square Press

WILSON, J. CHRISTIE
1959   *Introducing Islam.* New York, Friendship Press

YANG, C.K.
1957   "The Functional Relationship between Confucian
            Thought and Chinese Religion" in *Chinese Thought
            and Institutions.* (J.K. Fairbank, ed.) Chicago,
            Chicago Univ. Press   269-290

1970   *Religion in Chinese Society.* Berkeley, Univ. of
            California Press

YANG, Y.C.
1943   *China's Religious Heritage.* New York, Abingdon-
            Cokesbury Press

ZAEHNER, R.C.
1962   *Hinduism.* London, Oxford Univ. Press

ZWEMER, SAMUEL M.
1909   *Islam, A Challenge to Faith.* New York, Laymen's
            Missionary Movement

1920   *The Influence of Animism on Islam: An Account of
            Popular Superstitions.* London, Central Board of
            Missions & S.P.C.K.

CHRISTIAN MISSION

IN THE

ANIMIST WORLD

ANON   "Jungle Ordeal: (Motilone Indians) *Christian Life* April 35-45, 72-73, 80

BARRETT, DAVID B.
1968   *Schism and Renewal in Africa.* Nairobi, Oxford Univ. Press

BEEKMAN, JOHN
1957   "A Culturally Relevant Witness" *Prac. Anth.* 83-88 (also in 1960 Supplement)

DANHO, JOSUÉ
1958   "Encounter Between Christian and Non-Christian" *Ghana Assembly Report* 41-46   London, Edinburgh House Press for I.C.M.

EVANS, MELVIN O.
1971   "Spirit Possession Among Certain Southern Bantu Tribes in Relation to the Bible and Church Growth" M.A. thesis, School of World Mission, Fuller Theological Seminary, Pasadena

FRERICHS, A.C.
1957   *Anutu Conquers in New Guinea.* Columbus, The Wartburg Press (more particularly Part II, 107-216)

1957   "Problems and their Solutions" Part II in *Anutu Conquers in New Guinea.* Columbus, Wartburg Press

1962   "Cultural Symbols in the Service of the Church" *Pacific Journal of Theology.* Sept. 6-11

GROSS, DANIEL R.
1971   "Ritual and Conformity: A Religious Pilgrimage to Northeastern Brazil" *Ethnology* 10   129-148

GUSTAFSON, JAMES
    1970   "Syncretistic Rural Thai Buddhism" M.A. thesis,
                   School of World Mission, Fuller Theological
                   Seminary, Pasadena (Especially Parts II & III,
                   146-259)

HAYWARD, V.E.W. (ed.)
    1963   *African Independent Church Movements.* London,
                   Edinburgh House Press   (Symposium)

HERBERG, WILL
    1958   "The Christian Witness in an Emerging 'Other-
                   Directed' Culture" *Prac. Anth.* 5   211-215

HOOKER, J.R.
    1965   "Witness and Watchtower in the Rhodesias and
                   Nyassaland" *Jr. African Hist.* 6   91-106

ISICHEI, ELIZABETH
    1969   "Ibo and Christian Beliefs: Some Aspects of a
                   Theological Encounter" *African Affairs* 68,121-34

JOHNSON, HARMON A.
    1969   "Authority Over the Spirits: Brazilian Spiritism
                   and Evangelical Church Growth" M.A. thesis,School
                   of World Mission, Fuller Theological Seminary,
                   Pasadena

    1970   *The Growing Church in Haiti.* Coral Gables, West
                   Indies Mission

KERR, JOHN STEVENS
    1971   *The Mystery and Magic of the Occult.* Philadelphia,
                   Fortress Press

KOCH, K.
    n/d   *Between Christ and Satan.* Grand Rapids, Kregel
                   Publications

    n/d   *The Devil's Alphabet.* Grand Rapids, Kregel
                   Publications

    n/d   *Occult Bondage and Deliverance.* Grand Rapids,
                   Kregel Publications

    1965   *Christian Counseling and Occultism.* Grand Rapids,
                   Kregel Publications

LAWRENCE, P.
    1956   "Lutheran Influences on Madang Societies" (New
                   Guinea) *Oceania* 27   73-89

LOEWEN, J.
1969   "Mythology and Missions" *Prac. Anth.* 16   147-92

MAURIER, HENRI
1968   *The Other Covenant: A Theology of Paganism.* Glen
            Rock, Newman Press

MILLER, ELMER S.
1971   "The Argentine Toba Evangelical Religious Service"
            Ethnology 10   149-159

NIDA, EUGENE
1968   *Religion Across Cultures: A Study in the Communi-*
            cation of the Christian Faith. New York, Harper &
            Row

NOBLE, LOWELL L.
1962   "A Culturally Relevant Witness to Animists" *Prac.*
            Anth. 9   220-222

OOSTHUIZEN, G.C.
1968   *Post-Christianity in Africa: A Theological and*
            Anthropological Study. Grand Rapids, Wm. B.
            Eerdmans Publishing Co.

PAUW, B.A.
1960   "Patterns of Christianization among the Tswana &
            Xhosa-Speaking Peoples" Fortes & Dieterlen 1965
            240-253

SHEARER, ROY E.
1968   "Animism and the Church in Korea" M.A. thesis,
            School of World Mission, Fuller Theological
            Seminary, Pasadena

SHEWMAKER, STAN
1969   "A Study of the Growth of the Church of Christ
            Among the Tonga Tribe of Zambia" M.A. thesis,
            School of World Mission, Fuller Theological
            Seminary, Pasadena (Particularly Ch. 4, 38-62)

SHROPSHIRE, D.W.T.
1938   *The Church and Primitive Peoples.* London, S.P.C.K.

SMITH, EDWIN W.
1936   *African Beliefs and Christian Faith.* London,
            Lutterworth Press

SMITH, GORDON H.
1947   *The Missionary and Primitive Man.* Chicago, Van
            Kampen Press

SPRUTH, ERWIN G.
1970   "The Mission of God in the Warbag Area of New
            Guinea" M.A. thesis, School of World Mission,
            Fuller Theological Seminary, Pasadena

SUNDKLER, B.G.M.
1961   "The Concept of Christianity in the African Inde-
            pendent Churches" *African Studies* 2   203-213

TABER, CHAS. R.
1969   "Why Mythology?" *Prac. Anth.* 16   145-146

TIPPETT, A.R.
1967   *Solomon Islands Christianity.* London, Lutterworth
            Press (more particularly Part 6, 267-345)

1969   *Verdict Theology in Missionary Theory.* Lincoln,
            Lincoln Christian College Press

TURNER, H.W.
1967   *African Independent Church (The Church of the Lord:
            Aladura)* Oxford, Clarendon Press   2 Vols.

1969   "The Place of Independent Religious Movements in
            the Modernization of Africa" *Jr. Relig. in Africa*
            2   43-63

VICEDOM, G.F.
1961   *Church and People in New Guinea.* London, Lutter-
            worth Press

WARNECK, JOH
1954   *The Living Christ and Dying Heathenism.* Grand
            Rapids, Baker Book House

WILLIAMSON, S.G.
1965   *Akan Religion and the Christian Faith.* Accra,
            Ghana Universities Press

WELBOURN, F.B. & B.A. OGOT
1966   *A Place to Feel at Home: A Study of Two
            Independent Churches in Western Kenya.* London,
            Oxford University Press

SUPPLEMENTARY ITEMS ON ANIMISM

COCHRANE, GLYNN
  1970   *Big Men and Cargo Cults*. Oxford, Clarendon Press

ENDICOTT, K.M.
  1970   *An Analysis of Malay Magic*. Oxford, Clarendon
            Press

LEWIS, I.M.
  1971   *Ecstatic Religion: An Anthropological Study of
            Spirit Possession and Shamanism*, Harmondsworth,
            Penguin Books

TURNER, VICTOR W.
  1969   *The Ritual Process: Structure and Anti-Structure*.
            Chicago, Aldine Publishing Co

Research Methods

ANTHROPOLOGY, ETHNOHISTORY   AND MISSIOLOGY

Teaching Anthropology

ANTHROPOLOGY, ETHNOHISTORY, AND MISSIOLOGY

Books and articles which discuss the methods and tools for
anthropological, ethnohistorical and missiological research,
means of data-collecting, documenting, evaluating, classify-
ing and writing up, with a sub-unit on teaching.

ADAMS, R.N.
   1962   "Ethnohistoric Research Methods: Some Latin
              American Features" *Ethnohistory* 9,   170-205

ADAMS, WM. Y.
   1969   "Ethnohistory and Islamic Tradition in Africa"
              Ethnohistory 16,   277-288

THE AMERICAN BEHAVIORAL SCIENTIST
   1962   Volume 10, No. 9 was devoted to social research in
              Africa and No. 10 to Southeast Asia, and include
              useful bibliographies of the areas.

ARON, RAYMOND
   1961   *Introduction to the Philosophy of History*. Boston,
              Beacon Press   Trans. from French by G.J. Irwin

BACKSTROM, C.H. & G.D. HURSH
   1967   *Survey Research*. Evanston, Northwestern
              University Press

BARKER, R.G. & L.S.
   1961   "Behavior Units for the Compatative Study of
              Cultures" in Kaplan, 1961: 457-476

BARTON, A.H. & P.F. LAZERFELD
   1955   "Some Functions of Qualitative Analysis in Social
              Research" *Frankfurter Beiträge Zur Soziologie*
              Band 1, 321-361

BARZUN, JACQUES & HENRY F. GRAFF
1962   *The Modern Researcher*. New York, Harcourt Brace
            and World, Inc.

BEALS, RALPH L.
1967   "International Research Problems in Anthropology:
            Report from the U.S.A." *Curr. Anth.* 8,   470-475

BEATTIE, JOHN
1964   *Other Cultures: Aims, Methods and Achievements in
            Social Anthropology*. New York, Free Press of
            Glencoe

1965   *Understanding an African Kingdom*. New York, Holt,
            Rinehart & Winston

BERKHOFER, ROBERT F.,Jr.
1963   "Protestants, Pagans and Sequences among the North
            American Indians. 1760-1860" *Ethnohistory* 10,
            201-232

BEVERIDGE, W.I.B.
1957   *The Art of Scientific Investigation*. New York,
            Alfred A. Knopf Inc.

BIRCH, T.W.
1964   *Maps: Topographical and Statistical*. Oxford,
            Clarendon Press

BLALOCK, HUBERT M., Jr.
1964   *Casual Inferences in Non-experimental Research*.
            Chapel Hill, University of No. Carolina Press

BLOCH, MARC
1964   *The Historian's Craft*. New York, Vintage Books.
            Trans. from the French by P. Putnam

BOHANNAN, PAUL & FRED PLOG
1967   *Beyond the Frontier: Social Process and Cultural
            Change*. New York, Natural History Press

BREEN, QUIRINUS (ed.)
1940   *Survey of Social Science: An Introduction to a
            Science of Society*. Eugene, University of Oregon
            Co-operative Store

BROOKS, PHILIP C.
1969   *Research in Archives: The use of Unpublished
            Primary Sources*. Chicago, Univ. of Chicago Press

BROOM, L.; B.J. SIEGEL & J.B. WATSON
1954   "Acculturation: An Exploratory Formulation" The
            Social Science Research Council Seminar on
            Acculturation, *American Anthropologist*   56,
            973-1000; also in Bohannan & Plog,   255-286

BUCHER, R. & E.L. QUARANTELLI & C.E. FRITZ
1956   "Tape Recorded Interviews in Social Research"
            American Sociological Review 21,3   359-364

BUTLER, PIERCE
1933   *An Introduction to Library Science.*   Chicago,
            University of Chicago Press

CAMPBELL, W.G.
1954   *Form and Style in Thesis Writing.*   Boston, Houghton
            Mifflin & Co.

CARTWRIGHT, DORWIN (ed.)
1951   *Field Theory in Social Science: Selected Papers of
            Kurt Lewin.* New York, Harper Bros.

CASAGRANDE, JOSEPH B. (ed.)
1960   *In the Company of Man: Twenty Portraits of Anthro-
            pological Informants.* New York, Harper & Row

COHEN, MYRON L.
1968   "The Hakka of 'Guest' People" *Ethnohistory*   15,
            237-292

COHEN, RONALD, et al.
1970   "Entree into the Field" in Naroll & Cohen, 1970:
            220-245

COLLIER, JOHN, Jr.
1967   *Visual Anthropology: Photography as a Research
            Method.* New York, Holt, Rinehart & Winston,Inc.

COMMITTEE of ROYAL ANTHROP. INST.
1960   *Notes and Queries on Anthropology.* London,
            Routledge & Kegan Paul Ltd.

CONDON, RICHARD A. & BURTON O. KURTH (eds.)
1960   *Writing from Experience.* New York, Harper & Bros.

CORDASCO, FRANCESCO & ELLIOT S.M. GATNER
1963   *Research and Report Writing.*   New York, Barnes &
            Noble

CORRIS, PETER
1969   "Ethnohistory in Australia" *Ethnohistory* 16,
            201-210

CULSHAW, WESLEY A.
1964   "Four Santal Autobiographies" *Practical Anthro-
                 pology* 11   pp. 77-89

DARK, PHILIP
1957   "Methods of Synthesis in Ethnohistory" *Ethno-
                 history* 4.3 pp. 231-278

D'EPINAY, C.L.
1968   "Toward a Typology of Latin American Protestantism"
                 Rev. Relig. Res. 10   4-11

DODGE, ERNEST S.
1968   "The American Sources for Pacific Ethnohistory
                 Research" *Ethnohistory* 15   1-10

DOLLARD, JOHN
1938   "The Life History in Community Studies" *Amer.
                 Soc. Rev.* 3   724-737 (also in Kluckhohn & Murray,
                 1969,   532-544

1949   *Criteria for Life History, with Analyses of Six
                 Notable Documents*. New Haven, Yale Univ. Press

DRIVER, HAROLD E.
1961   "Introduction to Statistics for Compartive
                 Research" in Moore, 1961   303-331

DUNDES, ALAN (ed.)
1968   *Every Man His Way: Readings in Cultural Anthro-
                 pology*. Englewood Cliffs, Prentice-Hall Inc.

DUNDES, ALAN & R.E. PFEIFFER
1968   "Guide to Research in Cultural Anthropology" in
                 Dundes 1968: 537-551

DURKHEIM, EMILE
1962   *The Rules of Sociological Method*. New York, The
                 Free Press of Glencoe for the Univ. of Chicago
                 with Catlin's introduction.

EDWARDS, A.L. & F.P. KILPATRICK
1948   "A Technique for the Construction of Attitude
                 Scales" *Journ. of Appl. Psych.* 32,   374-384

EGGAN, FRED
1954   "Social Anthropology and the Method of Controlled
                 Comparison" *Amer. Anthro.* 56. 5   743-763

1961   "Some Anthropological Approaches to the Understand-
                 ing of Ethnological Cultures" *Ethnohistory* 8   1-11

EGGAN, FRED
    1962   "Some Reflections on Comparative Method in Anthropology" in Spiro's *Context & Meaning in Cultural Anthropology*. New York, Free Press 1965   357-372

EHRLIGH, EUGENE & DANIEL MURPHY
    1966   *Writing and Researching Term Papers and Reports*. New York, Bantam Books

EMBER, MELVIN
    1970   "Taxonomy in Comparative Studies" Naroll & Cohen 1970   697-706

EPSTEIN, A.L.
    1967   *The Craft of Social Anthropology*. London, Social Science Paperbacks in assoc. with Travistock Pub.

FENTON, WILLIAM W.
    1962   "Ethnohistory and its Problems" *Ethnohistory* 9 1-23

    1966   "Field Work, Museum Studies & Ethnohistoric Research" *Ethnohistory* 13   71-85

FICHTER, JOSEPH H.
    1957   "The Marginal Catholic: An Institutional Approach" in J.M. Yinger's *Religion, Society and the Individual*   423-433

FRIEDLANDER, FREDERICK
    1968   "Behavioral Research as a Transactional Process" *Hum. Organ.* 27   369-379

GANNON, F.X.
    1967   "Bridging the Research Gap: C.A.R.A. Response to Vatican II" *Review of Religious Research* 9.1 3-10

GARRETT, ANNETTE
    1966   *Interviewing: Its Principles and Methods*. New York, Family Service Assoc. of America

GLASER, BARNEY G.
    1963   "Retreading Research Materials: The Use of Secondary Analysis by the Independent Researcher" *American Behavioral Scientist* 6   11-14

GLUCKMAN, MAX & FRED EGGAN, et al.
    1965   *The Relevance of Models for Social Anthropology*. A.S.A Monograph 1, M. Banton, ed., New York, F.A. Praeger

GOLDFRANK, VICTOR
1970   "Anthropological Informants and the Achievement of
            Power in Chan Kom" *Sociologus* 20   17-41

GOODE, WM.J. & P.K. HATT
1952   *Methods in Social Research.*   New York, McGraw-Hill

GOTTSCHALK, LOUIS, CLYDE KLUCKHOHN & ROBT. ANGELL
1945   *The Use of Personal Documents in History, Anthro-
            pology and Sociology.*   New York, Soc.Sci.Res.Coun.

GUSTAVSON, CARL G.
1955   *A Preface to History.*   New York,McGraw-Hill Bk.Co.

HAISER, TRAVIS L. & L.L. GRAY
1965   *Writing the Research and Term Paper.*   New York,
            Bell Publishing Co.

HAMILTON, GORDON
1964   *Principles of Social Case Recording.*   New York,
            Columbia Univ. Press for the New York School of
            Social Work

HAMMOND, PHILLIP E.
1967   *Sociologists at Work: Essays on the Craft of
            Social Research.*   New York, Doubleday & Co.

HANSON, R.H. & E.S. MARKS
1958   "Influence of the Interviewer on the Accuracy of
            Survey Results" *Journ. American Statistical Assn.*
            53   635-655

HARING, DOUGLAS G. (ed.)
1956   *Personal Character and Cultural Milieu.*   Syracuse,
            Syracuse Univ. Press.   Part I (1-121) deals with
            methods of research in Culture & Personality.   See
            also 127-128 for editorial article on "The Use of
            Ethnographic Reports on Cultural Behavior in
            Different Societies."

HASELBERGER, HERTA
1961   "Method of Studying Ethnological Art" *Curr. Anth.*
            2   341-384

HENRY, FRANCIS & S. SABERWAL
1969   *Stress and Response in Field Work.* New York, Holt,
            Rinehardt and Winston

HENRY, JULES & M.E. SPIRO
1953   "Psychological Techniques: Projective Tests in
            Field Work" Kroeber   1953: 417-429

HENRY, WM.E.
  1961   "Projective Tests in Cross-Cultural Research"
              Kaplan 1961: 587-596

HICKMAN, JOHN M.
  1965   "Vicos and Tama: Implications for Community Devel-
              opment and Missionary Research" *Practical Anthro-
              pology* 12.6   241-249

HOCKETT, HOMER CAREY
  1960   *The Critical Method in Historical Research and
              Writing*. New York, The Macmillan Co.

HOLMBERG, A.R.
  1958   "The Research and Development Approach to the
              Study of Change" *Human Organization* 17.1   12-16;
              also in Bohannan & Plog   307-318

HONIGMAN, JOHN J.
  1970   "Sampling in Ethnographic Field Work" Naroll &
              Cohen 1970:   266-281

HORAN, HUBERT
  1968   "Sociology in the Bush" *Pract. Anth.* 15   258-268

HUBBELL, GEORGE SHELTON
  1966   *Writing Documented Papers*. New York, Barnes &
              Noble Inc.

HUDSON, CHARLES
  1966   "Folk-History and Ethnohistory" *Ethnohistory* 13
              52-70

HYMAN, H.H.; G.N. LEVINE & C.R. WRIGHT
  n/d   *Introducing Social Change in Developing Communi-
              ties: An International Survey of Expert Advice*.
              New York, U.N. Res. Inst. for Soc. Development

JACKSON, M.
  1959   "An Account of Religious Sociology in France"
              Sociological Rev. 7   19-21

JANES, ROBERT W.
  1961   "A Note on Phases of the Community Role of the
              Participant-Observer" *Amer. Sociological Rev.*
              26.3   446-450

JEFFREYS, M.D.W.
  1956   "Some Rules of Directed Change Under Roman Catholi-
              cism" *Amer. Anthro.* 58   721-731

JUNKER, BUFORD H.
1968   *Field Work: An Introduction to the Social Sciences.*
            Chicago, Univ. of Chicago Press

KAHN, R.L. & C.F. CANNELL
1959   *The Dynamics of Interviewing: Theory, Technique
            and Cases.* New York, John Wiley & Sons Inc.

KEESING, ROGER, et al.
1970   "Models for Ethnographic Analyses" (Regional
            models) Part IV, Naroll & Cohen 1970: 423-578

KINCAID, H.V. & M. BRIGHT
1957   "The Tandem Interview: A Trial of the Two-Inter-
            viewer Team" *The Pub. Op. Quar.* 21   304-312

KLEBE, JOHN
1966   "A Suggested Schema for the Study of Complex
            Societies" Complex Societies Seminar paper, Univ.
            of Oregon

KOBBEN, ANDRE J.
1952   "New Ways of Presenting an Old Idea: The Statis-
            tical Method in Social Anthropology" *Journ. Royal
            Anthrop. Inst.*   82   126-146

1970   "Comparativists & Non-Comparativists in Anthro-
            pology" Naroll & Cohen 1970: 581-596

KROEBER, A.L. (ed.)
1953   *Anthropology Today: An Encyclopedic Inventory.*
            Chicago, Univ. of Chicago Press

LANGNESS, L.L.
1965   *The Life History in Anthropological Science.*
            New York, Holt, Rinehart & Winston, Inc.

LARSON, DONALD N.
1964   "Making Use of Anthropological Field Notes"
            Pract. Anth. 11   142-144

LAZARFELD, PAUL F.
1944   "The Controversy over Detailed Interviews" *The
            Pub. Op. Quar.* 8   39-60

1948   "The Use of Panels in Social Research" *Proc. Amer.
            Philos. Soc.* 42   405-410

1958   "Evidence and Inference in Social Research"
            Daedalus 4   87-130

LE VINE, ROBT. A.
1970   "Research Design in Anthropological Field Work"
             Naroll & Cohen 1970   183-195

LEACOCK, E., et al.
1958   "Social Stratification and Evolutionary Theory"
             Symposium   *Ethnohistory* 5   193-249

LEFCOWITZ, MYRON J. & ROBERT M. O'SHEA
1963   "A Proposal to Establish a National Archives for
             Social Science Survey Data" *Amer. Behav. Sci.* 6
             27-30

LESSA, W. & E. VOGT
1965   *Reader in Comparative Religion.* (2nd Edition)
             New York, Harper & Row   Part 12

LEWIS, OSCAR
1953   "Controls and Experiments in Field Work" Kroeber
             1953   452-475

1956   "Comparisons in Cultural Anthropology" in *Current
             Anthropology: Supplement to "Anthropology Today"*
             Chicago, Univ. of Chicago Press   W.L. Thomas (ed.)
             259-292

1962   *Five Families.* "The Setting" 1-19   New York,
             Science Editions

1970   *Anthropological Essays.*   Part 1 "Theory & Method"
             New York, Random House

LINDZEY, GARDNER
1961   *Projective Techniques and Cross-Cultural Research.*
             New York, Appleton-Century-Crofts

LOEWEN, JACOB A.
1965   "Missionaries and Anthropologist Co-operate in
             Research" *Pract. Anthro.* 12   158-190

LOWIE, ROBERT H.
1940   "Native Languages as Ethnographic Tools" *Amer.
             Anth.* 42   81-89

LUOMALA, KATHARINE
1947   "Missionary Contributions to Polynesian Anthro-
             pology" in the Symposium: *Specialized Studies in
             Polynesian Anthropology.* Bull. 193 5-31
             Honolulu, Bishop Museum

LURIE, N.O.
1961   "Ethnohistory: An Ethnological Point of View"
             Ethnohistory 8   78-92

LUTZ, R.R.
1949 *Graphic Presentation Simplified.* New York, Funk
     & Wagnalls

MACRIDIS, ROY C.
1962 "The Area Concept" *The American Behavioral*
     Scientist 5 3-4

MADGE, JOHN
1965 *The Tools of Social Science.* New York, Doubleday,
     Doran

MALINOWSKI, B., et al.
1965 *Methods of Study of Culture Contact in Africa.*
     London, Oxford Univ. Press for International
     African Institute. Reprinted from *Africa* V.7,8,9

MAQUET, JACQUES J.
1964 "Objectivity in Anthropology" *Curr. Anth.* 5
     44-55

MARKMAN, ROBERTA H. & MARIE L. WADDELL
1965 *Ten Steps in Writing the Research Paper.* New York,
     Barron's Educational Series, Inc.

McEWAN, W.J.
1963 "Forms and Problems of Validation in Social Anthro-
     pology" *Curr. Anth.* 4 155-183

MEAD, MARGARET
1939 "Native Languages as Field Work Tools" *Amer.*
     Anthro. 41 189-205

1968 "The Application of Anthropological Techniques to
     Cross-National Communication" A. Dundes 1968:
     518-536

MENZEL, DONALD H.: H.M. JONES & L.G. BOYD
1961 *Writing a Technical Paper.* New York, McGraw-Hill
     Book Co.

MERTON, R.K. & P.L. KENDALL
1946 "The Focused Interview" *Amer. Journ. of Soc.*
     51,6 541-557

MOORE, FRANK W.
1961 *Readings in Cross-cultural Methodology.*
     New Haven, Human Relations Area Files Press

1961 "Cross-Cultural Documentation" Editorial article
     in item above. 277-282

MOORE, FRANK W.
1970 "The Human Relations Area Files" Naroll & Cohen
    1970: 640-648

MURDOCK, GEORGE PETER
1940 "The Cross-cultural Survey" *Amer. Soc. Rev.* 5.3
    361-370

1953 "The Processing of Anthropological Materials"
    Anthro. Today (ed. Kroeber) 467-487

1965 *Culture and Society.* Pittsburgh, Univ. of
    Pittsburgh Press

MURDOCK, G.P., et al.
1961 *Outline of Cultural Materials.* New Haven, Human
    Relations Area Files Inc.

MURRA, JOHN F.
1968 "An Aymara Kingdom in 1567" *Ethnohistory* 15
    115-151

MYERS, JAMES E.
1969 "Unleashing the Untrained: Some Observations of
    Student Ethnographers" *Hum. Organ.* 28 155-159

MYERS, JOHN H.
1958 *Statistical Presentations.* Ames, Littlefield,
    Adams & Co

MYRDAL, GUNNAR
1969 *Objectivity in Social Research.* New York,
    Pantheon Books

NAROLL, RAOUL & R. COHEN (eds.)
1970 *A Handbook of Method in Cultural Anthropology.*
    New York, The Natural History Press

NEUMAN, S. & S. SINGMAN
1962 "The Southeast Asia Specialist" *The American
    Behavioral Scientist* 5 9-14

NUNEZ, THERON A., Jr.
1958 "Creek Nativism & the Creek War of 1813-1814"
    Ethnohistory 5 1-47, 131-175, 292-301

O'HARA, ALBERT R.
1963 "Sociological Errors through Insufficient Data"
    Nat. Taiwan Univ. Journ. of Soc. 1 99-100

PASTERNAK, BURTON
1968   "Atrophy of Patrilineal Bonds in a Chinese Village
            in Historical Perspective" *Ethnohistory* 15
            293-327

PAUL, BENJAMIN D.
1953   "Interviewing Techniques and Field Relationships"
            A.L. Kroeber 1953   430-451

PAULSON, I.
1961   "Scientific Method in Monographs on Religion"
            Amer. Anth. 63   862-833

PELTO, PERTTI J.
1970   *Anthropological Research: The Structure of Inquiry*
            New York, Harper & Row

PERT ORIENTATION & TRAINING CENTER
1963   Pert Fundamentals. Vol. 1: Networking; Vol. 2:
            Scheduling & Planning   Washington, D.C., Pert
            Orientation & Training Center

PESHKIN, ALAN
1968   "The Use of Trained Native Observers in Field Work"
            Hum. Organ. 27   266-272

REDFIELD, R., R. LINTON & M.J. HERSKOVITS
1936   "Memorandum for the Study of Acculturation" *Amer.*
            Anthro. 38   149-152: also in Bohannan & Plog
            181-186

RENIER, G.J.
1965   *History: Its Purpose and Method.* New York,
            Harper & Row

RICHMOND, MARY E.
1965   *Social Diagnosis.* New York, The Free Press

RIVERS, W.H.R.
1910   "The Genealogical Method of Anthropological
            Enquiry" *The Sociol. Rev.* 3   1-12

ROSS, E.J.
1950   "The Sociology of Religion in France Today" *Amer.*
            Cath. Sociol. Rev. 9   3-14

1954   "Modern Studies in the Sociology of Religion in
            France and Belgium" *Amer. Cath. Sociol. Rev.*
            15   115-140

ROTH, WARREN J.
1964   "Maryknoll Fathers and Anthropology" *Pract.*
            Anth. 11 238-240

SALER, BENJAMIN
1965   "Religious Conversion and Self-Aggrandizement: A
            Guatemalan Case" *Pract. Anth.* 12 107-114

SCHNEIDER, BEN R., JR. & HERBERT K. TJOSSEM
1964   *Themes and Research Papers.* New York, The
            Macmillan Co.

SCHUSKY, ERNEST L.
1966   *Manual for Kinship Analysis.* New York, Holt,
            Rinehart & Winston

SCHWARTZ, MORRIS & CHARLOTTE
1955   "Problems in Participant Observation" *Amer. Journ.*
            of Sociology 54.4 343-353

SEARS, ROBERT D.
1961   "Transcultural Variables and Conceptual Equi-
            valence" Kaplan 1961: 445-455

SEWELL, WM. H.
1949   "Field Techniques in Social Psychological Study in
            a Rural Community" *Amer. Sociological Rev.* 14.6
            718-726

1956   "Some Observations on Theory Testing" *Rural*
            Sociology 21 1-12

SHELTON, AUSTIN J.
1964   "The 'Miss Ophelia Syndrome' in African Field Re-
            search" *Pract. Anth.* 11 259-265

SIMEY, T.S.
1962   "Social Research Today: An Evaluation" *Frontier*
            5 401-405

SORENSON, E.R.
1967   "A Research Film Program in the Study of Changing
            Man" *Curr. Anth.* 8 443-469

SPINDLER, GEO. & W. GOLDSCHMIDT
1952   "An Example of Research Design: Experimental Design
            in the Study of Culture Change" *SW. Journ. Anth.*
            8 68-82, also Naroll & Cohen 1970: 210-219

STERN, FRITZ (ed.)
1963   *The Varieties of History.* Cleveland, The World
            Publishing Co.

STEWARD, J.H.
1943   "Acculturation Studies in Latin America: Some
     Needs and Problems" *Amer. Anth.* 45 189-206

STRICKLAND, D.A. & L.E. SCHLESINGER
1969   "'Lurking' as a Research Method" *Hum. Organ.* 28
     248-250

STURTEVANT, WM. C.
1966   "Anthropology, History and Ethnohistory"
     Ethnohistory, 13 1-51

TATJE, T.A.
1970   "Problems of Conceptual Definition for Compara-
     tive Studies" Naroll & Cohen 1970: 689-696

TAX, SOL
1945   "Anthropology and Administration" *Amer. Indigena*
     5.1 (1945) also in *Readings in Anthropology*
     (Hoebel et al.) 383-393

TEXTOR, R.B.
1962   "A Statistical Method for the Study of Shamanism:
     A Case Study from Field Work in Thailand" *Hum.*
     Organ. 21 56-60

TIPPETT, A.R.
1965   "Shifting Attitudes to Sex and Marriage in Fiji"
     Pract. Anth. 12 85-91

1967   *Solomon Islands Christianity.* London, Lutterworth
     Press ch. 19-21, 286-318

1968   *Fijian Material Culture: A Study of Cultural Con-*
     text, Function and Change. Honolulu, Bishop
     Museum Press 1-34, especially the section on
     "Ethnohistory "

TURABIAN, KATE L.
1965   *A Manual for Writers of Term Papers, Theses and*
     Dissertations. Chicago, Univ. of Chicago Press

TURNER, H.W.
1965   *Profile Through Preaching.* London, Edinburgh
     House Press

TYLOR, E.B.
1899   "On a Method of Investigating the Development of
     Institutions Applied to Laws of Marriage & Descent"
     Journ. Roy. Anth. Inst.   18 245-272

UNIVERSITY OF CHICAGO PRESS
        A Manual of Style. Chicago, Univ. of Chicago
        Press

VALENTINE, C.A.
  1960   "Uses of Enthnohistory in an Acculturation Study"
        Ethnohistory 7 1-27

VANSINA, JAN
  1962   "Ethnohistory in Africa" *Ethnohistory* 9   126-136

WASHBURN, WILCOMB E.
  1961   "Ethnohistory: History 'in the Round" *Ethno-*
        history 8 31-48

WEBB, E.J., D.T. CAMPBELL, R.D. SCHWARTZ & L. SECHREST
  1966   *Unobtrusive Measures: Nonreactive Research in the*
        Social Sciences. Chicago, Rand McNally & Co

WELTFISH, GENE
  1959   "The Question of Ethnic Identity" *Ethnohistory*
        6 321-346

WESTERMANN, D. & R. THURNWALD
  1948   *The Missionary and Anthropological Research.*
        London, Oxford Univ. Press for Intl. African Inst.

WHITE, D.R.
  1970   "Societal Research Archives System: Retrieval,
        Quality Control and Analysis of Comparative Data"
        Naroll & Cohen 1970: 676-685

WILLIAMS, THOMAS RHYS
  1967   *Field Methods in the Study of Culture.* New York,
        Holt, Rinehart & Winston, Inc.

WHITING, JOHN W.M.
  1954   "The Cross-cultural Method" in Lindzey's *Handbook*
        of Social Psychology 523-531; also in Moore
        1961   283-291

WHITING, J.W.M., et al.
  1966   *Field Guide for the Study of Socialization.*
        New York, John Wiley & Sons

WONDERLY, WILLIAM L.
  1967   "Social Science Research and the Church in Latin
        America" *Pract. Anth.* 14   161-173

WORLD VISION MAGAZINE
  1966   "New Tools for World Evangelism" Special Issue
        Oct. Number

WOUK, JONATHAN
1967   "Studying a Society's Secrets" *Prac. Anth.* 14
            214-221

YOUNG, FRANK W. & RUTH C.
1961   "Key Informant Reliability in Rural Mexican
            Villages" *Hum. Organ.* 20   141-148

YOUNG, PAULINE
1935   *Interviewing in Social Work: A Sociological
            Analysis.*   New York, McGraw-Hill Book Co.

1946   *Scientific Social Surveys and Research.*   New York,
            Prentice-Hall Inc.

TEACHING   ANTHROPOLOGY

ALBERT, E.M.
1963   "Value Aspects of Teaching Anthropology"
            Mandelbaum, et al.   1963 (a)   559-581

ARENESBERG, CONRAD M.
1963   "Courses in Ethnological Subjects"   Mandelbaum,
            et al.   1963 (a)   159-170

BARNETT, HOMER G.
1963   "Materials for Course Design"   (Applied Anthro-
            pology)   Mandelbaum, et al.   1963 (a)   373-391

BEALS, RALPH L.
1963   "Personnel Resources: Building Up the Anthro-
            pology Department"   Mandelbaum, et al.   1963 (b)
            37-47

BEATTIE, J.H.M.
1963   "Techniques of Graduate Training"   Mandelbaum
            1963 (a)   439-453

BOHANNAN, PAUL; M.S. GARBARINO & E.W. CARLSON
1969   "An Experimental Ninth-Grade Anthropology Course"
            Amer. Anth.   71   409-420

BUSWELL, JAMES O.
1954   "Anthropology & the Christian College Curriculum"
            Prac. Anth.   2   142-156

CASAGRANDE, J.B.
1963   "The Relations of Anthropology with the Social
            Sciences"   Mandelbaum, et al.   1963 (a)   461-474

CUTHBERT, M.
1965   "Anthropology in Missionary Training" *Prac. Anth.*
            12   119-122

EWING, J.F.
1957   "Anthropology and the Training of Missionaries"
              Catholic Educational Review 55   300-311

FIRTH, RAYMOND
1963   "Aims, Methods and Concepts in the Teaching of
              Social Anthropology" Mandelbaum, et al. 1963 (a)
              127-140

FORTES, MEYER
1963   "Graduate Study and Research" Mandelbaum 1963
              (a)   421-438

FRENCH, DAVID H.
1963   "The Role of the Anthropologist in the Methodology
              of Teaching" Mandelbaum, et al. 1963 (a)   171-78

GIVENS, G.D.
1964   "Books Available for Anthropology Courses" (USA)
              Curr. Anth. 5   332-338

HEWES, GORDON W.
1963   "Course Design" (Cultural & Social Anthropology)
              Mandelbaum, et al. 1963 (a)   153-157

JUNOD, HENRI PHILIPPE
1935   "Anthropology and Missionary Education" *I.R.M.*
              24   213-228

KEESING, F.M.
1963   "Experiment in Training Overseas Administrators"
              Human Organ. 8

KRAFT, C.H.
1960   "Preliminary Report on Correspondence Courses in
              Anthropology" *Pract. Anth.* 7   43-44

1961   "Correspondence Courses in Anthropology" *Prac.
              Anth.* 8   168-175

LEIGHTON, A.: J. ADAIR & S. PARKER
1956   "A Field Method for Teaching Applied Anthropology"
              Human Organ. 10   5-11

LIENHARDT, MAURICE
1953   "The Need for Anthropologically Trained Mission-
              aries" (Translated by George R. Horner) *Prac.
              Anth.* 1   93-97

LITTLE, KENNETH
1963   "The Context of Social Change" Mandelbaum 1963
              (a)   363-371

LURIE, NANCY O. & J.W. WHILING
  1954   "A Technique for Teaching Ethnology" *Amer. Anth.*
             56   442-445

LUZBETAK, LOUIS J.
  1961   "Toward an Applied Missionary Anthropology" *Anth.*
             Quar. 34   165-176

  1963   "The Nature and Scope of Applied Missionary
             Anthropology" Chap. 2 in *The Church and Cultures.*
             Techny, Divine Word Publishers (See also
             Bibliography   364-409)

MANDELBUAM, D.G.
  1963   "A Design for an Anthropology Curriculum"
             Mandelbaum, et al.   1963 (a)   49-64

MANDELBUAM, D.G.; G. LASKER & E.M. ALBERT (eds.)
  1963 a   *The Teaching of Anthropology.* Berkeley, Univ. of
             California Press

  1963 b   *Resources for Teaching Anthropology.* Berkeley,
             Univ. of California Press

MERRIAM, A.P.
  1960   "Anthropology in the Interdisciplinary Course"
             Whiteford 1960   38-43

NELSON, HAROLD
  1963   "Teaching Anthropology in Junior Colleges"
             Mandelbaum, et al.   1963 (a)   525-528

PETERS, GEO. W.
  1965   "Training Missionaries for Today's World" *E.M.Q.*
             2   19-28

RAPOPORT, R.N.
  1963   "Aims and Methods" (Applied Anthropology)
             Mandelbuam, et al. 1963 (a)   339-352

ROSENSTIEL, ANNETTE
  1959   "Anthropology and the Missionary" *Journ. Roy.*
             Anth. Inst. 89   107-115 (Reprinted in *Prac. Anth.*
             1961 8   15-24)

ROWE, JOHN H.
  1963   "Library Problems in the Teaching of Anthropology"
             Mandelbuam, et al. 1963 (b)   69-316 (Includes a
             fine Bibliography)

SMALLEY, WM. A.
  1960 a   "Anthropological Study and Missionary Scholarship"
             Prac. Anth. 7   145-152

SMALLEY, WM. A.
1960 b "Selected & Annotated Bibliography of Anthropology for Missionaries" New York, *Occasional Bulletin,* Missionary Research Library v. 11

TABER, C.R.
1967 "The Training of Missionaries" *Prac. Anth.* 14 267-274

TAYLOR, R.B.
1967 "Training Facilities in Anthropology" *Prac. Anth.* 14 73-83

THOMPSON, LAURA
1963 "Concepts and Contributions" (Applied Anthropology) Mandelbaum, et al. 1963 (a) 353-361

TIPPETT, A.R.
1960 "Probing Missionary Inadequacies at the Popular Level" *I. R. M.* 49 411-419

1968 "Anthropology: Luxury or Necessity for Missions?" *E. M. Q.* 5 7-19

WHITEFORD, ANDRED H. (ed.)
1960 *Teaching Anthropology.* Beliot, Logan Museum of Anthropology Symposium